Kingston upon Hull City Libraries
WITHDRAWN
FROM STOCK

FOR SALE

THE JEWS OF EXETER

AN ILLUSTRATED HISTORY

HELEN FRY

HALSGROVE

First published in Great Britain in 2013

Copyright © 2013 Helen Fry

All rights reserved. No part of this publication may be reproduced, stored in a retrieval system, or transmitted in any form or by any means without the prior permission of the copyright holder.

British Library Cataloguing-in-Publication Data
A CIP record for this title is available from the British Library

ISBN 978 0 85704 198 2

HALSGROVE
Halsgrove House, Ryelands Business Park,
Bagley Road, Wellington, Somerset TA21 9PZ
Tel: 01823 653777   Fax: 01823 216796
email: sales@halsgrove.com

Part of the Halsgrove group of companies
Information on all Halsgrove titles is available at: www.halsgrove.com

Printed in China by Everbest Printing Co Ltd

*Dedicated to
my exceptional and special sons
Jonathan, David and Edward*

CONTENTS

Acknowledgements		6
Introduction		9
Chapter 1	The Jews of Medieval Exeter	11
Chapter 2	Foundation of the Community from 1720s	22
Chapter 3	The Synagogue	31
Chapter 4	Synagogue Restorations	46
Chapter 5	The Burial Grounds	53
Chapter 6	The Community 1800-1880	61
Chapter 7	Decline and Revival	74
Chapter 8	Two World Wars	87
Chapter 9	Revival and the Community Today	101
Appendix 1	List of Tombstones in the Old Jewish Cemetery	113
Appendix 2	List of Tombstones in the New Jewish Burial Ground, Exwick	124
Appendix 3	Census Returns 1841-1901	126
Appendix 4	List of Rabbis and Ministers	143
Appendix 5	Pedlar Certificates 1871-74	144
Appendix 6	Congregation Ledger September 1827	145
Appendix 7	Jewish Creditors and Christian debtors in Medieval Exeter	146
Appendix 8	List of Hebrew Congregation: 1896-1999	154
Bibliography		157
Index		159

ACKNOWLEDGEMENTS

I WISH TO THANK the members of Exeter Hebrew Congregation and its committee for first suggesting that I write this history for the synagogue's 250th anniversary. It is a huge honour and privilege. My close relationship with the community goes back to the 1990s and has a special place in my heart from the ten years when I lived in Exeter. My heartfelt thanks to Brana Thorn, Frank Gent, Renee Smithens, David Cohen, Bill Boam, Richard Halsey and Tony Reese for all their practical support during the writing of this book. Frank has acted as a historical consultant during the production of this book and readily answered many questions pertaining to the history of the congregation and provided illustrations. Brana Thorn and Renee Smithens have generously conducted interviews for me and also researched material in the synagogue's newsletters for the 1980s and 1990s.

Huge thanks to Simon Butler and his enthusiastic team at Halsgrove for agreeing to publish this special history, for their dedication to recording provincial history and providing such an excellent high quality production.

Descendants who have generously given material and photographs are Judith Hornung and Barbara Fainlight for extensive information about the Samuels family, and Eric Smith and the Glynn sisters for information on their ancestors and their own memories of religious life in Exeter around the time of the Second World War. Bill Boam has not only helped with his own family material but accompanied me on trips to the cemetery and synagogue. I am indebted to Judy Wilson in Australia, as well as Audrey Vaughan, Carol McFadzean, Eve Richardson and Giles Croft for material and illustrations relating to the Silverstone, Lazarus, Laurance or Elsner families of Exeter. Thanks to Wayne Ezekiel of Newfoundland for making contact with me about his Ezekiel ancestors. I am grateful to Clive Henley for sending details of the Woolf family from 1790s onwards. My thanks also to Doris Black of London, formerly of Plymouth Jewish community, for her enthusiastic support of this book.

My thanks to Malcolm Wiseman, Harry Freedman and Elkan Levy for providing extensive memories of their pastoral work and the religious services that they conducted during the periods that they ministered to the Congregation.

Writing this history would not have been possible without the dedicated scholarship of those figures who have gone before me and recorded aspects of the community's history which has already been lost. In this respect I wish to pay tribute to the late Revd Michael Adler who in the 1930s recorded all the pre-1940 tombstones in the old cemetery. Today many of those early tombstone inscriptions are illegible or do not exist which makes Dr Adler's work so valuable for the community's history. Much of Exeter's Jewish history would have also been lost without the work of the late Rabbi Dr Bernard Susser, former rabbi of Plymouth synagogue who frequently visited Exeter. He carried out years of dedicated research for a Ph.D thesis which he published as a book in 1993 called *The Jews of South-West England*. He should be honoured also for rescuing some of the community's 19th century records from a builder's skip. I knew Rabbi Susser well and after I moved to London he would often meet to discuss his exciting new research discoveries. Since his untimely death in 1997, his daughter Hannah Jaffe has continued to offer her support in things connected to South-West Jewry. Tribute must also be paid to Frank Gent, former President of the congregation, who took up Bernard Susser's mantle and filled in many of the remaining gaps in the congregation's history, especially on key figures like the Ezekiel family and Jewish silversmiths of the city.

I would like to thank Eddie Sinclair (conservator, researcher and analyst of historic polychromy) for generously granting copyright permission for me to quote extracts from her report on the 'Exeter Synagogue: Polychrome Survey.' Eddie is currently undertaking the restoration of the Bishop's Throne in Exeter Cathedral. During the conservation of the synagogue in the 1990s, consultation and joinery was provided by Hugh Harrison, analysis Catherine Hassall, gilding Judith Wetherall and Clare Timings, and graining Frank Gent.

I would like to thank Rabbi David Katanka for translating inscriptions on the Exeter silver and providing translations of some of the Hebrew headstones in the cemetery. Thank you to my friend and mentor Mary Curry for reading some draft chapters and providing material. I have also been lucky with support from archivist Jan Wood at Devon Heritage Services; Staff at the West Country Studies Library; and Ellie Jones, the archivist at the Exeter Cathedral Archive. I am indebted to Elizabeth Selby at The Jewish Museum, London for help with illustrations and the use of material from the archives in this book. Also to The London Metropolitan

ACKNOWLEDGEMENTS

Archives as well as Charles Tucker, archivist to the Chief Rabbi and Beth Din; and to my friend Evelyn Friedlander of The Hidden Legacy Foundation for her enthusiasm and support of recording Devon Jewish life. Thank you to Petra Laidlaw who provided material about Jews in Exeter in 1851. Also my thanks go to Dr Anthony Joseph of The Jewish Genealogical Society of Great Britain for checking genealogical material on Exeter Jewish families in the 1800s.

To my circle of friends and family who enable me to carry out this work: my husband Martin, our three sons and my mother Sandra Doney; also my father-in-law David Fry. Thanks too go to staff at The London Jewish Cultural Centre, most especially Trudy Gold and Judy Trotter for their enthusiastic support. So too to other friends: Claudia Rubenstein, Colin Hamilton, Susan Ronald, Louisa Albani and especially to Sheila Hamilton who has provided much support on the writing journey. To my writing partner in fiction James Hamilton, my thanks for his creative ideas and indefatigable support of my work as a historian. Further information about my books can be found on the official author website: www.helen-fry.com

Special commendation

A special commendation goes to my 14-year old son Jonathan Fry for providing a substantial number of photographs for the book. All photographs in the chapter on the Jews of Medieval Exeter were taken by him at the National Archives when we arranged a special visit to see the 800-year old surviving Jewish business transactions and medieval documents from the Exeter *Archae*. It was a memorable day for both of us. Jonathan has also aided with other research and the compilation of the census returns. He also took a trip to Exeter with me and photographed the synagogue, old cemetery and other artefacts pertaining to the history of Exeter Jews. Jonathan is marvellous company and my special thanks for his participation in this project.

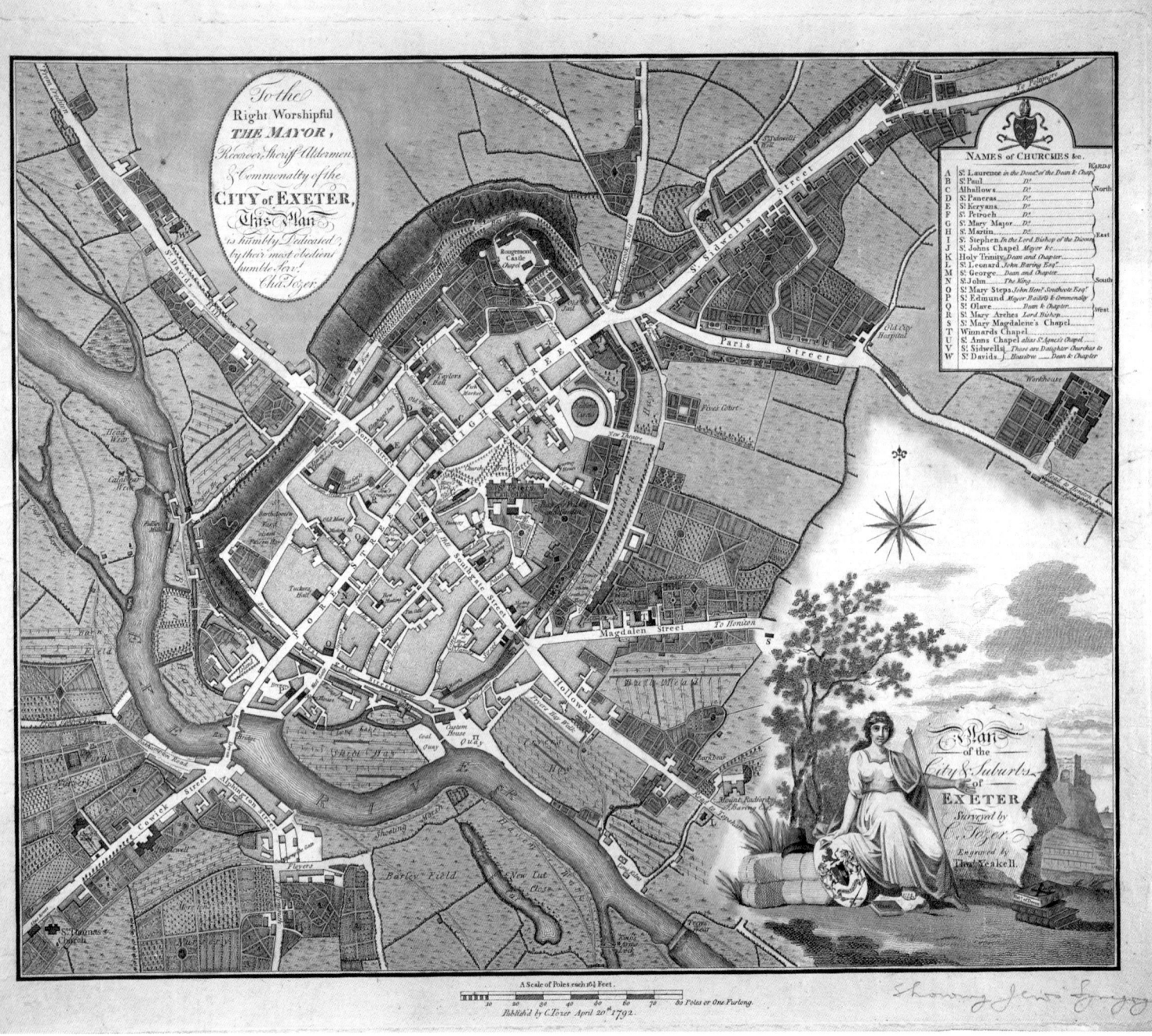

Map of Exeter, COURTESY OF JEWISH MUSEUM LONDON

INTRODUCTION

IN 2013 EXETER SYNAGOGUE reached an historic landmark with the celebration of it 250th anniversary. As the second oldest extant synagogue outside London it has a rich history that stretches back to the early 18th century. Evidence exists too for a much older Medieval worshipping Jewish community in Exeter before their expulsion from England in 1290. By the mid-eighteenth century Exeter possessed a viable Jewish community like Plymouth, Falmouth and Penzance, and looked to the future. During this period the four communities all acquired a burial ground and constructed their own purpose-built synagogue. Plymouth synagogue is still in use as a place of worship, built a year before Exeter in 1762, and also has two burial grounds.[1] The Jewish cemeteries of Falmouth and Penzance are still in existence, albeit fallen into disuse;[2] and their former synagogues are extant but no longer in use as places of worship. The Falmouth synagogue is an artist's residence and the Penzance synagogue has been subsumed into a Public House. During the eighteenth century the busy port and market town of Barnstaple in North Devon also had a practicing Jewish community, although with no purpose built synagogue.[3] Orthodox Jewish services were held in the house of Abraham Ralph house for over forty years; indicating that there were enough Jews living in Barnstaple to form a *minyan*, but not sufficient numbers to warrant the construction of a synagogue or have its own burial ground. Naturally there was cross-over and interaction, as well as inter-marriage between the Jewish communities of Devon and Cornwall.

While much information is available on Exeter's Jewish history in Bernard Susser's seminal book *The Jews of South-West England*, there is place here for an updated and fully illustrated history. *The Jews of Exeter* offers a window into the different centuries of Exeter's Jewish history: from periods of birth and growth to decline and revival. It focuses on the personalities and figures who shaped the community and kept the beautiful Georgian synagogue going through difficult eras as well as times of expansion and renewal. Exeter's gem of a purpose-built synagogue which dates to 1763 is now a Grade II Listed building and hugely significant in terms of Britain's wider heritage. The old Jewish burial ground in Magdalen Street on the edge of Bull Meadow was acquired in 1757, with until recently the earliest legible tombstone dating to 1807. Included in this book for the first time is a full list of those buried in the two Exeter Jewish cemeteries, thus providing important information for genealogists and family historians.

Exeter's Jewish community has seen its share of notables: from Alexander Alexander, optician by Royal Appointment to William IV to Herchel Smith in the 20th century who patented the contraceptive pill and was one of those chemists to profoundly influence the course of history. Over a period of two and a half centuries the Jews of Exeter have contributed significantly to the wider Devon and Exeter community, including aspects of commerce, business, the arts, politics and civic life. It is hoped that this book will highlight the importance of preserving this unique history and heritage for posterity.

---

[1] For a history of Plymouth synagogue see, see Bernard Susser, *The Jews of South-West England*.
[2] Inscriptions of the tombstones have been published in a book *The Lost Jews of Cornwall* (ed. Keith Pearce and Helen Fry).
[3] See Helen Fry, 'The Jews of Barnstaple and Bideford', in *European Judaism*, autumn 2001, p.4-13.

Medieval manuscript of transactions by Jews in Exeter

Medieval manuscript from the Exeter Archae, period of Edward I

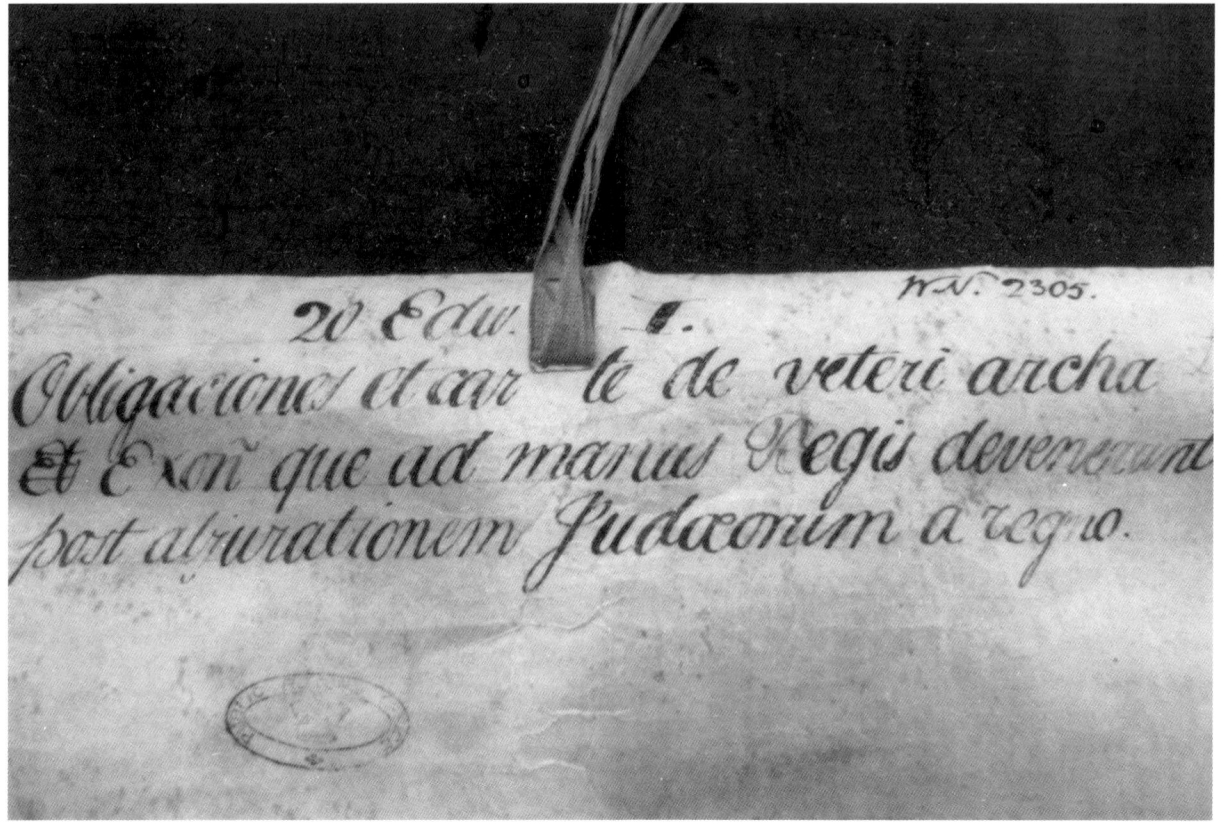

CHAPTER 1
THE JEWS OF MEDIEVAL EXETER

THE FIRST JEWS to settle in England came with William the Conqueror in 1066. Although there may have been itinerant Jews living in Britain since Roman times there was no organized community or settlement until the Norman period. William the Conqueror brought Jews with him from France to England, although there is no indication of any Jewish presence in Exeter during his reign. Precisely when Jews arrived in the city is not recorded. The earliest evidence for Jews living in Exeter dates to 1177 when a law was passed which granted them a cemetery beyond the city walls. Before that, corpses had to be escorted to London for burial.[4] Historian Alexander Jenkins writes that in the reign of Henry II: "The liberty of burial in Exeter was at this time given to the Jews, many of whom were then resident therein".[5] There is no longer a precise reference to the location of the burial ground, but it is safe to assume that Jews were already established in the city well before 1177 because they would not have been granted a burial ground on immediate arrival in the city. Their own burial ground was only necessary when the community was well-established. The worshipping Jewish community of Medieval Exeter once had its own synagogue although, like the burial ground, its precise location is now unknown. The community appointed a Rabbi and lay leaders to conduct regular services.

The first surviving financial transaction for Jewish business in the city dates to 1181. Official documents pertaining to the Jews in Medieval Exeter have survived in several archives: the British Museum,[6] Exeter Cathedral archives, Royal Archives at Windsor and the Public Record Office in Kew.[7] During this period there was no parliamentary administration and so England's Jews became the direct property of the Crown. It was a mixed blessing. On the one hand they came under the King's protection; on the other, they were useful to him because periodically he could demand money from them to fill the empty Royal coffers. The money of the King's Jewish subjects was often used to fund wars or campaigns, including the Crusades. Jews had no choice but to oblige with Royal demands if they were to live freely and enjoy the King's protection.

From the Exeter Archae

In spite of the anti-Jewish teaching of the Church, there was a degree of religious tolerance for Jews living in England during The Conqueror's reign. According to protection under the Crown, they enjoyed freedom to practice their religion and were permitted to set up their own Law Court, or Beth Din, to decide on matters of religion. A Beth Din was established in Exeter but its use entailed a heavy levy to the Royal Exchequers, necessitating its convening only in the most serious of legal cases. In carrying out their transactions, Jews were allowed to swear an oath on their Torah (Scroll of the Law) rather than the customary Christian Bible which included the New Testament. However, that religious tolerance did not extend to freedom of employment. According to Canon Law (the law of the Church) and civil law, Jews were restricted to the practice of usury only, i.e. lending money as a loan and charging interest on it. Usury was an occupation forbidden to Christians. Many of the medieval legal documents which survive today are financial transactions for money-lending to Christians by Jews.

Profits from usury could be significant, but Jewish money-lenders bore an enormous amount of taxation to the King from their profits, as well as the burden of other

---

[4] Jacobs, *The Jews of Angevin England*.
[5] Alexander Jenkins, *Civil and Ecclesiastical History of the City of Exeter and its Environs*.
[6] Cartulary of the Priory of St Nicholas and Lansdowne MSS.
[7] TNA: E101, No. 249, 27 is a report upon property. E101, No. 260, 2, gives a list of bonds in the Archa.

tallages imposed at the King's whim. Jews were permitted to own land as shown in the cases of three notable Exeter Jews Abraham (son of Moses), Fauntekin Bonenfant and Jacob of Exeter who in 1235 were pledged land by Gentiles against debts that were owed to them. In 1250 land in the High Street next to the house of Bartholomew Boschet was pledged to Jews against debts.[8]

In the Pipe Rolls of 1181, the twenty-seventh year of Henry II, an Exeter Jew by the name of Piers Deulesalt paid the sum of 10 marks for the king to take charge of his financial bonds. Deulesalt's original Hebrew name was Isaish ('May God save him') which when translated into French was Dieu-le-saut. This is the name that the money-lender assumed. In his article *The Medieval Jews of Exeter* Michael Adler comments that the name was: "characteristic of the manner in which a large number of Jewish men and women of the time assumed Norman-French names." The official system of registering bonds was not yet in practice so Piers of Exeter was compelled to pay for handing his documents into safe custody with the king's officers. Within seven years the Jews of Exeter were noted to be quite wealthy. According to Jacobs in *The Jews of Angevin England*: 'In the Plea Rolls of the year 1188, it is recorded the Jews of Exeter render count of one mark gold for a fine for pleas which were between them in common. The amount they paid was equivalent in value to about £2,006 in 1931.'

Centres of Archae

Henry II's reign ended in 1189. He was succeeded by Richard I ("the Lionheart"). But the position of Jews in England was always a precarious one. The following year while the new king was in France preparing for the Crusades, anti-Jewish riots were unleashed against the Jewish communities in England which resulted in Jews being massacred in the cities of Lincoln, Bury St Edmunds and Norwich. The worst riot culminated in a massacre in York. The West of England, including Exeter, escaped the riots. After one murderous uprising in London, the mob destroyed any documentation and evidence of money owed to Jews. This led to the loss of vital revenue for the Crown. When the king eventually returned to England he would instigate centres of Archae, discussed below, which would solve the problem of loss revenue from theft of Jewish business transactions. His return to England was at least two years away. In December 1192 he was captured by fellow Christian prince Leopold of Austria and held for over a year.

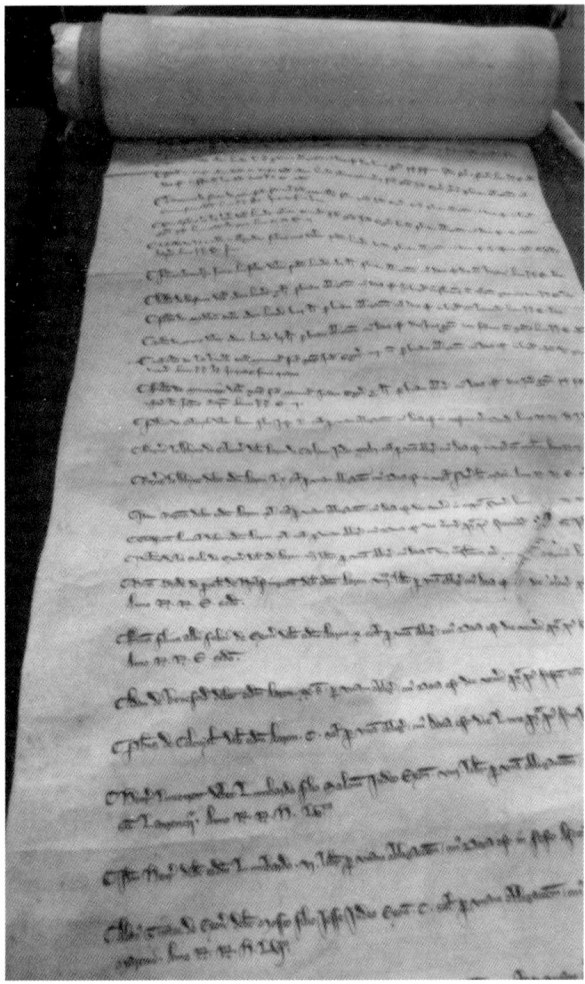
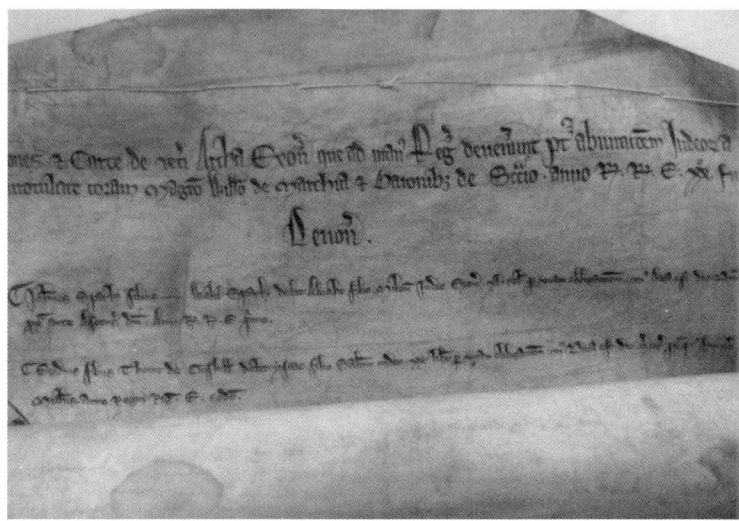

Manuscript from the Exeter Archae

---

[8] Archives of the Dean and Chapter of Exeter. As well as official archives, the works of Tovey (18th century) and Adler (1931) have also been helpful.
[9] Amiot is called Amideus in the Latin text of the Cartulary of the Priory of St. Nicholas of Exeter.

Examining the Exeter Archae at the National Archives

During 1193 England was preoccupied with collecting the ransom due for King Richard's release from prison. The Jewish communities of England were called upon to contribute a total sum of 5,000 marks towards the ransom which amounted to three times the amount paid by the whole city of London. Details of their payments survive in documents in the National Archives. Exeter Jews were also required to make their own contribution, although they cannot have been very affluent since only Amiot appears to have contributed anything.[9] He sent the sum of £1 3s. 3d. (less than 2 marks out of the 5,000 demanded). Amiot appears to have been the only local money-lender in the city that year. In 1204 he is recorded as loaning the sum of £5 to Sir Henry de la Pomeroy, a member of the famous Devonian family. The King was entitled to exact a tax of one bezant, or 2 shillings, for every £1 of the debt.

In early 1194 Richard I was released from captivity and returned to England. One of the first changes he initiated was the creation of Centres of Archae to preserve Jewish business transactions. Exeter was to become one of the first six or seven permitted Centres of Archaes. The centres formed branches of the newly-established Exchequer of the Jews or *Scaccarium Judeorum* and ensured the survival of Jewish documents by acting as a depository for existing and future transactions. Each centre had a bureau to administer the Archa, managed by two reputable Jews and two Christian clerks who were known as Chirographers. An Archa was an official chest with three locks and seals for depositing all business documents and transactions carried out by Jews. Local Archaes were overseen by the central authority of the Exchequer of the Jews. Whenever the King demanded money or a Jew died or converted to Christianity, an order was issued to the Sheriffs to inspect the Archa. Any debts owing to that Jew were then collected for the King's coffers. The names of many of the local Chirographers of the Exeter Archa have been preserved.[10]

In the same year as the Archae were established, Richard I decreed that Jews could only live in designated centres. These official settlements formed branches of the newly-established Exchequer of the Jews. England eventually had twenty-six centres of Archae, including London, Lincoln, Oxford, Canterbury and Norwich; all major settlements of Medieval Jewry. Exeter was one, demonstrating the importance of the city. Although in most cases, the precise location of Jewish residency in Exeter is not recorded, it is thought they settled near the High Street. A Jew by the name of Amiot occupied a house in the High Street in 1211 and a Jewess named Comitissa also in 1290. Amiot was recorded as living in a house belonging to Godekniht, near land possessed by a well-known Exeter figure, Peter de Palerna. Two other houses are also mentioned as belonging to Jews of the city in 1280 but the locality is not stated.[11]

Deulecresse le Eveske

By 1205 there were other Jewish money-lenders living in the city. They were Deulecresse le Eveske (Samuel and Juetta his wife), Jacob the son of Yveling and Deulecresse's brother and sister Sarah. The latter three probably formed a limited liability loan office from

---

[10] In the National Archives and also the Exeter Cathedral Archives. They have been reproduced as appendices at the end of this book.
[11] Michael Adler, *The Jews of Medieval England*.

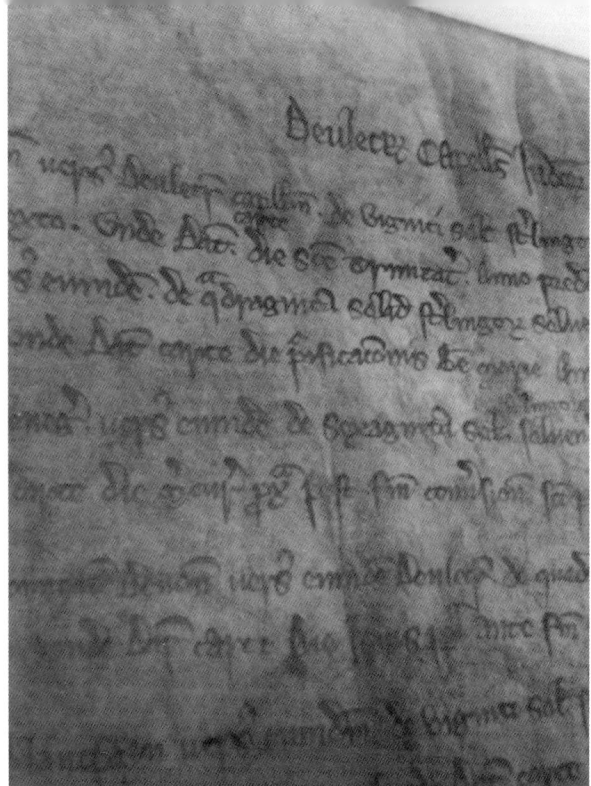

Reference to Deulecresse le Eveske

which to operate. In 1212 Henry de Nunant (Devonian landlord of Cliston Manor, Broadclyst) borrowed money from local Jews, against which he pledged his manor. The property was later confiscated by the King.

Deulecresse le Eveske was a notable Exeter Jew who became leader of the community and designated as 'the bailiff (ballivus) of the Jewry'.[12] He was in trouble in 1220 with another Jew, Solomon of Exeter. They were accused by William de Esse of demanding a debt from him that was not owing. They were summoned by the Sheriff to London to answer the charge before the Justices at Westminster. They gave a satisfactory defence and were acquitted.

Jews during this period were required by Canon Law of the Church to wear two broad strips of white linen or parchment in the shape of the Tables of the Law on their outer garments. Deulecresse le Eveske and Solomon of Exeter complied with these regulations when they travelled to London for the summons.

Two important monetary transactions by Deulecresse are recorded in the document *The Cartulary of the Priory of St. Nicholas* (Exeter). The first dates to 1224, the second to 1233. He was closely connected with the leaders of both the Jewish and Christian communities, and relations between them appear to have been good. The first monetary entry of 1224 concerns William Bozun of Clist who gave Deulecresse five shillings which a Martin Rof had paid him for rent of land in Clist.[13] Rof was a notable figure too who held office as Bailiff from 1224 for four years, and Mayor of Exeter eleven times during his career from 1234. The Jewish witnesses to the transaction were the Chirographers Moses le Turk and Ursell the son-in-law of Amiot,[14] Jacob of Gloucester, Bonefei the son of Isaac and Moses of Burdell. The Christian witnesses were Martin Prodome (Mayor) and his brother William, a priest. Jewish witness Moses le Turk originated from Tuarz in Normandy. Other members of his family lived elsewhere in England: Solomon in Bristol, Jacob in London and Samuel his brother in Kent. Moses le Turk eventually died in Hereford in about 1270 and left a small estate. His widow Genta paid the usual death duty to the Crown of one-third. Jacob of Gloucester, the second Jewish witness, occurs frequently in the records of Exeter Jewry as sharing leadership of the community with Deulecresse Episcopus. Jacob was selected as the official Exeter representative to collect the first tax levied by the regency of King Henry on "his" Jews in 1219.

The second entry in *The Cartulary of the Priory of St. Nicholas*, dating to 1233, is during the mayoral office of Hilary Blund and contains a personal declaration by Deulecresse. In it Deulecresse sells to Martin Rof the rent which he had originally received from William Bozun. In return Rof was to pay Deulecresse in the form of either a pair of white gloves or the sum of threepence per annum. Deulecresse was paid £2 by Rof for the transaction which the Jewish bailiff then passed to Joseph of Bristol. As representative of King Henry, Joseph of Bristol had come to Exeter with royal letters "to compel the Jews to pay debts owing to our Lord, the King". The principal Christian witness to this deed was Mayor Hilary Blund. The Christian Chirographers were Philip de Stokes and Henry Picot and Jewish Chirographers were Jacob of

---

[12] Also called Episcopus; or Hebrew name Gedalya Cohen.

[13] No. 371 in Nichols' *Collectanea Topographica et Genealogica*. Here Deulecresse is named here Deulecresse Episcopus Judeorum.

[14] Amiot of the Northampton Donum or "Northampton Tallage".

arrears with the payment of the Bristol Tallage. The Jews of Exeter, together with other brethren in England, were arrested and imprisoned for a time in Bristol Castle. Exeter Jews who owed money to the King at this time were Samuel of Wilton (deceased) and his widow Iveta; Deodatus the son of Amiot; Jacob of Gloucester; Samuel Episcopus (Cohen) and Samson cum ore. Strict orders were given to seize their property.

That same year (1221) King Henry III arranged the marriage of sister Princess Joan to King Alexander of Scotland and called upon "his" Jews to contribute towards the dowry. From seventeen centres of Jewry came the total sum of £564. Exeter could only gather £8 5s. 8d. The two richest Exeter contributors were Jacob of Gloucester (£3 11s. 0d) and Deulecresse le Eveske (£2 10s. 0d). Others who gave money were Ursell (18s.), Ursell son-in-law of Amiot (15s.), Moses le Turk (6s.) and Moses of Exeter (5s.).

Two years later the community had increased in number and wealth because they were able to pay to a royal tax the sum of £78 10s. 6d. out of a total collection of £1,680 from the whole Jewish community of England. This time three Exeter Jewish women contributed. They were Bona daughter of Abraham who paid £1 10s. and Chera (Chère) and Hanot (Hannah) who together paid £1 11s. 8d. The list of twelve men was once again headed by Jacob of Gloucester (£17 and 14 marks) and Deulecresse (£13 18s 10d.). Other Jewish men of Exeter also contributed: Moses le Turk (£9 6s 8d), Bonefei, the son of Isaac (£4), Ursell (£4), Ursell, the son-in-law of Amiot (£3 19s. 8d.), Sampson (£1 7s 4d) and Moses, son of Solomon (13s. 4d.). New Exeter Jewish residents mentioned for the first time are Solomon of Dorchester who, together with his son-in-law Deulecresse, subscribed £2 10s. 0d; also Jacob of Norwich (5 marks) and Lumbard, the son of Deulecresse Episcopus (13s.)

In other aspects of their lives England's Jews were heading for a tough time. The Church's Fourth Lateran Council had already decreed in 1215 that Jews had to wear a distinctive badge on their clothing. This measure would reappear centuries later when in the 1930s Nazi dictator Adolf Hitler forced Jews in Germany's Third Reich to wear a yellow badge with Star of David. When Henry came of age in 1227 he intensified the anti-Jewish measures against the Jews in his land by forbidding them to leave England because they had become such a valuable source of income to him. There was further bad news in 1230 when Henry levied on the Jews another tax which amounted to a third of their property. The following year in 1231 Henry gifted the city of Exeter and its castle to his brother Richard, Earl of Cornwall and Count of Poitou. Although the city now belonged to the Earl of Cornwall, the status of the Jews of Exeter remained the same: they were still the sole property of the Crown.

Gloucester and Moses le Turk who both sign the document. Martin Rof later gave his Clist [Clyst] property to the Priory of St. Nicholas as recorded in the *Cartulary*.

The Bristol Tallage

The names of Jewish witnesses occur in the numerous Receipt Rolls of tallages preserved in The National Archive.[15] In 1216 King John demanded payment of 60,000 marks (the "Bristol Tallage") from the Jews of England. King John died that same year and his nine year old son succeeded him as Henry III.

By 1221 the Jews were struggling to pay the Bristol Tallage imposed by John before his death and were in arrears. The earliest entry in the Receipt Rolls of Tallages is for 1221 and gives a list of local Jews who were in

---

[15] TNA, E. 401, 8.

Bonenfant, Joseph Crespin and the Jewish Parliament

Ten years later in February 1241 the King called for a *Parliamentum Judaicum* ("Jewish Parliament") to be assembled which he would address personally. It was convened on the pretext of improving relationships with "his" Jews. In reality Henry III was in desperate need of money again. He issued orders to the Sheriffs of the Jews that delegates should attend the parliament. The Sheriffs were threatened with dire penalties if they failed to carry out his command. A hundred and nine Jews from twenty-one Jewish centres assembled in Worcester for the "Jewish Parliament". It was then that Henry told them they must find ways to raise a new tallage of 20,000 marks which had to be paid within a year. It became known as "The Worcester Tallage".

Reference to Jacob Crespin

Jewish Assessors and Collectors were appointed to help the Sheriffs raise the tax from fellow Jews "under pain of forfeiting their goods and estates and the severest penalties, to the terror of all others". Four representatives from Exeter attended the parliament in Worcester. They were Jacob of Gloucester, Deulecresse Episcopus (the two most prominent members of the Exeter Jewish community), Bonenfant the son of Judah who was an active moneylender and Joseph Crespin the son of Abraham. In 1244 Bonenfant became a Chirographer for the Exeter Archa and was joined in office by Joseph Crespin.

England's Jews struggled to keep up with the King's demands. The Worcester Tallage had scarcely been paid when the King inflicted a further tax of 60,000 marks on all the Jews of England. Henry claimed it was punishment for the murder of a child in London whose death was blamed on "the Jews". Blaming Jews for the death of Christian children was a common anti-Jewish motif in the Medieval Ages and subsequent centuries. The Jews of Exeter gave its contribution towards the new tax and when they struggled to pay the balance of their due, it was generously settled by Joseph Crespin, the Chirographer. Around this time another Exeter Jew by the name Deulegard is mentioned. He moved from Exeter to Winchester where he became a Chirographer.

When Henry could not raise any more money for the coffers from the Jews of England he turned to his brother Richard, Earl of Cornwall. In 1251 the King sold the whole of English Jewry to Richard for the sum of 5,000 marks. Henry III deemed the Jews to be the property of the Crown and as such he could sell them. The sum received from Richard was paid straight into the Royal Exchequer. Now the Jews of England, including the Jews of Exeter, belonged to the Earl of Cornwall.

But the King's taxation of the Jews did not cease. There was further taxation exacted against them. An Exeter Jew by the Hebrew name of Isaac, son of Abraham, paid the sum of £5 5s. In 1254 Exeter Jews gave £2 from community funds, whilst a local debtor Aaron (the son of Abraham of London) paid the noteworthy sum of £10. Bonenfant the Chirographer paid 12 marks. In total Exeter Jews gave £20 to the King, a significant sum of money at that time.

A year later in 1255 Bonenfant gave a pledge for another Royal tallage that had been ordered to be paid this time to Richard the Earl of Cornwall, under whose protection all Jews now were. The Jews must have wondered how long they would keep having to pay random taxes to the Crown and the King's brother.

By 1260 Bonenfant was no longer in office as Chirographer in Exeter and was succeeded by Lumbard Episcopus, the son of a prominent community member Deulecresse Episcopus. As men of wealth Bonenfant and his brother Samuel had been pledged to Edward Prince of Wales. It was common practice for wealthy Jews to be given by the King as sources of private income to various members of the royal family. Bonenfant died about 1270. His wife Comitissa and son-in-law Vives (Hayim) carried on his business affairs. Concerning her house in the High Street in Exeter, the Expulsion Report of 1290 shows there were four bonds for the sale of corn due to her and one tally for the sum of 2/- (a bezant).

The wealth of Exeter's Jewish community had dwindled significantly by 1260. A Receipt Roll of that year details a new tallage of 500 marks that was demanded from all Jewish subjects of King Henry. The document shows that key Exeter Jews could no longer afford the high taxation exacted upon them. The once wealthy Jacob of Gloucester could only give the sum of 13s.[16] Lumbard Episcopus paid 6s. 8d; Bonenfant only 4 marks, whilst his brother Samuel gave 2½ marks. Joseph, the son of Moses, gave 4s. The total given by Exeter Jews amounted to only £8 6s. 4d. A second tax of 2,000 marks was levied against the Jews that same year. Such was their decline that Exeter's Jews were unable to contribute anything at all. As a result local Sheriffs, Mayors and Bailiffs were ordered by the Crown to open the Exeter Archae to check what money was owing to the city's Jews for land and rents or goods, chattels and jewels or pledges. In 1266, maybe due to severe financial hardship, Bonenfant's brother Samuel converted to Christianity. It was no saving grace for him because all his property still reverted to the Crown. It was the role of the Sheriff of Exeter to ascertain whether any debts were owing to Samuel, and if so, they were to be collected for the Prince of Wales.[17]

The Jews of Medievel Exeter lived peacefully with their Christian neighbours and conducted business very well as demonstrated in a document entitled "An Anglo-Norman Custumal of Exeter".[18] From the city records, the document quotes the local custom that a plea from a Christian against a Jew could not be heard unless in the presence of a Jew and Christian. Likewise a plea from a Jew against a Christian could not be heard except in the presence of a Christian and Jew. It displays a rare equality and justice before the law for the Jew. When the barons led by Earl Simon de Montfort revolted against Henry III from 1262-67 and brought disturbances to Jews in London, Canterbury and Bristol, the riots did not touch Devon or its capital Exeter. During the revolt the seal of *The Exchequer of the Jews* in London was stolen and consequently six important deeds were placed in the Exeter Archa for safe-keeping. However during the revolt one Exeter Jew, Jacob Baszyn, was staying in Oxford and was murdered there by soldiers of the rebellious barons. No justice was ever meted out for his death.

Jacob Copin

A new Jewish celebrity appeared on the Exeter scene in 1266. He was Jacob Copin, appointed Chirographer in place of Lumbard who had died. A good reference of conduct for him was given by Bonenfant and Deulecresse le Chapleyn (ie. the Chazan/cantor or Precentor of the synagogue). This is one of the rare mentions of a synagogue in Medieval Exeter. Jacob Copin was joined in office by Jacob Crespin, son of Joseph Crespin who had also died. Jacob Crespin continued to be one of the leaders of the local worshipping community and the most prominent money-lender until a few years before the

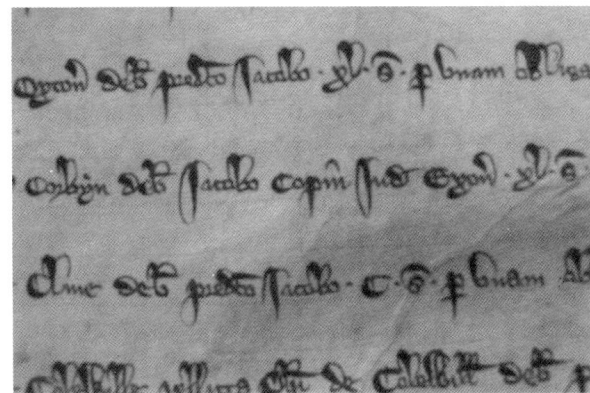
Reference to Jacob Copin

Expulsion of Jews from England in 1290.

Jacob Copin became one of the wealthiest money-lenders in Exeter. His clients included Sir Robert le Denys, Richard Bullock the goldsmith and a Christian Chirographer, two priests Roger de Moleyns and Arnulf of Hunecroft, and numerous residents of Devon and Somerset. To one debtor he lent £169 10s. 0d in two years. In 1270 he was assaulted during a visit to the village of Newton where he was carrying out a business transaction. The Sheriff was ordered to arrest the assailants because King Henry III would not allow any of his Jews to be ill-treated because they continued to be a valuable source of income. The assailants Robert of Buleshill, Christiana his wife and William Le Layte, fled and evaded justice.

The three principal Jewish financiers in Exeter at this time were Copin, Deulecresse le Chapleyn and Samuel, son of Moses. In the same year that Copin was assaulted, a charge was brought against him and the other two financiers concerning a debt. The plaintiffs failed to appear and they were fined.[19] In 1272 Copin is the only Exeter Jew listed in the Receipt Roll as contributing towards King Henry's new tallage of 20,000 marks. Copin was able to give £20 to the Royal coffers. Since it came only from him, he probably gave it on behalf of the whole Exeter Jewish community.

In 1272 Edward I ascended to the throne after the death of his father Henry III. His reign was to be a tragic turning point for medieval English Jews. By now the Jews of England had lost much of their wealth because of the excessive heavy taxation levied by Henry III. Edward could no longer use the Jews as bankers because they had nothing left to give. His response was to ban Jews officially from the practice of money-lending which had been one of the few occupations permitted to them by law. Now the Jews of England, including the Jews of Exeter, faced total catastrophe. Little did they know that there was worse to come.

---

[16] He died in about 1267.
[17] No record has survived to give more precise details about Samuel's unfortunate finances.
[18] Published by Professor J. W. Schopp and R. C. Easterling for the History of Exeter Research Group of the University College of the South-West.
[19] TNA: E.401,1567.

In 1273 Copin of Exeter paid 6 gold bezants to the royal coffers on a promise to settle arrears of a previous tallage. The following year the Prior of St Nicholas of Exeter collected a hundred pounds demanded by Edward from the Jewish community. The next year six of Exeter's Jews paid a further £20 towards a royal tax and this time Copin's name was absent from the list of contributors. The only donors were Jacob Crespin the Chirographer (£9) and Samuel son of Moses (£7), and also named were Lumbard (son of Deulecresse), Isaac (son of Moses), and Benedict Bateman (Hayim) and his daughter Juetta (or Iveta) from Bridgwater, Somerset.

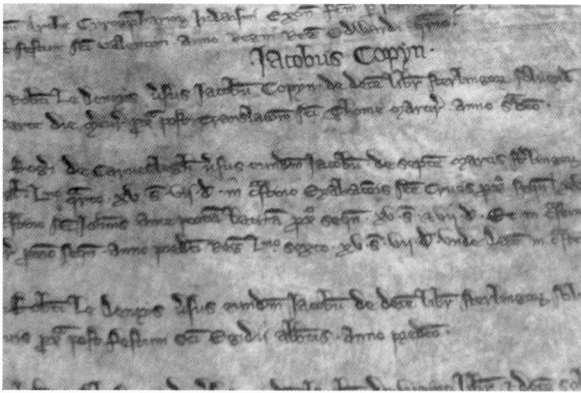

Transactions of Jacob Copin

In 1276 Copin and his brother Leo found themselves accused with others of clipping coins; in effect tampering with money and therefore guilty of fraud.[20] As with many accusations against Jews during the medieval period, there appears to have been no actual evidence to justify the charge. Nevertheless all the Jews of England would pay heavily for it. Amongst the accused were Aaron of Caerleon (living in Bristol), Deulecresse le Chapleyn and Solomon (son of Solomon). They were granted bail but there is no surviving record of any conclusion, except that two years later all the Jews of England were imprisoned in one night and brought to trial. In London alone 293 Jews were condemned.

The Statute de Judasimo

In 1275 Edward's imposed levy of 25,000 marks on the Jews of England was met with complete failure. They were unable to pay. In response Edward I passed the Statute de Judasimo (Jewish Law) which prohibited usury by the Jews. The statute also required Jews to live only in towns where *archae* were held. Now Exeter became one of the few centres left where the Jews of medieval England were allowed to live. The new law also required all Jewish males over the age of seven to wear a distinctive yellow Jewish badge. Jews were forbidden to build new synagogues or appear in public without their distinctive badge. However they were permitted to trade in wool and corn. In Exeter this soon became a profitable industry for the local Jews. A short time later, the Statute de Judasimo was modified to allow Jews to lend small amounts of money.

The last record of any tax paid to the King by England's Jews is for the year 1277. Edward received as much as £40 from Exeter's Jews out of a total levy of £1,000 throughout the country. It is thought the Exeter Jews could afford the sum of £40 because their financial position had improved with the wool trade and after the usury laws were relaxed.

The Exeter Jewish congregation at this time still benefited from the leadership of Chirographers Copin and Crespin. Later in 1277 these two men found themselves unexpectedly at the centre of a serious charge of fraud when Robert Fichet of Spaxton in Somerset died owing £80 to Exeter Jew Solomon (son of Solomon). Hugh Fichet, the deceased's son, was a minor so his guardian

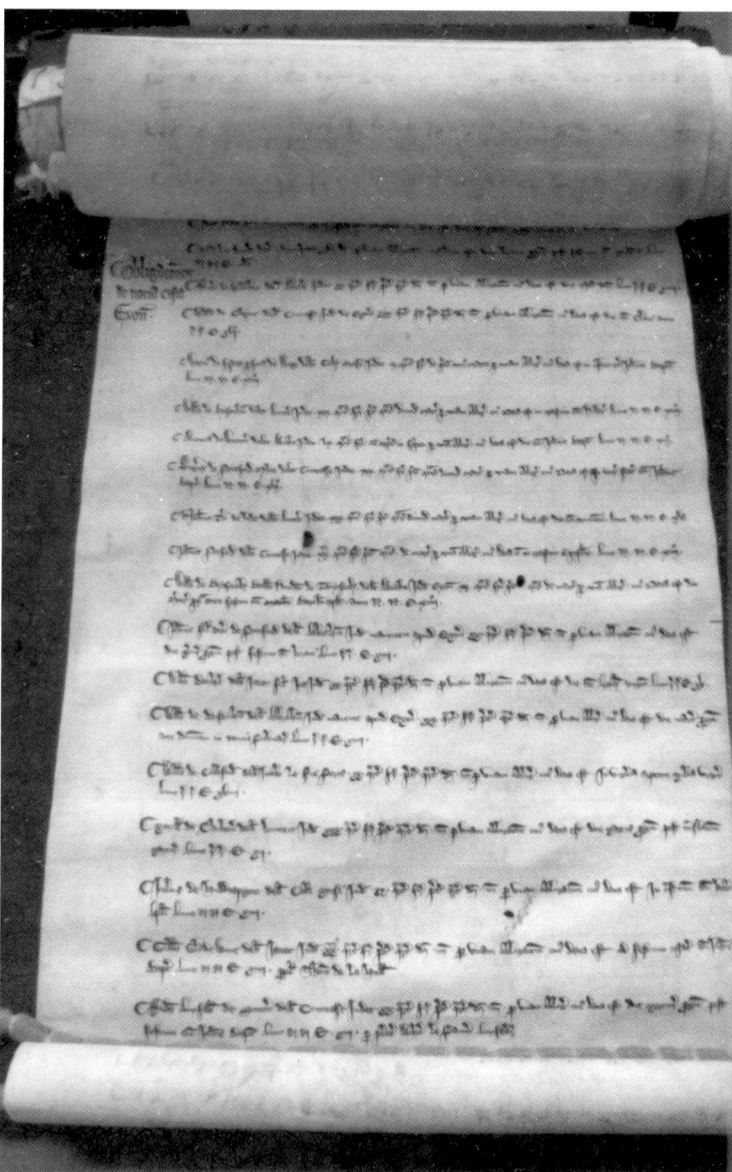

Portion from the Exeter Archae

---

[20] Clipping a coin rendered it worth less than its face value. The culprit thus accrued enough clippings to make an overall profit in value. It was a very serious offence.

took care of matters. Fichet's guardian claimed that the debt of £80 was not owing and that Adam, a clerk to the Chirographers, had forged the document at the suggestion of Solomon the money-lender after Robert Fichet's death and had placed it in the Exeter Archa. Action was taken first against the two Jewish Chirographers Copin and Crespin. Before it came to trial Copin and Crespin paid a mark to the Royal Exchequer to be bailed until Christmas. Their assurors were Aaron of Winchester, Moses Babelard of Wilton, Elias of Hereford and Pictavin (son of Isaac) of Nottingham. Copin and Crespin's defence was that Christian Chirographers David Taylor and Richard Bullock should also be brought to trial. If the two Jewish Chirographers were equally guilty, said their argument, then so were the two Christian ones because an archa could only be opened in the presence of all four Chirographers.

A Gentile by the name of Andrew of Pouderham [Powderham] and other Christian witnesses testified to the truth of Copin and Crespin's defence, along with Jewish witnesses Isaac (son of Moses), Deulecresse le Chapleyn, Ursell (son-in-law of Deulecresse), Solomon of Dorchester, Lumbard (son of Solomon) and Solomon (son of Samuel). The defendants were granted bail with assurity given by five of the most prominent Jews in England: Benedict of Winchester, Bonefey of Oxford, Jacob le Clerk, Elias of Cornhill, Aaron (son of Yves of London) and Isaac of Southwark. Copin and Crespin were acquitted. Hugh Fichet's guardian was fined for bringing false charges. For the next two years Jacob Copin continued to lend money to Devon and Somerset's gentry, clergy and local farmers. He often partnered with Samuel (son of Moses) for business transactions.

After 1280 the Exeter Jewish community began to decline quite rapidly. A number of anti-Jewish measures hastened their end. It was also the year that Jacob Copin of Exeter was hanged. No evidence has survived to give any idea what charge led to his terrible fate. That same year there was mention in the Exeter Cathedral records about premises not to be mortgaged to Jews, possible because of the whole Copin situation.[21] After his death Copin's house was confiscated by the Crown. One of his young daughters Claricia converted to Christianity and entered the *Domus Conversorum* (House of Converts) in London's Chancery Lane. Twenty-eight years later she returned to live in Exeter with her son Richard and daughter Katherine. After nineteen years she left the city to live in the House of Converts again. She died there in the year 1356 at a great age.

Claricia was not the only Exeter Jew to convert to Christianity. Other Jewish converts were Alice of Exeter, Richard the elder (a tailor), brothers Samuel and Solomon (the sons of Leo) and Henry of Exeter.

In 1284 the Archbishop of Canterbury John Peckham issued a decree that all synagogues in London except one should be demolished. No synagogues should be allowed in private houses. In 1286 Pope Honorius IV added his voice and addressed a Papal Bull to the Archbishops of Canterbury and York denouncing the "accursed and perfidious" Jews of England who have done "unspeakable things and horrible acts to the shame of our Creator and the detriment of the Catholic faith."

Then came the Synod of 1287 held at Exeter in which Bishop Peter Quivil roused his clergy to protect their congregations against "the insidious wiles of their Jewish neighbours".[22] Bishop Peter passed various edicts which aimed to segregate Christians and Jews socially. Jews and Christians were forbidden to attend each other's religious festivals, Jews could not build new synagogues, and on Easter Day no Jew of Exeter was allowed on the streets of the city. Exeter's Jews were ordered to pay taxes to parish clergy and forbidden to hold public office. They had to strictly adhere to wearing the distinctive badge that had been first decreed at the Fourth Lateran Council. No documentation has survived to suggest what the local Jews thought of these new measures. What is known is that they continued to trade with their Christian neighbours. As with previous difficult times they rode the storm until it blew over, but they could not foresee their expulsion from England within just three years.

The Expulsion

In 1290 unexpected catastrophe struck the Jews of England, and that included the Jews of Exeter. On 18 July King Edward I passed a decree to expel all Jews from the land. Jews were no longer legally allowed to live in England. Edward's timing of the expulsion may not have been arbitrary because it was the fast day of 9th of Av in the Jewish calendar which commemorates the destruction of the First and Second Temples in Jerusalem. The Jews of England were given three months to leave the kingdom before All Saints Day on 1st November 1290. Edward's action drove 16,500 Jews into exile. Most made their way to France, only to be expelled again in 1306. Around ten

---

[21] This has survived in Exeter Cathedral archives. Correspondence between the author and the Cathedral archivist.
[22] G. Oliver, *Lives of the Bishops of Exeter*, p. 48.

per cent went to Flanders (modern day Belgium). They were only allowed to take with them moveable property. Their homes and synagogues became the property of the Crown. Any debts still owing to them was also transferred to the King. The debts alone amounted to some nine thousand pounds in medieval money.

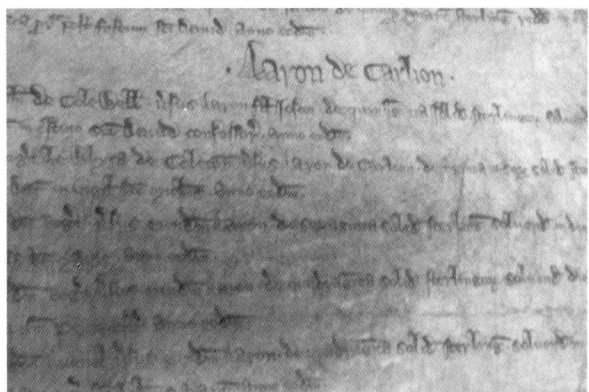

Reference to Aaron of Caerleon

To establish the amount of debts owing to the Jews at the time of the Expulsion, the Archae from each centre had to be opened. Surviving records in the National Archives and British Museum provide valuable information on the state of the finances of Exeter Jews at this time. In the presence of the Sheriff of Devon, twenty-five Exeter Christians took oath and testified that their former Jewish neighbours possessed no lands or dwelling places. The only exception was Comitissa, the widow of Bonenfant the Chirographer. She herself was a prominent financier who occupied a tenement in the High Street which she had bought without the attached shop from Joan (daughter of Adam the writer) for the sum of 11/- a year.[23] The Exeter Archa was opened in Westminster and its contents analyzed. In the chest were:

1. A hundred and forty-three unpaid bonds for money lent by Exeter Jews, dating from 1237-1275. The highest amount was for £60 in a transaction carried out by Jacob Copin. The total amount of debts owing to Exeter Jews was £1,058 4s. 2d.

2. Twenty-four tallies which were inscribed wooden sticks used as vouchers for loans. These recorded sums from 2/- to £3 13s. 3d. Some are dated, and in those cases are between the years 1286 to 1289.

3. Twenty-one receipts for advances on corn. These receipts date from 1284-1290 and amounted to a total value of £180 13s. 4d.

The total amount owing to Exeter Jews at the time the Archa was opened was amongst the largest owed to any Jews in England. The wealthiest creditor was Jacob Copin with unpaid debts of £357 owing to him from the period 1266-1275. After his execution in 1280 his transactions in the Exeter Archa should have reverted to the King but were forgotten or overlooked. The transactions were still in the chest when it was opened in 1290. Exeter Jewess Amité (widow of Samuel son of Moses) ranked next to Jacob Copin in the amount of business transactions. There are 36 deeds in her name with total debts owing to her amounting to £215. One of her clients was John Quynel, Rector of Shobrooke Church, near Crediton. Next on the list came Jacob Crespin the Chirographer with £114 owed to him. Also listed are Isaac (the son of Moses) owed £89; Deulecresse le Prestre (the Synagogue official) who had 17 debtors with bills for £75. That included clients such as Sir Philip of Uppecote and a Christian chaplain. Aaron (son of Jose of Caerleon) was owed £34 and Solomon (son of Solomon of the Fichet case) the sum of £26. Comitissa who lived in the High Street and dealt in

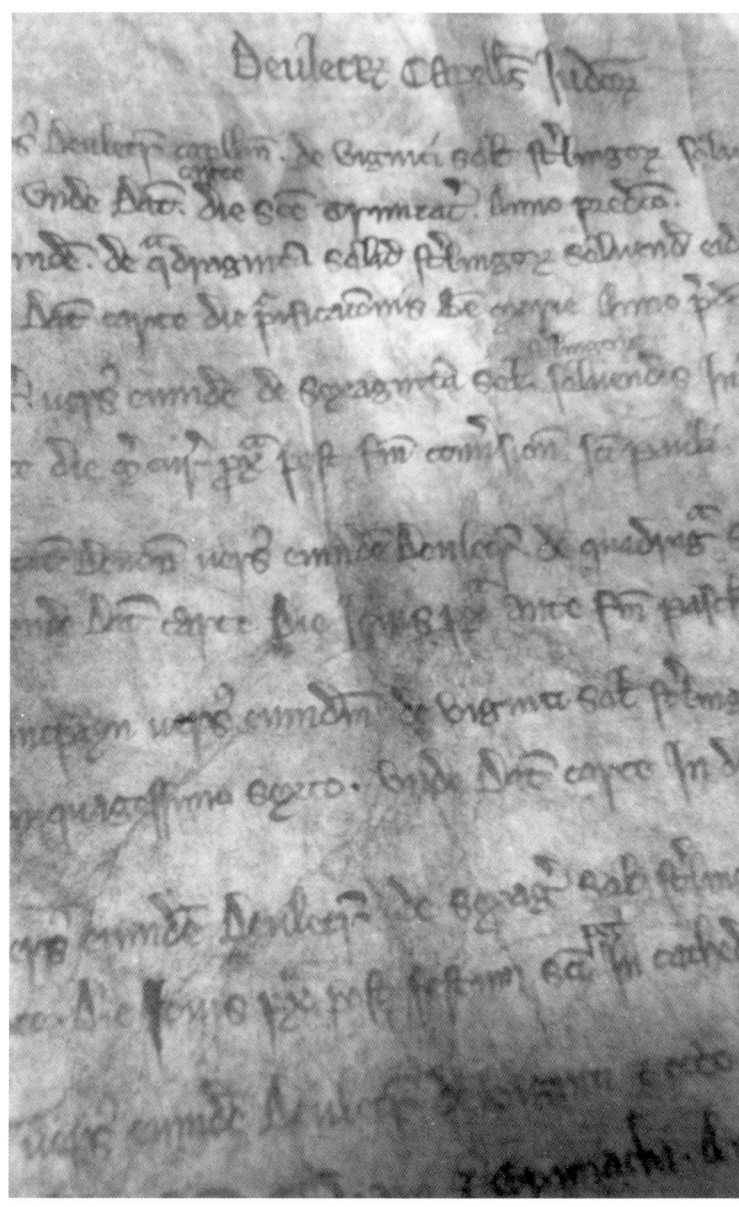

---
[23] Of that rent, 10/- was for the Hospital of St John of Exeter and 1/- for the candles of the Church of St Lawrence.

corn to the value of £33 6s. 8d. also had a tally of 2/- (2 bezants) entered in her name. The 800 year old Exeter Archa which survives in the National Archives today contains the names of 25 men and four women who were among the richest Jews in England in the latter half of the 13th century.

The story of the Jews of medieval Exeter and England is a tragic one. They lived constantly at the mercy of the King. Without complaint the Jews of England accepted their position, got on with their lives and lived as law-abiders in the land. Wherever financially possible they gave the full monetary dues demanded by the King, but no amount of loyalty could ultimately appease a monarch who chose to turn his back on his Jews. When their usefulness was over they were cast out of England on pain of death. It was a stark forerunner of other European expulsions, most notably Spain and Portugal in 1492. After two hundred years of peaceful living in the city the medieval Jewish community of Exeter ceased to exist. Exeter would not see another settled Jewish community for nearly 400 hundred years.

After the Expulsion of 1290, Jews were not legally permitted to live in England for over three hundred and fifty years. However there is evidence of a small number of Jews unofficially living in the kingdom in Tudor Times in the 15th and 16th centuries. In 1492 after Jews were expelled from Spain and Portugal, some Marranos (Jewish Catholics who practiced Judaism secretly) and Conversos (Jews who chose to convert to Catholicism for political motives) came into England through places like Cornwall, Wales and Ireland. The two main centres of Marrano settlement were to be found in London and Bristol. The most notable Marrano figure was the wealthy Jewess Dona Gracia, a prominent business woman whose ship put into Plymouth. She remained in England until it was safe for her to sail for Antwerp. The Marrano community placed agents in the port of Plymouth and possibly Exeter to promote trade for their textile houses in London and to inform Marranos who had fled to Spain and Portugal whether or not it was safe to land in England. In Elizabethan times Elizabeth I's own doctor Dr Lopes was a Jew, but he met a tragic end. He was executed after his enemies convinced the Queen that he was a traitor.

It appears that there may have been Jews living unofficially in Exeter in the 17th century because the Bishop of Exeter complained of 'Jewism' affecting his flock in the diocese.[24] From this it is possible to deduce that some Exonian Christians were being attracted to Judaism and this ruffled the feathers of the Establishment and local clergy. In 1617 a Marrano called Antonio Dacosta Doliveira was known to be living in Plymouth as a commercial agent acting on behalf of Count Gondomar, the Spanish ambassador to London. Marranos began to feel comfortable enough in England during the 17th century to openly practice their faith even though they still could not officially live in England. Monarchs from the Tudor period onwards turned a blind eye to their presence and did not enforce the expulsion order.

[24] Bernard Susser, *The Jews of South-West England*, p.29.

CHAPTER 2
FOUNDATION OF THE COMMUNITY FROM THE 1720s

THE EXETER JEWISH community today traces its roots directly back to the 1720s. After almost four hundred years of no official presence in the city Jews were once again free to live and prosper there. The community comprised both Sephardi Jews of Spanish and Portuguese origin and Ashkenazi Jews from Eastern Europe and Germany, in sufficient numbers to form a coherent community in Exeter. The common language amongst the immigrants who originated from Poland, Russia and Germany was Yiddish. Jews were officially readmitted to England in 1656 under Oliver Cromwell. After the Readmission there are isolated references to Jews in Exeter in the late 17th century. The Exeter Cathedral Archives contain references to 'Rabbi Moses the Jew' who in the years 1676, 1677 and 1679 was given sums of money by the Dean and Chapter of Exeter. Charitable money was also given to 'Abraham Chittleby a poor Jew' in 1734. Although it was thought that Exeter possessed no organized Jewish life until the 1750s, an address given at the re-dedication of the synagogue in 1853 stated that the congregation had been founded in 1728. It was also noted at that dedication service that an inscription dating to the 1720s could still be deciphered in the burial ground and a place of worship had been dedicated around 1734. No trace of the inscription has survived in the old Jewish burial ground today, nor are there records of where the original place of worship had been. It is not clear whether the pre-1763 synagogue was purpose-built or premises converted for worship.

Early Settlers circa 1720s

The early Jewish settlers in Exeter were predominantly skilled traders and educated Jews from the professions and trades, including jewellers, spectacle makers, quill makers, watch makers and shopkeepers. They were not poor itinerant pedlars and hawkers, as commonly thought, although there were nevertheless lots of Jewish commercial travellers operating throughout Devon and Cornwall from the 1720s. One of the first Jews known to have settled in Exeter was Jacob Monis. Originally from Padua in Italy, he came to Exeter at the turn of the eighteenth century and advertised his services in the *Flying Post* in 1724 as a teacher of languages:

> 'Jacob Monis, a learned Jew, born in Padua, Who, after many years travels in most Parts of Europe, has attained to the perfect Knowledge of the following Tongues, viz: Hebrew, Italian, Spanish, and Portuguese, now teaches the same, both as to Speaking, Reading and Writing Grammatically. He will attend any Gentleman at his own Apartments, if desired. Inquire for him at Peter's Printing House.'

Painting of synagogue façade by John White, c.1900.

FOUNDATION OF THE COMMUNITY FROM THE 1720s

Interior of synagogue and bimah

Another Italian Jew, snuff-merchant Gabriel Treves arrived in the city sometime prior to 1734. A short time later he brought his nephew Joseph Ottolenghe over from Italy to join him in business with the intention of marrying his daughter. Ottolenghe's conversion to Protestant Christianity caused a serious and very public family rift, discussed in more detail below.

During the 1740s two silversmiths Abraham Ezekiel and his brother Benjamin Ezekiel became prominent in Exeter Jewish life and later in the foundation of the synagogue. Together with clockmaker Samuel Jonas they were largely responsible for the consecration of the synagogue in 1763-4. Other Ashkenazi Jews in the city at this time were Simon Nathan who is known about because he was declared bankrupt in 1741.[25] There was also mention of Manele b. Zalman (Emanuel Solomon) of Exeter who was admitted as a member of the Great Synagogue, London in 1763/4; and Joseph Abrahams who placed an advert in the *Trewman's Flying Post* on 17 January 1799.

Of Sephardi origin was a man by the surname of de Costa who had settled in the city by the 1770s and was known to have taught languages. Another, Samuel Lopes, lived in the White House in 1797 for a rent of £6.7s a year. Manasseh Masseh Lopes was another key local figure who later became a Baron and in 1818 secured the seat as MP for Barnstaple in North Devon. Lopes was linked primarily with the Plymouth Hebrew Congregation, although his wife's name was entered in the Exeter Meat Tax Book for the purchase of 2lbs of kosher meat.

Also in the city were silversmiths Emanuel Levy and Francis Lyon (1752-1837); the latter apprenticed as a watchmaker to John Lakeman of Exeter in 1767. Trading from premises in Fore Street Emanuel Levy made large quantities of good quality domestic silver which were assayed at Exeter Assay Office with his mark EL.

Will of Emanuel Levy

His work included twenty-four bells registered on 7 May 1811, presumably for the Exeter synagogue. His will of 1818 bequeathed ten pounds to the Exeter congregation. Other beneficiaries were his wife Elizabeth and daughters Sarah, Briny and Charlotte, and son Jonas and Simon, also grandson Lyon Jacobs (son of his daughter Esther who had married Jacob Jacobs). Emanuel Levy's son Simon also practiced as a silversmith and registered his mark SL with the Exeter Assay Office. In 1811 Simon Levy made a beautiful set of silver *rimmonim* (bells) for use on a Torah scroll in Exeter synagogue. Like his father he primarily made silver for local families and gentry, and frequently engraved it with a family crest. In October 1818, for example, he had hallmarked '17 dozen teaspoons, 42 salt spoons, 14 dessert spoons, 4 mustard spoons, 4 butter

---
[25] *London Gazette*, 24 October 1741.

knives, 12 forks, 2 sugar tongs, 1 jug, 1 coffee pot, 6 teapots and 2 "nossels" (possibly candle-holders)'.[26]

Another Jew Isaac Gompertz (1773-1836) was one of 15 children. In 1818 he converted to Christianity and married out of the Jewish faith to Florence Wattier. He is best known for his famed poem "Devon" which was published in Teignmouth in 1825. An extract from the poem is inscribed on his brother Barent Gompertz's tombstone in the old Jewish cemetery, but is now illegible. Lazarus Cohen (1763-1834) became an active member of the synagogue during the late 18th century. He traded from premises in Fore Street. With an inventive mind he designed an improved reaping machine which was exhibited before the Leeds Agricultural Society in 1790. By occupation he had a shoe and pattern warehouse in Exeter from 1796 until his death in 1834. He wrote two works: *Sacred Truths* (1808) and *A New System of Astronomy* (1825) and is buried in the old Jewish cemetery.

Details of Jews living in Exeter during the eighteenth century can be ascertained from insurance policies on their businesses. These documents have survived in the archives at the Guildhall, London. Jewish businesses at this time included Abraham Solomon Davis, slopseller and dealer in plate at Westgate, Mary Arches parish; Isaac D'Israeli on the Lime Kiln House, Exeter, in August 1794; Joseph and Leah Isaac on premises in St David's Hill in September 1800; Jacob Jacobs, quill manufacturer in North Street, taken out in January 1807; Samuel Jacobs in August 1776 on 'The Plume of Feathers Inn' at the bottom of North Street and adjoining house; Moses Mordecai and Bernard Joel jointly on premises in St Mary Arches Lane – pawnbrokers, silversmiths and salesmen; and Bernard Joel in his sole name on Little Style, South Street – again premises of pawnbrokers and silversmiths. Moses Mordecai had policies on several addresses in central Exeter around Fore Street and Mary Arches as well as East Town, Crediton. Mordecai was a practicing silversmith in the last decade of the eighteenth century and his name occurs on the title deeds to the cemetery lease in 1801. He made fine silverware, including a pair of tea leaf diamond cut spoons which were hallmarked in Exeter circa 1800.

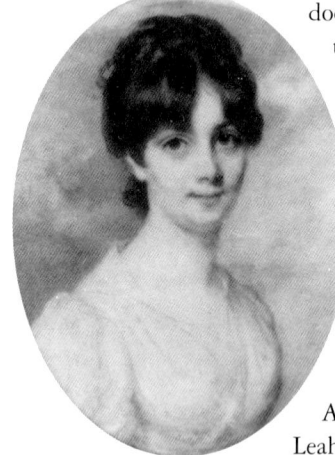

Miss Ezekiel (either Catherine or Amelia) by her brother Ezekiel Ezekiel

Insurance policies also exist for Sarah Nathan Levi who traded in the city as a linen-draper and dealer in clothes, taken out in October 1793; Samuel Benedict, glasscutter, engrave and dealer in chinaware who took out a policy on premises at the bottom of Fore Street in February 1808; and London merchants Lewis Schuman and John Lew Stephani on premises in Idle Lane, Exeter in 1765. As early as 1730 Mary Moses took out insurance on an address in Shycott [?] Hill, St John's, Exeter.

The Ottolenghe Affair

Sometime prior to 1734 Gabriel Treves brought his nephew Joseph Ottolenghe over from Italy to marry his daughter. On the surface the problem between uncle and nephew initially appears to have arisen when Ottolenghe converted to Christianity. However the problem went much deeper. Their rift became the subject of a very bitter argument that was played out in public. The details are recorded in two publications by Treves and a lengthy response by Ottolenghe. The publications reveal something of Jewish life in Exeter in the 1730s. Treves' two publications were entitled: *A Vindication of the Proceedings of Gabriel Treves against Joseph Solomon Ottolenghe, now a Prisoner in Southgate, Exon*; and *An Advertisement*. In his response, *The Answer of Joseph Ottolenghe to his Uncle Treves's Vindication etc*, Ottolenghe gives a detailed account of his conversion and his interpretation of the argument. He also provides an interesting insight into the wider Jewish community at that time. He tells how there were enough Ashkenazi Jews residing at a public house (not named) in the city for him to earn a decent living as their *shochet* or kosher slaughterer. As a new convert Ottolenghe had the local Christian community on his side. His publication was printed for Edward Score in the Guildhall, Exeter and sold by Samuel Birt in Ave-Maria Lane, London.

Not only did Treves expect Ottolenghe to marry his daughter but also to follow in the snuff trade. Both expectations were unlikely. Instead Ottolenghe preferred to spend his time reading and studying. The rift was so

St. Paul, *when he was a Prisoner in* Rome:
Exemplified in a
DISCOURSE
Preach'd before the Inhabitants of the
Parifh of St. *Petrock* in EXETER,
On *SUNDAY* the 6th of *July*, 1735:
Occafioned by their
Delivering *Jofeph Ottolenghe*,
A Poor Convert *Jew*, out of *South-gate* Prifon;
Into which he was caft by a *Jew*, after his Converfion to Chriftianity.
Publifhed at the Requeft of the Parifhioners of St. *Petrock's*.
For the Benefit of the faid Poor Convert Jew.

By LEWIS STEPHENS,
Archdeacon of Chefter, *and Canon-Refidentiary of the Cathedral-Church of* St. Peter, Exon.

Unam omnes rempublicam cognofcimus Mundum.
Tertull. Apol.

EXON: Printed by *E. Farley* for *E. Score*, Bookfeller; And *S. Birt*, at the Bible and Ball in *Ave-Mary* Lane, London.
(Price One Shilling.)

AN
ANSWER
TO
TWO PAPERS
Lately publifh'd by
GABRIEL TREVES,
A
JEW of the City of *Exeter*.
The one intituled,
A Vindication of the Proceedings of *Gabriel Treves* againft *Jofeph Solomon Ottolenghe*, now a Prifoner in *Southgate, Exon*;
The other is intituled,
An ADVERTISEMENT.
Wherein is contain'd the faid *Jofeph Ottolenghe's* Vindication of himfelf, againft the Afperfions caft on him in the faid Papers.
Together with
An Account of his Converfion from the *Jewifh* to the *Chriftian* Religion.
AND ALSO
Of the HARDSHIPS which he hath fuffer'd from the faid *Gabriel Treves*, his Uncle, &c. fince his Converfion.

By *JOSEPH OTTOLENGHE.*

LONDON:
Printed for EDWARD SCORE, over-againft the *Guild-Hall*, in *Exeter*; and fold by SAMUEL BIRT, in *Ave-Maria-Lane*, *London*.

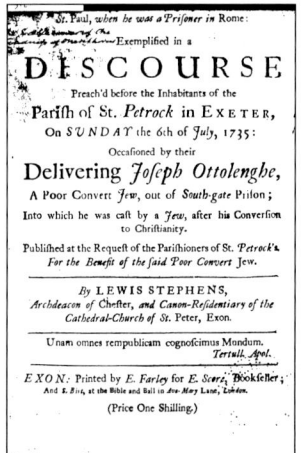

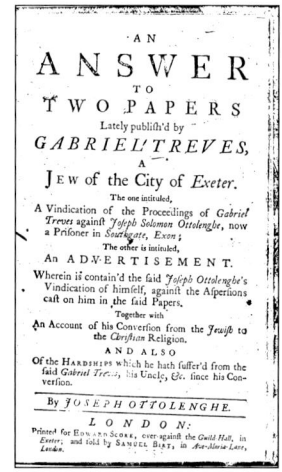

[26] Frank Gent, quoted from catalogue *The Jews of Devon and Cornwall*, p. 111.

FOUNDATION OF THE COMMUNITY FROM THE 1720s

bitter that Treves had his nephew imprisoned in Exeter's Southgate Prison on charges of debts for passage from Italy to England, clothing and lodgings. In September 1735 local Gentiles gave testimony to Ottolenghe's good character on oath before John Belfield in Exeter. The witnesses included Elizabeth Angell, Mary Rice and Samuel Lichigaray.

In *A Vindication*, Ottolenghe reveals that he had been brought up in a strictly Jewish household and attended the synagogue regularly in Casal and Leghorn in Italy. When he arrived in London he discovered his cousin was already married and his uncle had been busy trying to dissolve the marriage through the Rabbinical Court. The court did not rule in his favour and the marriage was not dissolved. Ottolenghe had effectively arrived in England to marry his cousin, only to find her already married. Treves was a bit of a rogue because he tried to accuse his son-in-law of buying snuff on the Sabbath, hence enabling the court to rule against the marriage on the grounds of breaking the Law. This also failed. Even though his daughter's marriage was not dissolved, Treves then tried to persuade Ottolenghe to marry her in Church but Ottolenghe was still a strictly observant Jew at this point and refused. Treves promised Ottolenghe that he had made him his sole heir and would disown his daughter if she did not marry Ottolenghe. Why Treves was so obsessed with Ottolenghe marrying his daughter is not clear. It all ended in bitter dispute with Ottolenghe leaving his uncle's household and his uncle finally getting him behind bars in the local prison for a period.

In his publication Ottolenghe explains that his conversion to Christianity came about through reading the New Testament in English. This he had done to enable him to learn the new language of the country he settled in. He writes: 'I was confirmed by the Bishop of Exeter, and soon after I received the Blessed sacrament of the Lord's supper, and continue to be a partaker thereof.' The subsequent fate of Treves is not known, but Ottolenghe emigrated to South Carolina and began a new life as a Christian preacher and teacher.

Abraham Ezekiel and Benjamin Ezekiel

During the 1740s Abraham Ezekiel and Benjamin Ezekiel came to Exeter as young men in their twenties from the Rhineland and became founding members of the synagogue. Abraham was a silversmith, engraver, optician, watchmaker and print-seller. Well respected for his craftsmanship, he was recognised and accepted by the Exeter gentry and bourgeoisie, as was his brother Benjamin. Very little is known about Benjamin Ezekiel except that his untimely death in October 1785 earned him the unusual honour of a brief obituary in the *Flying Post*:

> 'Last week died suddenly, as he was walking near St Bartholomew's yard, Mr Benjamin Ezekiel, for many years a respectable inhabitant of this city...'

Cameo of Henry Ezekiel

It is likely that Benjamin Ezekiel is buried in the old Jewish cemetery which opened in 1757, although no tombstone for him has survived today.

In 1763 Benjamin's brother Abraham Ezekiel and Kitty Jacobs leased a plot of land behind St Mary Arches Church in Synagogue Place for the purpose of building a synagogue. The lease was transacted through an intermediary because in the 1760s by English Law Jews could not directly lease land. Abraham Ezekiel's name also appears on the first lease for the Jewish burial ground in Magdalen Street a few years earlier in 1757. Little else is known about Abraham Ezekiel except that he contributed to Exeter's poor and is recorded as paying paid 2d a week to Exeter's Poor Rate in the 1750s.[27] In 1760 he was granted the administration of the goods of Mordecai Solomon, deceased, as creditor.

Synagogue interior, 1910

---

[27] Exeter Poor Rate Book, 1752-6, p.125.

Abraham Ezekiel lived in Exeter for fifty years and moved to Portsmouth around 1796 to live with his daughter Rosy after separating from his wife Sarah, with whom he had had six children. He died there in 1799. In his obituary that year he was described as a 'respectable tradesman of Exeter.'[28] Two of his daughters Amelia and Catherine and two sons Henry and Ezekiel are known to have remained in Exeter and are buried in the old Jewish cemetery.

Ezekiel Abraham Ezekiel

Ezekiel Abraham Ezekiel became one of the most prominent members of the Exeter Jewish community during the late 1700s.[29] Born in 1757 to Abraham and Sarah Ezekiel, he was one of the first Jews to be born in the city since the Expulsion of 1290. He was the eldest of at least six children, and at the age of fifteen in 1772 he was apprenticed to Exeter goldsmith Alexander Jenkins. Towards the end of the apprenticeship Ezekiel produced his first engraving which was a view of Bideford. An advertisement for the engraving appeared in the *Flying Post* on 23 July 1779:

'A Perspective of Bideford is just published by Subscription. Engraved by Ezekiel. Sold by Mr Henry Mugg, Bookseller, and the Engraver, at Mr Ezekiel's, Silversmith, Exon; also by Mr John Jewell the Author,

Ezekiel Ezekiel's trade card

Ezekiel engraving of Chichester Family Arms

at Bideford, by whom Youth are genteelly Boarded and instructed in all the Branches of Practical Mathematics. Price 10s 6d in Colours 12s 6d.'

In February 1784 Ezekiel placed a large advertisement in the *Flying Post* listing his skills:

'...by constant Supply of new Patterns from London, executes Perspective and Ornamental Copper Plate engraving, Shop Cards, Draughts, Bills of Exchange, Household Plate, Seals in Steel, Silver, and Stone, Merchants and all other stamps, in the newest and most elegant taste:- Neat Copper Plate Printing, on reasonable Terms, Jewellery Work in general, with curious Devices in Hair, done in the most pleasing Manner. Mourning Rings and all Funereal Engraving, on the shortest Notice.'

Perhaps not unsurprisingly the nature of Ezekiel's work meant that he was prolific. He published his own ornately engraved trade card dating to around 1797 which advertised him as an engraver and optician. He also sold spectacles, telescopes, gold seals, plate, watches, cutlery and prints.[30] Spectacles he sold in silver, tortoiseshell and steel as well as reading glasses, microscopes and magic

---

[28] *Sherborne and Yeovil Mercury*, 2 December 1799.
[29] Much of what appears about Ezekiel Abraham Ezekiel is due to the years of dedicated research carried out by Frank Gent who has generously granted permission for it to be used in this book.
[30] *Trewman's Flying Post*, 13 March 1800.

Ezekiel clock   *Ezekiel engraving of Exeter surgeon John Patch*

lanterns. He engraved bookplates,[31] and produced many trade cards for other people and local gentry.[32] Perhaps the finest works are his portraits of Thomas Glass in 1788, Exeter surgeon John Patch in 1789,[33] Major General Stringer Lawrence c.1790, William Holwell and John Marshall in 1798. His portrait and stipple engraving of Micaiah Towgood 1794 (dissenting Minister of Exeter 1700-92) are now in the British Museum. Ezekiel engraved the headline used for a time by the *Flying Post* and also the breastplate of the Third Exeter Volunteer Corps. By 1795 Ezekiel added the skill of optician to his profession and claimed to be the first expert in the field in the Westcountry. His microscope with slides is displayed in the Exeter Museum. On 27 April 1796 he took out an insurance policy on business premises in Fore Street as 'engraver, clock & watchmaker, optician, printseller and dealer in plate'.

In 1799 Ezekiel advertised as a miniaturist and achieved quite a reputation in this field. His self-portrait was exhibited at the end of the nineteenth century but its whereabouts are now unknown. As a silversmith Ezekiel registered eight pieces of work at the Exeter Assay Office. Although the record is brief it mentions eight silver medals, all hallmarked in February 1801, and one seal hallmarked the following year in September 1802. Ezekiel employed James Richard, a Gentile, as an engraver and pupil. It was after Ezekiel's death that Richard carried on the business.

Another advert was placed by Ezekiel in the *Flying Post* in June 1805, but by now his health was already failing. He was discharged from the Militia List on grounds of health releasing him from any duty of military service in the war with France. Just eighteen months later on 13 December 1806 he died. The *Flying Post* carried a lengthy obituary which shows the affection and standing he had not only acquired amongst his own people in the Jewish congregation but also the wider Exeter community:

'On Saturday last died aged 48, Mr E. A .Ezekiel, of this city, engraver and jeweller. He had long lingered under the complaint of dropsy and contemplated his

---

[31] Fourteen of which are recorded in publications. One exists in the Jewish Museum and seven more in the British Musuem.
[32] Five are in the British Library and his own trade card in the Victoria and Albert Museum.
[33] Now in the British Museum.

dissolution with a most religious resignation. He was followed to the grave by many respectable persons, who have for several years, passed enjoyed the pleasure of his agreeable conversation, and the attachment of his unshaken friendship. In the profession of an engraver, he possessed a correct taste, a happy facility in making designs, to meet the ideas of his employers, and as a workman, he was certainly unequalled out of London. His portraits of several distinguished characters in this city and neighbourhood will always be admired for their faithful execution... In a word there are few men whose loss will be more felt, not only by his immediate friends and connections, but by the public at large. A discourse was delivered at the grave, previous to the interment, by the chief priest of the Synagogue; who, truly and affectingly, held up the deceased as a pattern for imitation, both as a good son and brother, a good man and a good citizen of the world.'

Ezekiel never married. He had lived in Exeter with his brother Henry and unmarried sisters Kitty and Amelia at 179 Fore Street, just a short walk from the synagogue which their father had founded. He requested to be buried in the Jewish cemetery in Magdalen Street next to his mother Sarah who had died at the age of 70 in June of that same year. Today there is no official burial register for either of them, neither is there a tombstone to mark their resting places. The oldest extant headstone in the burial ground dates to 1807.

Ezekiel's original will dated 18 September 1806 was destroyed along with other wills at the Exeter Probate Registry during the blitz on Exeter in 1942. Fortunately a copy had already been made and a transcript survives. Ezekiel appointed as trustees his brother Henry and brother-in-law Benjamin Jonas (of Plymouth Dock).[34] It was witnessed by Emanuel Levy and Samuel Benedict of Exeter. When probate was granted in January 1807 the estate was valued at just under £600, not an insignificant sum for that time. In the will, Ezekiel requested that the synagogue minister Rev. Moses Levy say *Kaddish* (the mourner's prayer) for him for eleven months, usually the duty of a son. Ezekiel bequeathed the sum of eight pounds to the synagogue for the purchase of 'a good Time Piece Clock to be erected and put up in the said Synagogue'.[35] His eldest sister Rosy Nathan in Portsmouth, who had taken in their father after their parents separated in 1796, received only one shilling. His other sister Anne Jonas of Plymouth Dock received five pounds in recognition of her 'great attention of duty to our dear mother and to me.' For brother Henry there were all his Hebrew and English books 'to be delivered to him on his marriage by either of my sisters Kitty or Amelia and in the interim to have them occasionally'. The rest of the estate was bequeathed equally to sisters Kitty and Amelia. Nearly thirty years later Ezekiel Ezekiel's eminence was still remembered amongst a list of names in 1830 of 'Persons of Eminence, Genius and Public Notoriety, Natives of Exeter'.[36] Today some of his engravings survive in the Devon and Exeter Institution and once hung in its main entrance as a fitting reminder of one of Exeter's finest artists.

Henry Ezekiel

Henry Ezekiel, COURTESY OF JEWISH MUSEUM LONDON

Born in 1773 to Abraham and Sarah Ezekiel, Henry Ezekiel was the younger brother of Ezekiel Ezekiel. Henry traded as a watchmaker in the city and seems to have made a good living and prospered as a middle class gentleman. Two surviving portraits in the Jewish Museum, London of Henry Ezekiel and his wife Betsy testify to a well-attired and comfortable couple. He married Betsy Levy in Exeter on 14 March 1810 at the age of thirty-eight. Their ketubah (religious wedding document) survives in the Jewish Museum, London. Betsy was ten years younger than Henry. They had three daughters, all of whom eventually married. Their second daughter Georgiana married John Levi on 6 March

---

[34] Today called Devonport.
[35] Today there is no trace of this clock.
[36] A series of biographies of distinguished Exonians written by Revd Dr. George Oliver.

FOUNDATION OF THE COMMUNITY FROM THE 1720s

Betsy Ezekiel, COURTESY OF JEWISH MUSEUM LONDON

Below left: *Tombstone of Henry Ezekiel*
Below right: *Tombstone of Betsy Ezekiel*

1839;[37] and youngest daughter Eleanor married Isaac Mosely on 21 June 1843.[38] The eldest daughter, Selina, was the last to marry. On 19 October 1841 she wedded Arthur Wellington Hart at 129 Fore Street, Exeter.

Henry Ezekiel was one of the main characters in the life of the Exeter Jewish community for around thirty years. In October 1818 he placed an advert thanking those in the city who had aided and assisted the warden, elders and congregation after a calamitous fire. No report of the event itself seems to have appeared in the local newspapers.

Henry Ezekiel did not live to see any of his daughters marry. He died on 10 November 1836 and is buried in the cemetery in Magdalen Street. His wife Betsy died on 16 September 1851 at the age of 68. She is also buried in the cemetery in Magdalen Street. After Henry's death, the two sisters Kitty (Catherine) and Amelia continued to run the business. Their names are given in the Trade Directories as carrying on the business as "C & A. Ezekiel, Engravers and Opticians" at 179 Fore Street until 1830. According to the headstone in the cemetery, Catherine Ezekiel died on 3 July 1837 aged 69;[39] and sister Amelia Ezekiel according to the Hebrew calendar on 13th Sivan 1839 aged 60. They are also buried in the old Jewish cemetery. Three dedicated generations of the Ezekiel family contributed to the synagogue and the city for three-quarters of a century.

---

[37] Their marriage is No.4 in the synagogue marriage register. Georgiana as Mrs Levy died at the age of 50 on 12 September 1874 at 7 Augustine Road Camden. She is buried in the Willesden Jewish Cemetery, London.
[38] No.11 in the synagogue marriage register. Eleanor died on 13 February 1896 aged 78.
[39] Although the death certificate says 6th June = 23rd-24th Sivan.

Moses Mordecai Hart

The 1780s saw the arrival of Moses Mordecai Hart, a goldsmith who registered his mark at the local Assay Office in 1788. Hart worked as an engraver in seals, stamps, plate, copper and pewter. He had registered his mark at the Exeter Assay Office and ran a jewellers shop in Fore Street, Exeter. In the *Exeter Directory* for 1792 he is mentioned as one of the principle traders of the city. Moses Hart was one of the names on the renewed lease of 1803 for the old Jewish cemetery, and again in 1807. His illustrated a family pedigree dating to 1799 appeared as Item 761 in the *Anglo-Jewish Historical Exhibition Catalogue* of 1888 but has since been lost. He died in 1809 and is probably buried in the old Jewish cemetery, although today the earliest surviving tombstone dates to 1827. His original will of 1808 was written in Yiddish and contained an unusual clause:

'I solemnly prohibit my wife to marry Mr Bendix, nor shall she take him as a lodger and in case of her doing it nevertheless, then she shall have no more money than her ketubah (marriage settlement) £20, or to arrest her £1,000.'[40]

Hart may well have suspected his wife of improper behaviour with Bendix (a member of the synagogue) and wanted to prevent a relationship between them after his death.

By the end of the late 18th century and into the 19th, the Exeter Jewish community was at its height. It was no longer made up predominantly of immigrants but Exeter-born Jews as the 1841 census reveals.[41] This was a well-settled viable community.

Above: *Seats with scrolled armrests, ground floor of synagogue*
Below: *View of the bimah, reading desk*

---

[40] Susser, *The Jews of South-West England*, p.83.
[41] The 1841 census shows that only 20 Jews were foreign; over 106 were born in Exeter or England.

CHAPTER 3
THE SYNAGOGUE

EXETER'S GEORGIAN synagogue is one of the rare gems of Anglo-Jewish heritage. The Grade II Listed building with stucco white front that has survived for nearly three centuries has changed little since its foundation two hundred and fifty years ago. As the third oldest synagogue in the country and second oldest outside London, regular services are still held and it is a thriving community today. The discreet unassuming place of worship is located in Synagogue Place, the only Jewish named street in the city. The synagogue was built in 1763, within a decade of a bitterly contested Parliamentary election when a local MP was unseated for supporting Henry Pelham's unpopular Jews' Naturalisation Bill. The so-called 'Jew Bill' was eventually repealed. The general anti-Jewish feeling at this time may explain the synagogue's modest, plain exterior and the fact that it is tucked away down a lane. 'The exterior in times of mob riots was anonymous and originally devoid of windows, although some were later added,' wrote the architect Edward Jamilly in *The Georgian Synagogue*.[42]

On 5th November 1763 a lease was taken out for a piece of land behind St Mary Arches Church near Fore Street. It was on this land that the synagogue was built. The lease for a 'parcel of ground in the parish of St Mary Arches' was granted to Abraham Ezekiel and Kitty Jacobs via an intermediary because in English Law at that time Jews were not permitted to directly lease land. The Ezekiel family went on to lead and support the community for the next seventy-five years. After almost a year in construction the newly-built synagogue was consecrated on 10th August 1764. A description of the opening ceremony survived in a family Bible from the period, although the whereabouts of the Bible is unknown today. The description survives in a letter in the synagogue archives:

> *'August 10th, 1764: This day the Jews consecrated their new synagogue in the City of Exeter. The service began with prayers for the King and Royal Family. As soon as those prayers were ended, the music which consisted of two violins, a hautboy and bassoon played God save the King. They then carried the Law of Moses seven times round their reading desk and between the times of carrying it the following psalms were sung: 1-7, 30, 24, 84, 122, 132 and 100. After these psalms and some prayers they stopped about half and hour and then said the first service of their Sabbath, the whole lasted above three hours.'*[43]

Exeter synagogue exterior, c.1910, facing a mattress factory. To the right of the synagogue is a building that housed the minister and religion school

---

[42] Edward Jamilly, *The Georgian Synagogue*, p.18.
[43] Letter dated 17 July 1929 in the synagogue archives at the Devon Record Office.

Exterior of synagogue today

behind the original building was purchased and the building extended to meet the needs of the growing community. The expansion programme meant that the synagogue could seat around 80 to 90 and the Ark was again located on the north wall. A ladies' gallery was added and an octagonal glass roof to light the interior. The Greek Revival porch which is flanked by Doric columns was also added in 1835/6.

Today this beautiful interior gives witness to almost three centuries of continuity and worship. It is a simple yet intimate and charming house of prayer. Above the gilded Ark which houses the scrolls of the Torah is the Decalogue (the Ten Commandments of Moses) inscribed in Hebrew. Architectural synagogue historian Dr Sharman Kadish comments that 'Exeter's Ark is much simpler than Plymouth's and was probably made by local naval joiners or travelling craftsmen. Both share the use of gilding and *scagliola*.'[47] It has been suggested that the Ark was crafted in Europe, possibly Germany, or made in England along the continental style. In the centre of the synagogue is the wooden *bimah*, or central dais, from where services are led. The *bimah* has an elegant rail and candelabra which have been converted to electricity. Along the north and south walls are wooden seats, traditionally reserved for male worshippers. The back pews have beautiful scrolled armrests and tilting book-

During the opening ceremony the scrolls of the Torah were paraded seven times around the Bimah and was followed by the singing of the National Anthem. Over the double entrance doors from the lobby into the main sanctuary is a Hebrew inscription which reads 'Pray according to the law towards Jerusalem'. The original synagogue may have been single-storey and consisted only of the area which today is occupied by the vestibule, side room and toilet.[44] It seated around 30 people and the Ark was located on the north wall, probably free-standing as in the case of most Georgian synagogues.[45] During her 1998 survey on the Ark Eddie Sinclair, conservator and analyst of historic polychromy, discovered that the original Ark of 1763 presented a colour scheme of blue which gave it an altogether different appearance which was much richer. She comments: 'Blue was once the most expensive colour available, and its use highlights the status of the Community at the earlier period... The use of blue ties up with the polychromy of the Ark in the Plymouth Synagogue.'[46]

The perimeters of today's synagogue building was the result of extensive work in 1835/6 when a piece of land

Doric porch entrance to the synagogue

---

[44] Discussions with Frank Gent.
[45] Sharman Kadish, *The Synagogues of Britain and Ireland*, p, 26.
[46] Eddie Sinclair, 'Interim Polychromy Report. Exeter Synagogue: Ark Polychromy, 1998.
[47] Sharman Kadish, *op.cit*, p. 26.

THE SYNAGOGUE

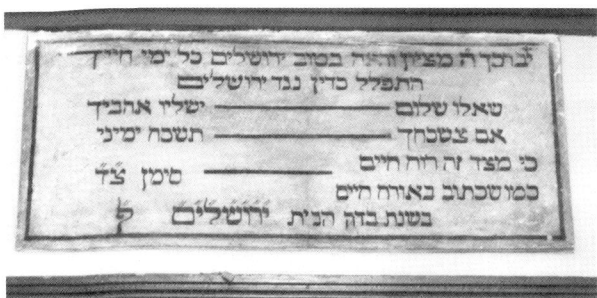

Inscription over interior lobby entrance to synagogue

rests for the use of prayer books during the service. Above is the ladies' gallery which is supported on slender, stencilled pillars and plain panelled fronts. The same beautiful interlocking curved metalwork surrounds the ladies' gallery as the central dais below.

The synagogue once housed a mikveh, or ritual bath, on the second floor for use by women of the congregation according to Jewish tradition.[48] There is no second floor today, having been destroyed when an incendiary device exploded at the side of the building in the Second World War. The mikveh had fallen into disuse long before that, however during its existence it was known to have been used for the conversion of two Gentile women to Judaism, three children and one male. One of the women was 'Miriam daughter of Abraham', wife of Jonah Solomon. Her conversion and use of the mikveh for the occasion took place in 1810. Since her son Baruch was born prior to her conversion, he was not legally Jewish. He needed to undergo formal conversion which took place on 7 October 1811. Two years later a mother and two daughters were immersed in the mikveh for the purposes of conversion. The mother was the 'mistress of Menachem Mendel ben Ze'ev Wolf of Exeter, and her four year old daughter Rebecca and two year old daughter Leah.[49] In the late 1830s the synagogue's mikveh fell into disuse and for religious ritual purity Exeter' Jewesses preferred to use a natural spring at a pub at the North Gate. In 1838 the congregation tried to regulate the situation by specifying that the women could only use a mikveh of specific requirements and size, thus excluding the natural spring as falling outside those requirements. The situation became the subject of correspondence between community members and the Chief Rabbi in London. The community replied to the Chief Rabbi:[50]

> *One {a mikveh} was formed on the same building as the shul {synagogue} at a cost of not less than £80, but from necessity of being built on the second floor and the apparatus to heat the water being above that again and the difficulty of obtaining a supply of water and the injury it produced to the premises we were reluctantly*

View from the ladies' gallery

> *impelled to abandon its use within the last eighteen months and consequently the Public Baths are now resorted to where there is a bath constructed which on investigation is found to be within two inches of the prescribed rule for size as being kosher. But we regret to add that on account of a trifling extra expense it is not generally used.*

By 1844 the use of the mikveh had been abandoned. The spring at North Gate had failed when the railway cut through to Central Station. Today, no mikveh exists in the synagogue and the practice has fallen into disuse.

Scrolls and Ritual Silver

Exeter Hebrew Congregation has six scrolls of the Torah. One is Sephardi, possibly Yemeni, with a suggestion that it is as old as around 1450. Historian and former president Frank Gent suggests it is more likely to date to 1850. The oldest item of ritual silver owned by the Exeter Jewish community pre-dates the synagogue itself. It is a silver *kiddush* cup with no hallmark but bears the date 1732 and the initials RS. It was used by the earliest settlers in Exeter to say a blessing over wine. It is now in the Jewish Museum, London. An exquisite set of *rimmonim* (ceremonial bells to adorn the Torah scroll) was made for the Exeter synagogue by Simon Harris of Plymouth Dock in 1813. Harris registered his hallmark SH at the Exeter Assay Office at the turn of the 19th century. The 1813 rimmonim consist of 'three open-work crowns in a tier, surmounted by a pineapple. The bells

---

[48] Susser, *The Jews of South-West England*, p. 134.
[49] Susser, op. cit, p.237.
[50] Chief Rabbinate Archives, MSS 104, p.37.

THE JEWS OF EXETER

Torah scrolls and adornments

Simon Levy wine strainer, 1823
COURTESY EVELYN FRIEDLANDER

Below left: *Rimmonim, Simon Levy, 1811*
COURTESY EVELYN FRIEDLANDER

Below right: *Exeter rimmonim, Simon Harris, 1813*
COURTESY EVELYN FRIEDLANDER

are inside the crown.'⁵¹ The inscription reads: 'Donated to the Exeter community in the year 573 (=1813).' No record appears to have survived for who donated them.

Exeter possesses a second pair of equally exquisite silver rimmonim, made in 1811 by Simon Levy and hallmarked SL at Exeter Assay Office. They each consist of several tiny bells on a stem-like tree with velvet cushion crown on the pinnacle and were given in the name of seventeen local Jewesses. It may be that the women collected money for the bells to be made or that they were donated because of exceptional worth of these women in the community. The beautiful Hebrew inscription engraved by a member of Birmingham Jewish community reads in translation:⁵²

> *These bells are a gift in the name of the following women and maidens of Exeter in honour of God who merited his blessing in the holy congregation of Exeter; the intermediate Shabbat Chol haMoed 9ᵗʰ Nissan. I engrave and sign my name Avigdor the son of Chaver Yishai, in the holy congregation of Birmingham:*
> *Kaila the daughter of Chaver Abraham*
> *Sarah the daughter of Shimi*
> *Malka the daughter if Chaver Abraham*
> *Baila the daughter of Shumuel the Levite*
> *Gitcha the daughter of Yechiel*
> *Rachel the daughter of Mchor Abraham*
> *Bryna the daughter of Gershon*
> *Motta the daughter of Yehuda*
> *Kaila the daughter of Shimon the Levite*
> *Yochebed the daughter of Yehuda*
> *Esther the daughter of Menachem*
> *Gulta the daughter of Chaver Nathan*
> *Gela the daughter of Moshe*
> *Hannah the daughter of Moshe*
> *Gresla the daughter of Moshe*
> *Esther the daughter of Chaver Isaac*
> *Sarah the daughter of Menachem*

The community has several *yadim*, or pointers, for use during the reading from the scroll. A *yad* was made for the congregation by Simon Harris in 1814 and has 'a barley twist shaft with an octagonal handle, divided by an incised knop with matching finial.'⁵³ The Hebrew inscription shows it to have been a gift from Reb Shmuel, son of Zvi Hart minister. For the Falmouth synagogue in 1815 Harris made a silver pointer with 'spirally fluted shaft and an octagonal handle, divided by a basketwork knop with a matching finial.'⁵⁴ It is engraved with a Hebrew inscription dating to 1836 which reads: Israel son of Naphtali Hirsch, Truro 5596'. Today it is in the collection of the Jewish Museum, London. In 1864 a silver shield, or breastplate, used to decorate the scroll of the Torah was given by Solomon Elsner in memory of his wife Rosina. It was made in Birmingham in 1863-4 by George Unité and bears the hallmark GU. In September 1941 a perpetual lamp was given to the synagogue in memory of the late Andrew Block by his sons. In 1986 a pair of fine blue velvet Ark curtains were received from Kingston Synagogue and are still in use today. In September 2000 two new sets of Rimmonim were given to the synagogue, thanks to the Redstone Family and the Ralph Collett Family Trust. Today the valuable objects of ceremonial silver are not used for services but have been distributed between the Jewish Museum and the bank vault.

Festivals, Services and Marking Royal Occasions

On 20 August 1854 the community marked the first ever visit from a Chief Rabbi to the synagogue. Chief Rabbi Rev Dr Nathan Adler had been staying in Torquay and arranged to travel by train to Exeter where he was met at the station by the President Alexander Alexander, the minister Rev. Meyer Mendelssohn and members of the committee. The Chief Rabbi was escorted to Alexander's home in a carriage and pairs for a breakfast. Afterwards he visited the old cemetery as well as other places owned by the community. At around 1pm he arrived at the synagogue to conduct the wedding ceremony of Rev. Albu and Miss Silverstone which he did in full ceremonial robes. The *Jewish Chronicle* reported that the synagogue was 'crowded to excess; the ladies' gallery particularly so.'⁵⁵ After the service an elegant sit-down lunch for around 70 people was provided in an inner

---

⁵¹ Exhibition catalogue of The Hidden Legacy Foundation: *The Jews of Devon and Cornwall*.
⁵² Kindly translated by Rabbi David Katanka.
⁵³ Catalogue of *The Jews of Devon and Cornwall*, p.91.
⁵⁴ Exhibition catalogue of The Hidden Legacy Foundation: *The Jews of Devon and Cornwall*.
⁵⁵ *Jewish Chronicle*, 1 September 1854.

Interior for High Holy Days

chamber of the synagogue. The room was decorated with flowers and foliage, and confectionary was provided by Mrs Wolfe of North Bridge in Exeter. Afterwards Alexander Alexander offered a toast to the Queen and the Royal Family. This was followed by a toast to the health of the Chief Rabbi. Alexander was ably supported that day by other prominent community members: Mr M Lazarus, B Myers, Mr Elsner, Mr Wolffe, Mr Barnard, Messrs Jonas, D Lazarus, J Lyons and J Alexander. The Chief Rabbi returned thanks and expressed a desire to see a continuation of community harmony and hoped that a school would soon be founded under their new minister Rev Mendelssohn. He spoke of the 'spirit of religion and harmony which seemed to pervade the congregation. He was happy to find that they were now a united congregation.'

Speaking on behalf of Christians present at the synagogue for the Chief Rabbi's visit, Mr Latimer expressed hope that Jews would soon receive equal status in the law as their Christian brethren. In the vestry afterwards he told them: 'it was both un-Christianly and unjust to exclude the Jew from the several privileges which were attached to citizenship... The time could not be far distant when the exclusive laws which disgraced the Statute Book would be removed.'[56]

Offering up a toast to the Queen and Royal Family that day was not unusual. The loyalty of Jews in England to the Crown over successive centuries has never been in doubt. Every Sabbath in synagogues across England a special Prayer is recited for the Royal Family. Exeter is no exception. The Exeter congregation has also marked moments of national importance. In 1821 a special service took place in the synagogue led by Revd Levy to mark the Coronation of George IV. It was reported that Revd Levy gave 'an excellent lecture' before the congregation sat down to a 'handsome dinner'.[57]

On the occasion of Queen Victoria's visit to Exeter in 1845 Alexander Alexander, the then president of the Jewish community, forwarded an address to Her Majesty and received a generous reply. On the tragic death of Queen Victoria's husband Albert on 23 December 1861 the community chose to mark a period of official mourning. Within a fortnight of Albert's death a special service was held in the synagogue during which an impressive discourse was given by the minister Rev Mendelssohn. The synagogue's interior was 'draped in black and had a most mournful appearance'.[58]

For the festival of Pentecost in May/June each year the synagogue was decorated with flowers and shrubs. For the autumn Feast of Tabernacles a *succah* (temporary dwelling)

---

[56] Ibid.
[57] *Trewman's Flying Post*, 26 July 1821.
[58] *Jewish Chronicle*, 3 January 1862.

was erected by honorary officers in the synagogue yard. One year it was reported in the *Jewish Chronicle*: 'The public Succah attached to the synagogue is completed in all its decorations and will, it is hoped, impress all who visit it with solemnity.'[59]

Charity

Charity box

The *mitzvah* (good deed) of giving to charity is an important part of Jewish life and includes giving to non-Jewish causes. Throughout its history the Exeter synagogue has been conscious of its duty in this respect. Wealthier Jews provided for poor Jews of the city and the Minute Book of 1832 gives provision for poor relief in times of illness.[60] On occasion, poor Jews of the city were each 'provided by their more fortunate brethren with a good meal of meat and bread, together with a shilling in money.' Funds were also raised for the wider community. In June 1815 services were held in the synagogue by Mr Lightindale, Solomon and Braham (probably travelling officials) in aid of the Devon and Exeter Hospital, with an invitation to attend extended to non-Jews.[61] A donation of £30 was sent to the hospital and legacies from individual members received. It made such an impression that six further services were arranged. Good relations had existed between the Jewish community and hospital management since 1797 when the 'warden of the Jews' was granted two votes in the election of a new surgeon: one vote as an official representative; the other in a private capacity.

Circa 1830 the congregation founded a Society for Charity to the Poor. In 1860 the congregation, at the behest of its then president Myers Solomon, responded to a crisis facing Christians in Syria. On 23 September a lecture was given in the synagogue and a collection taken for the British Syrian Relief Fund. Those who contributed to the fund included Mr M. Solomon, S. Elsner, H. Davis, B. Myers, Asher Barnard, Rev D. Rooks, Emanuel Jacobs and Lionel Bernum.[62] That same year donations were also sent to the Jews of Morocco Relief Fund. Today the community continues to undertake work for charitable causes. Today a charity box originally from a non-conformist chapel is mounted on the left hand side wall in the vestibule entrance of the synagogue.

Marriages: 1838-1872

In 1837 parliament passed a law requiring all civil and religious marriages in England and Wales to be entered in a Marriage Register. Exeter synagogue was issued with its own Register for marriages which took place according to the rites and ceremony of Jewish tradition. Some of the weddings mentioned below were also announced in the *Flying Post*. Prior to 1838 marriages were often announced in the local newspaper. Notice of the following Jewish weddings appeared in the *Flying Post*: A. Abraham married in March 1824; R. Abraham in September 1830; Alexander Alexander in October 1830; P. Jacobs in June 1832 and Joseph Marks in June 1833.

Between 1838 and 1872, after which the community began to decline, there was a total of thirty weddings. The first entry in the register was for 10 January 1838 for the wedding of Moses Lazarus of Exmouth to Rebecca Schultz, second daughter of Lewis Schultz. Rev Green officiated in the ceremony which took place in the synagogue.

The second marriage took place on 13 June 1838 when Hyman Davis of 2 Wellington Place, St Sidwell's

Oil painting of Henry Ezekiel,
COURTESY OF JEWISH MUSEUM LONDON

---

[59] *Jewish Chronicle*, 14 October 1870.
[60] EHC Minute Book, 1832, p.27.
[61] *Trewman's Flying Post*, 22 June 1815.
[62] *Jewish Chronicle*, 12 October 1860.

married Rebecca Jacobs, second daughter of the late Jacob Jacobs. It took place in the bride's mother's home at 8 Lower North Street. The third entry in the register is for the marriage in the synagogue on 7 November 1938 between Abraham Barnett of London and Caroline Lazarus, the eldest daughter of Eleazar Lazarus. On 6 March 1839 John Levi, a comb manufacturer, married Georgiana Ezekiel, the daughter of the late Henry Ezekiel of Exeter. They were married by Revd Green at the Ezekiel home at 135 Fore Street Hill, Exeter. The next five weddings also took place in private houses rather than the synagogue. On 28 July 1839 Jacob Lyons of Plymouth married Phoebe Solomon, the eldest daughter of jeweller Woolf Solomon at 18 Bartholomew Street. Again Revd Green officiated. The next marriage took place in North Street on 6 September 1840 when 52-year old Eleazer Lazarus, who already had a family and a widower, married 50-year old Esther Jacobs. They are listed the following year on the 1841 census.

Another wedding did not take place for nearly a year when the congregation's minister Revd Michael Levy Green married Rosetta Davis on 23 June 1841 at 165 Fore Street. On 18 August that year the marriage of 26-year old Henry Jacobs to Anna Harris took place at 67 South Street. Ten years later they are listed on the 1851 Census with their children. Another daughter of Henry and Betsy Ezekiel married on 19 October 1841 when Selina Ezekiel was wedded to Arthur Wellington Hart at 129 Fore Street, Exeter. A copy of the wedding invitation has survived which states the couple request 'no gifts'. Eighteen months later Abraham Moses Rosenberg married Fanny Solomon in the synagogue on 5 April 1843. The *Flying Post* records a third Ezekiel family marriage when Ellen Ezekiel, another daughter of Betsy and Henry Ezekiel, married Abraham Mosely at 8 Friars Walk on 21 June 1843.

The only wedding to take place during 1844 was on 31 July at Fore Street Hill between Israel Mordecai Levy and Selina Schultz. Almost a year later on 8 June 1845 Abraham Kestenberg, who originated from Poland and had been living in Plymouth, married Phoebe Jacobs of Penzance at 11 North Street, Exeter. On 22 June 1845 the Temperance Hotel was the location for the next marriage of Solomon Zamoiski to Priscilla Aaron, daughter of Caroline and Samuel Aaron of Exeter. Samuel Aaron was a jeweller of 69 High Street. Solomon Zamoiski's father Saul was a merchant. The ceremony was witnessed by Moses Lazarus and Simon Levy, both prominent members of the synagogue.

It was seventeen months before another Jewish wedding took place in Exeter. On 16 September 1846 pedlar Samuel Joyful Lazarus, son of Eleazar and Julia Lazarus, married Nancy Lazarus in South Street. The next entry was three years later when, on 8 August 1849, Myers Solomon married Deborah Lazarus. Later that same month on 22 August the marriage took place at 173 Fore Street between Joseph Lazarus of London and Caroline

Alexander Bernard advertising his shop Hart & Co.

Davis, daughter of Morris Davis. The next thirteen marriage entries are tabulated below:

27 November 1850: Mark Burstin of Bristol to Esther Solomon, daughter of W. Solomon, married at 4 Friernhay Street.

13 August 1851: David Kauffman to Caroline Solomon, daughter of Isaac Solomon, married at 125 Fore Street Hill.

3 December 1851: Abraham Levy to Ann Lazarus in the Synagogue.

28 September 1853: Solomon Elsner, optician of 5 North Street, to Rosina Silverstone, lace manufacturer, resident at 107 Fore Street and daughter of silversmith Israel Silverstone, married in the Synagogue.

20 August 1854: Rev Berthold Albu, living at 39 Bartholomew Yard, minister, to Bella Silverstone, daughter of Israel Silverstone, witnessed by Moses Lazarus and Solomon Elsner. Chief Rabbi Dr Adler officiated at the ceremony.

16 June 1858: Myer Mendelssohn of Bartholomew Street, minister, to Rebecca Silverstone, daughter of Israel Silverstone, married in the Synagogue, witnessed by Alexander Alexander.

10 April 1861: Jacob Harris, widow and broker, to Emilie Mendelssohn, sister of the minister, married in the Synagogue and witnessed by Moses Lazarus and Lewis Saltz (sic).

1 October 1861: Abraham Samuel of Rotterdam, widower and merchant of 6 High Street, to Lavinia

38

Johnson, third daughter of Moses Johnson, in the synagogue, witnessed by Alexander Alexander and Asher Barnard.

22 October 1862: Maures Dyte, herbalist, to Esther Lazarus, dressmaker resident at Waterbeer Street and daughter of David Lazarus, in the Synagogue, witnessed by B Myers and Solomon Elsner.

3 April 1867: Aaron Aarons, jeweller of Waterbeer Street and son of Solomon Aarons, to Julia Lazarus, daughter of David Lazarus, in the Synagogue, witnessed by Alexander Alexander and Barnet Jonas.

23 April 1867: Jacob Abel, jeweller of 15 South Street, son of Isaac Abel a jeweller, to Esther Jacobs of Bartholomew Place, daughter of Henry Jacobs, in the Synagogue, witnessed by B Meyers and Gershon Grunbaum.

19 May 1869: Jacob Lowenthal, draper of Market Street to Esther Zamoisky of Paragon Place, daughter of Solomon and Priscilla Zamoisky, in the Synagogue, witnessed by Alexander Alexander and Barnet Jonas.

4 September 1872: Solomon Alexander, Jewish minister of Leeds, son of Wolf Alexander (teacher of languages), to Sarah Solomons, daughter of optician and jeweller Myers Solomons, married at 60 High Street, Exeter, by Revd A Barnett of London (her uncle) and witnessed by Julia Solomon and Aaron Aarons.

Some weddings were fairly lavish as in the case of Solomon Elsner's marriage to Rosina Silverstone in 1853. It was reported that there were 'numerous in attendance, including non-Jews, most of whom sat down to a rich dinner.'[63] When Rosina's sister married Revd Albu the following year, the ceremony was performed by Chief Rabbi Adler who was visiting Torquay on holiday at the time and afterwards the guests returned to 'an inner chamber of the synagogue … where dejeurner for about 70 persons was served.'[64]

An example of another spectacular Jewish wedding was the marriage in Dawlish on 9 January 1872 of Hannah Solomon, second daughter of Leon Solomon of Dawlish, to Lewis Samuel of Edgbaston, Birmingham. The ceremony was conducted by Rev. M.B. Levy and Rev. L. Canter of London's Western Synagogue. The bride's father was a prominent figure in Dawlish and a member of three synagogues: Plymouth for which he generously paid for extensive repairs to it in the 1800s; Western Synagogue, London to which he donated a stunningly beautiful mantle for the Torah; and Exeter with reference to him in the congregation's account book for 1855. A long account of his daughter's wedding appeared in the Exeter & Plymouth Gazette:

Marriage of Maudie Gabrielson to David Jacobson at Cedars, Exeter 1907

---

[63] *Jewish Chronicle*, 30 September 1853.
[64] *Jewish Chronicle*, 1 September 1854.

'On the wedding day the Post Office, hotels and principal shops, and parts of the town were decorated with banners and crowds collected at the house in which the marriage was performed. The munificence of the bride's family occasioned an intense effect in Dawlish. Mr Solomon presented £10 to the vicar of Dawlish for distribution among the needy. A dinner was given to workmen, railway employees and ringers (who had peeled church bells loudly all day).'[65]

Rose Solomon, wife of Leon Solomon of Dawlish

Local people were not the only ones to benefit from Leon Solomon's celebrations of his daughter's wedding. At Westminster Jews' Free School in London he paid for entertainment at the school. Solomon eventually moved from Dawlish to London where he died at 60 Hogarth Road, South Kensington on 12 November 1879 at the age of 68.

In some cases, the daughters of local Jews married outside Exeter as in the case of Caroline Hort, daughter of Abraham Hort of Exeter, who married Montague Alex of Cheltenham on 23 December 1863.[66]

Rabbis and Ministers

In the course of its 250 year history the community has engaged seventeen paid rabbis or ministers. Records survive for some of them, whilst for others, very little is known about their ministry. The records which do survive often describe a rocky relationship with the community. A cantor was appointed for services; and sometimes this could also be the minister or shochet [kosher slaughterer]. The Congregation Regulations of 1823 insisted that the cantor wore a formal uniform which consisted of a mantel, biff and hat. Failure to do so would land him with a fine of 2/6d for each offence.[67] In 1844 the shochet was paid 19s. 6d per week by the congregation.[68] Until the Second World War, the Rabbi or Minister wore a dog-collar during services like Christian clerics.

The first minister to be engaged at Exeter synagogue was Rev. Moses Horowitz Levy who originated from Danzig. He arrived in the city in 1792 and served the community for 44 years. He died in office in 1837 and is buried in the old Jewish cemetery. He became the longest serving of minister of the Exeter Hebrew Congregation. Moses Levy was succeeded by twenty-eight year old Rev. Michael Levy Green whose tenure lasted just two years. He came on the recommendation of Chief Rabbi Dr Solomon Herschell whose disciple he had been. Green was described as 'a man of striking personality, great force of character and wide culture.'[69] He had been educated at Jews' Free School in London and his younger brother Aaron became chazzan at Bristol Orthodox Synagogue. On 23 June 1841 Rev. Green married Rosetta Davis, the daughter of M. Davis, at 165 High Street, Exeter. To supplement his low pastoral salary Rev Green set up a clothes shop in the city. His actions did not bode well with the Jewish community who objected. When he refused to give up the shop they forced his swift exit from the community. The Exeter Minute Book records:

'Mr Green having opened a shop in opposition to the wishes of the members, unless he give it up in three months, that he have notice to quit the situation ... Mr

---

[65] Doreen Berger, *Jewish Victorian: 1871-1880*, p. 537.
[66] *Jewish Chronicle*, 25 December 1863.
[67] EHC Regulations, 1823, no.22.
[68] EHC Minute Book 1843-63.
[69] *Jewish Chronicle*, 25 March 1910.

Green's answer is "I have no intention of giving up my shop."

With the experience of Exeter well behind him, Green moved to London and went on to establish a successful career in business.

That same year Polish-born Rev. Samuel Hoffnung arrived as Exeter's new minister. He served the synagogue for twelve years but his service was overshadowed by disputes and financial problems. The shul's finances became impoverished due to the beginnings of a decline in membership and the office of Beadle as a separate position had to be abolished. The committee suggested that Hoffnung should take a reduction of £10 p.a in salary, however the resolution was not passed. Instead Hoffnung agreed to undertake the role of minister and Beadle for an extra £2 p.a, to which the community agreed. The relationship between Hoffnung and the community was a rocky one. One of the disputes occurred between Hoffnung and President Alexander Alexander. Their acrimonious dispute caused significant scandal at the time, centred on Hoffnung's whipping of Alexander's 15-year old son. It appeared that Hoffnung's resignation came after a dispute with community member Mr Marks which provoked Alexander Alexander to write a letter of complaint to the Chief Rabbi. The Chief Rabbi wrote directly to Hoffnung: 'Alexander the *parnas* [President] has written to me that you broke into a terrible passion in the Synagogue and said to Marks, "May you not reach the end of your journey". Is this true?'

Hoffnung's resignation was not the end of the matter. The community refused to pay his salary and he was left destitute. The Chief Rabbi intervened again and wrote to Alexander Alexander: 'no respectable leader will go now to Exeter to be exposed to such insults.' Respectfully, Hoffnung's service did not go unrewarded. However the Minutes from the Congregation for 1853 actually reveal a different dispute had broken out which caused Hoffnung's final resignation. It was alleged that during the funeral of the late Harris Jacobs, Hoffnung had refused to follow the corpse to the grave and given no defence for his actions. The synagogue committee accused their minister of 'great dereliction of duty'. Alexander proposed giving Hoffnung three month's notice of dismissal. The motion was passed by the following members: I. Silverstone, B. Jonas, D. Lazarus, A. Alexander and M. Solomon. Only J. Marks refused to vote. Hoffnung rose and told them he accepted their notice to leave. In spite of the difficulties which Hoffnung experienced at Exeter a brass plaque commemorating his ministry hangs on the wall of the synagogue and its inscription reads: 'This synagogue was renovated in memory of Rev S Hoffnung, minister 1840-1853, and of Sigmond Hoffnung his elder son.'[70]

Just prior to Hoffnung's departure those members who had remained faithful to him during the disputes organized a dinner in his honour. During the evening they presented him with a silver salver with the following inscription:

'Presented by Mr Moses Lazarus on behalf of the principal members of the Exeter Hebrew Congregation and friends to the Rev S Hoffnung, previous to him leaving this city, as a token of regard and esteem for his piety and zealous discharge of his duties during the last thirteen years. June 26th 5613 {1853}.'

In the speech which followed Moses Lazarus said, 'you have rejoiced in our rejoicings and mourned with us in our afflictions. I believe your opponents regret the step they have taken; and would willingly recall what they did if they could. If at any time you should remember the viper's sting in looking at this salver and the list of names attached to it, you will also remember your friends that were your support under unmerited persecution.' By 1860 Hoffnung was working in a synagogue in Montreal.[71]

Revd. Hoffnung was replaced in 1853 by twenty-eight year old Rev. Berthold Albu of Berlin, on the recommendation of President Alexander Alexander. At a special meeting convened on Sunday 3rd July 5613 [1853] members decided to approach Rev Albu. Present

---

[70] *Jewish Chronicle*, 25 March 1910.
[71] *Jewish Chronicle*, 23 November 1860.

at the meeting were Alexander Alexander, M. Solomon, E. Jacobs, B. Myers, Israel Silverstone, D. Lazarus and Mr. Marks. The Minutes of the Congregation record:

> *'The President having stated to the meeting that Mr. Albu, the candidate for the office of Cantor, Shochet, etc., having read in Synagogue yesterday, much to the satisfaction of the Congregation, we now come to the consideration whether he will be competent to fill the said office. Mr. A. Alexander proposes Mr. Albu for Shochet and Teacher. Seconded by Mr. M. Solomon. Carried unanimous.'*[72]

Rev. Albu, who had previously served as minister of Griqualand West Congregation, Kimberley, South Africa, stayed in Exeter for less than a year from July 1853-April 1854.[73] He was formerly invited to become the next minister after conducting a very satisfactory Sabbath service during which the synagogue committee were pleased with 'his great talent in correct reading and singing. He has a clear, distinct delivery, and having been a conductor of a choir in the synagogue at Berlin.'[74] During his ministry in Exeter Albu lived at 39 Bartholomew Yard and served not only as the rabbi but community shochet (kosher slaughterer) and chazzan (cantor). He left in April 1854 to become minister of the Cheltenham synagogue. On 20 August 1854 he married Bella Silverstone, daughter of Israel Silverstone of the Exeter, in the synagogue.[75] In 1858 he became brother-in-law to his successor at Exeter, Myer Mendelssohn, when Rev. Mendelssohn married Bella's sister.

Prussian-born Rev. Myer Mendelssohn arrived in Exeter in 1854 to replace Albu as the new minister. Aged just 22, he was the youngest minister to serve the community and enjoyed a stable and productive relationship with the congregation. On 16 June 1858 he married local Jewish girl Rebecca Silverstone, daughter of shopkeeper Israel Silverstone of 107 Fore Street in a ceremony that was conducted in the synagogue.

Side view of the synagogue

A son, Sidney, was born to them in Exeter in December 1860. Sidney Mendelssohn later distinguished himself with seminal works on Africa, including *South African Bibliography*; *The Jews of Africa*; and *The Jews of Asia*. The 1861 census shows that Mendelssohn's sister Emilie was also living with them at 2 Bartholomew Street and also a female servant. Mendelssohn taught Hebrew and German in local schools, and established his own school of languages in the city at 6 Maddock's Row. An advertisement for nine more male pupils appeared in numerous editions of the *Jewish Chronicle* in 1863, with the aim of attracting parents from London to send their sons to Exeter for study. One of the advertisements referred to Mendelssohn's school as the 'Devonshire Educational Establishment for Hebrew Youth.'[76] Mendelssohn's advertisement was quick to reassure interested parties that their son's studies would not be affected by strict adherence to the Sabbath and festivals, and 'the house is spacious and the salubrity of Exeter well-known.' The boys would receive moral and religious development while studying Hebrew and German. The following year Mendelssohn's advertisements

---

[72] Exeter Minute Book 1852-54.
[73] Albu died in 1899.
[74] *Jewish Chronicle*, 5 July 1853.
[75] *Jewish Chronicle*, 1 September 1854.
[76] *Jewish Chronicle*, 4 September 1863.

extended the languages on offer to include Latin, English and French.[77]

Mendelssohn stayed as minister until 1867 when, due to the community's decline, he moved to Bristol to become rabbi there. A copy of his resignation letter to the president and members of Exeter Hebrew Congregation exists in the Minute Books:

'Having been elected Minister of the Bristol Congregation I beg to resign my post in Exeter and tender you according to my agreement 3 months notice which will terminate on the 3rd September next. At the same time allow me to thank you most earnestly for the confidence you have placed in me and the kindness you have {...} to further my future prospects. I beg to assure you although I leave you I shall ever feel a deep interest for the welfare of this congregation where I have spent more than 12 years of my life. I entreat our heavenly Father to grant success to your community. I trust that peace and harmony may always reign among your members within the sacred walls of your synagogue for it is only in the fulfillment of these conditions that a place of worship is really hallowed before the God of Israel. Wishing you all long life, health and prosperity, I am, gentlemen, Yours very truly, M. Mendelssohn.'[78]

After Mendelssohn's office, subsequent ministers appointed to Exeter synagogue would not serve longer than six years, and often much shorter periods. In 1878 Mendelssohn moved from the Bristol community to Kimberley in South Africa. In 1909 Mendelssohn's two sons presented the Exeter synagogue with a set of curtains for the Ark in memory of their father's service to the community.[79] Between Rev. Mendelssohn and Rev Mark Harris, there were four ministers whose ministries were relatively short. They were Rev S. Alexander, originally from Poland who served from 1867-1869, then Joseph Lewis who was minister from 1869-1870, David Shapiro 1870-1871 and S. Bach 1871-1874. Joseph Lewis appeared to have departed Exeter by the autumn of 1870 because the High Holy Day services were conducted by Alexander Alexander as Alexander had done for 38 consecutive years. Additional services were led by the newly appointed reader Rev D. Shapiro who: 'has given great satisfaction since his recent appointment by his assiduity in discharging his duties.'[80]

Rev. Mark Harris, probably also known as Mordechai ben Eleazer Hertz, was appointed minister for only three months in 1874. His short period of service to the Exeter community is explained by an unfortunate accident that occurred whilst he was travelling on the Midland Railway line in 1874:

Memor Book (memorial)

First page of Memor Book

'The Rev. M. Harris of Exeter was among victims of the railway accident at Hornby Junction. Great kindness was shown to him by a Christian gentleman, Mr Cocking. When Mr Cocking ascertained Mr Harris was a Jew he went to Sheffield and obtained the services of Rev. Mr Tuchman, minister of the congregation.'[81]

During the 1870s the synagogue engaged a caretaker 67-year old Aaron Israel who, according to the 1871

---

[77] *Jewish Chronicle*, 15 April 1864.
[78] Congregation Minute Books (1860-1897), letter dated 3 June 5627.
[79] *Jewish Chronicle*, 22 October 1909.
[80] *Jewish Chronicle*, 7 October 1870.
[81] *Jewish Chronicle*, 18 December 1874.

Census, lived at 6 Synagogue Place and originated from Poland. The same census records the Reader of the congregation as David Shapiro, aged 45, who lived at Jubilee Place and also originated from Poland. It may be that they took over duties from Revd. Harris after his accident. Harris sustained severe spinal injuries in the accident which occurred near Sheffield and was taken to Holmes Station Hotel. From there he was transferred to London for appropriate attention and lay in a precarious condition.[82] Later that year Harris received £800 in compensation for injuries and losses due to the accident.[83] The following year he was well enough to be appointed minister to the Portsea Hebrew Congregation,[84] and by February 1889 he was resident in Kimberley, South Africa and appointed minister to the Witwatersrand Hebrew Congregation. It has not been possible to ascertain when he died, but he is buried in Bulawayo, Rhodesia (now Zimbabwe).

In January 1875 Harris was replaced Rev. Marcus Manovitz who came Oxford Hebrew Congregation. Very little is known about Manovitz's time in Exeter, except that he left the following year after the High Holy Day services in the autumn of 1876. He was succeeded at some point by Rev. Lazarus until 1878 when Rev M Davidson, late of Edinburgh, was appointed. The synagogue had been closed for several months in 1878 due to falling membership and it was regretfully reported that the synagogue did not open for its Passover services that year.[85] Davidson must have arrived after Passover because by the autumn he was there to officiate at the services for the New Year and Day of Atonement, assisted by Mr A. Greenbaum of Plymouth and B Jonas and Albert Myers.[86] In the interim period until the appointment of a new minister in 1895, the synagogue barely opened its doors except for High Holy Day services. In 1884 the New Year Services were provided by visiting minister Rev J. Fürst.[87]

In January 1895 the community held its first Sabbath service for seven years, although services had taken place each autumn for the High Holy Days only. This Sabbath service was officiated by Rev. I. Litovitch who had came from London to be the new minister and shochet. His ministry lasted less than two years and covered a period when the community had not recovered its former numbers. A committee was formed of president Charles Samuels, treasurer Samuel Fredman and Mr A Hyman as warden. In 1896 it was reported that the community had only four resident members and for High Holy Days had to rely on visitors to make up a minyan.[88] The community Minutes record a letter dated 20 March 1897 by president Charles Samuels to Rev. Litovitch giving his notice:

'On account of a few members declining to pay their weekly subscription, I am compelled to give you notice that your services as Minister and Shochet will not be required after six weeks ending May 1st and we shall want you to give up possession of the Synagogue House on that day. P. S. the reason of giving you 6 weeks notice is you should have time in obtaining another place, and wishing you every success.'

Tombstone of Rev Abraham Rosenberg

From Exeter Litovitch took up a post as chazan and shochet at Chester synagogue. Finances had barely recovered and the following two ministers served for less than a year. They were Rev. Rittenberg and Rev. Pearlstein. Rittenberg arrived in early 1898 and clearly made an impact because in appreciation of his services the community voted at the annual meeting on 3 April 1898 to increase his salary to £25 per annum and 'handed him a cheque as a mark of esteem'.[89] However he only remained in Exeter for six months before taking up post at Cardiff New Congregation.

Rev. S Pearlstein served at Exeter after Rev. Rittenberg until July 1899 when he left to join the newly

---

[82] *Jewish World*, 1 January 1875.
[83] *Jewish Chronicle*, 19 November 1875.
[84] *Jewish World*, 29 December 1876.
[85] *Jewish Chronicle*, 3 May 1878.
[86] *Jewish Chronicle*, 3 October 1879.
[87] *Jewish Chronicle*, 3 October 1884.
[88] 25 September 1896.
[89] *Jewish Chronicle*, 15 April 1898.

opened Yarmouth synagogue.[90] Rev H. Bregman replaced Pearlstein and served the community from 1899 to 1904 and lived at 2 Friars Hill. During his ministry he was instrumental in collecting funds for the relief of Russian Jews and encouraging local Christians to contribute.[91]

Rev Daniel Caplan, minister of Plymouth in 1906, served at Exeter for a short period until 1908. Caplan already had in mind to move from Exeter when he officiated at a Shabbat service for the Blackpool synagogue that year after which they offered him a post as their new chazan and shochet.[92] Abraham Rosenberg followed as Exeter's minister and served from 1908 until his death while in office on 12 May 1913 at the age of 61. He died at his home at 43 West Grove Road and is buried in the old Jewish cemetery.[93]

The last minister to serve the Exeter congregation in a full-time post was Shinerock from 1916-1917. Since Shinerock there has been no resident rabbi or full-time minister. For the past ninety-five years the community has relied on their own members to lead services or visiting rabbis and ministers. From the 1960s until the present day, Revd Malcolm Wiseman (minister for Small Communities) has periodically carried out services and marriages for the congregation. During the 1970s and early 1980s Rabbi Dr Bernard Susser, rabbi of Plymouth synagogue, travelled to Exeter to perform services. On 2 September 1964 when Exeter synagogue celebrated its 200th anniversary, a special ceremony for the occasion was led by Rabbi Susser. From the 1980s weekly Shabbat services were reinstated by Harry Freedman and drew in a revival in the community. After Freedman returned to live in London, services were periodically led by Rev. Wiseman and his colleague Elkan Levy until the latter's emigration to Israel in 2011.

Surviving records and archives

Inevitably over the last 250 years not all the synagogue records have survived. Those that have are housed today in the Devon Record Office. These include: the Exeter Minute Books of 1852-54 and 1860-1897 (parts of which are written in un-translated Yiddish), the Laws of Exeter Hebrew Congregation 1823, a Memor Book (a memorial book) dating to 1857,[94] two legers: 1818-1826 and 1827, and miscellaneous documents. Historian Cecil Roth wrote in the 1950s that 'the most important records and some interesting pieces of old silver are distributed between the Mocatta Library and the Jewish Museum, London'. An article in the *Jewish Chronicle* in 1910 reveals that the nephew of the synagogue's ex-minister Revd Michael Green gave a talk to The Jewish Historical Society on the subject of the Exeter Minute Books. In it the lecture he said that the Minute Books were originally in Hebrew but had been translated in 1823 by Henry Ezekiel, Eleazar Lazarus and Simon Levy so the members could understand obligations set upon them; for example, if a public meeting was called, all members must attend or be fined 5s.

Over the years, especially from the 1960s, Rabbi Dr Bernard Susser was dedicated to preserving and recording the history of the Jews of Exeter and Plymouth. After his sudden death in 1997 his daughter received a call from the caretaker of the block of flats where her parents lived, expressing concern about the number of black dustbin sacks which were lined up outside. Mrs Susser had been clearing out her husband's papers. Fortunately these papers were saved because of the foresight of the daughter and caretaker. The daughter telephoned the author [Dr Helen Fry] who had been in close touch with Rabbi Susser before his death. Helen went over to Brondesbury in North-West London to look at the piles of papers. The black sacks contained documents, letters, research papers and Minute Books that related either to Exeter and Plymouth, and one or two London communities. Helen notified Frank Gent of Exeter Hebrew Congregation who then made an immediate journey to London to view the papers. Rabbi Susser's daughter gave over the whole archive to Frank Gent who catalogued it and deposited it at the Devon Record Office where it remains today.

The value of keeping community records cannot be overestimated. What may appear to some people as scrappy notes or old minute books may be the key to understanding a community's early beginnings or the life of its people. Historic Jewish communities like Exeter need to be vigilant and mindful of ways of preserving its archives as a record for posterity. Consequently the Exeter synagogue's more recent documents, correspondence, newsletters from the 1980s and papers have been deposited at the Devon Record Office as part of the overall synagogue archive.

Frank Gent sorting through the Susser Archive

---

[90] *Jewish Chronicle*, 28 July 1899 and 8 September 1899.
[91] *Jewish Chronicle*, 5 July 1901.
[92] *Jewish Chronicle*, 27 March 1908.
[93] *Jewish Chronicle*, 16 May 1913.
[94] Survives in the collection of the Jewish Museum, London.

CHAPTER 4
SYNAGOGUE RESTORATIONS

THE SYNAGOGUE has been enlarged and modernised several times in the course of its 250 year history. Dealing with such an old building has its ongoing challenges. Rising-damp and ensuring adequate ventilation are amongst the most serious and have posed a major problem for at least the last hundred years. Repairs and implementing a solution to damp problems can be extremely costly, especially if the damp affects so much of the interior fabric of the building and its wooden furnishings. Eddie Sinclair, a conservator, researcher and

Line drawing by Mrs Cohen, presented to Elkan and Celia Levy 2011

analyst of historic polychromy, wrote, 'The building has not received the attention that it deserves; funding has long been a problem, in spite of a caring congregation, resulting in the current crisis'.[95] Her two surveys and conservation work in the late 1990s revealed some important facts about the history of the development of the building and the Ark in particular. These findings are interspersed in the text below and quoted with her kind permission.

The first major work to be undertaken was in 1835/6 when the community was able to purchase land immediately at the back of the synagogue to extend and rebuild the place of worship. The front entrance and façade changed too with the addition of a porch and two Doric columns. The sanctuary was no longer in the front vestibule area but built on land recently acquired at the back of the premises. The synagogue could now seat around 80 worshippers. During this phase of work the Ark was placed on the north wall and a ladies' gallery added. A plaque survives today over the door from the lobby into the synagogue with an inscription that was put up in 1836 when the Ark was moved. It reads in translation from the Hebrew:

> *'May the Lord bless you out of Zion,*
> *May you see the good of Jerusalem*
> *all the days of your life*
> *Pray according to the Law facing Jerusalem*
> *Seek the peace of Jerusalem*
> *If I forget you let my right hand*
> *forget its cunning*
> *for from this side is the spirit of life*
> *as it says in the Code of Jewish Law Chapter 94*
> *in the year of repairing the house*
> *Jerusalem.'*

During her Polychromy survey in 1998 Sinclair discovered that the Ark had undergone redecoration during 1835/6. She discovered a recurrence of 'a deep rich red colour, applied as a two layer structure [to the Ark]. The red itself is a mixed colour consisting of vermilion and ultramarine, combined together to make a rich crimson-red.' This was highly significant because artificial ultramarine was discovered in France in 1828 and would have been commercially available by the time of the 1835 restoration of the Exeter Ark. She writes, 'At this early date its use would have been quite significant in highlighting the status of the Community. It suggests that the Ark was painted according to the latest fashion.' The new enlarged synagogue was rededicated in a special ceremony in September 1836:

> *'A temporary orchestra was erected and the sacred music was well performed by Turner's band. An immense wax candle, in a splendidly gilt candlestick, was burning on each corner of the desk, which was enclosed within a circular railing; the pillars at the grand entrance door being tastefully entwined with flowers and evergreens for the occasion.'*

---

[95] Eddie Sinclair, 'The Restoration of the Ark Paintwork. Exeter Synagogue: Polychrome Survey,' 1996 and 'Interim Polychromy Report. Exeter Synagogue: Ark Polychromy, 1998.

Further renovations were carried out between 1853 and 1854 and the Ark moved to the south-east wall so worshippers could correctly orientate towards Jerusalem during prayer.⁹⁶ A re-consecration took place on the evening of 1 June 1854 and was attended by seatholders and their families, and some Christian friends. A special Hebrew prayer was composed for the occasion by the Chief Rabbi, Dr Nathan Adler and a collection was taken for the poor of Jerusalem. The *Jewish Chronicle* gave a full description of the occasion:

> 'Masters Alexander, E Lazarus and I Lazarus entered the synagogue bearing three wax candles decorated with the choicest flowers, and stood outside of the canopy, which was supported by Masters I Alexander, M Silverstone, H Davis and I Silverstone. And then followed the Reader the Rev Albu, the President Alexander Alexander, the Treasurer M. Solomon, the warden I. Silverstone and Mr S. Elsner, each carrying a scroll; when the Reader commenced the form of prayer, and continued the Psalms, making seven circuits around the synagogue. At the end, the sacred scrolls being placed in the ark, the Rev Albu read within the gates of the ark, the form of prayer and the prayer for the Royal Family, both in Hebrew and English; after which Mr Alexander, the President, gave an address; the service being concluded by the Reader. The whole ceremony occupied about a hour. The synagogue was beautifully decorated with the choicest flowers and certainly had a very lovely appearance.'⁹⁷

During his address on this occasion, Alexander Alexander interestingly referred to an earlier synagogue in Exeter: 'I find that as far back as a century and a quarter there existed in this city an assemblage of our brethren. Our burial ground contains monuments of that date of the time I have mentioned and about the year 5494 [1734] our brethren fulfilled the command given us in Exodus "let them build me a sanctuary". On this plot then they raised a miniature temple which stood for thirty years and in the year 5524 [1764]... that it is now ninety years since these present walls were raised.'⁹⁸

By 1854 a second storey had been added to the synagogue. A photograph dating to around 1910 given by President Charles Samuels to Exeter Museum, shows the imposing neo-classical three-storey façade of 1853/4. On the ground floor were three windows, one to the left of the main entrance and two to the right. On the first floor were three tall arched windows which were lost in the bombing. The windows were replaced with oblong windows when the war damage was finally sorted. The 1910 photograph also shows that the synagogue once faced a mattress factory in one of the poorest parts of central Exeter. At the end of Synagogue Place was the entrance to a court of overcrowded slum dwellings. At the side of the synagogue was a building that formerly belonged to the congregation and housed the *shammas* (religious official), the *cheder* (religion school) and the minister. It was sold at an unknown date and eventually demolished in the 1960s to make way for Elm House. The second storey was destroyed when a bomb fell at the side of the synagogue during the blitz on the city in the Second World War.

View from the ladies' gallery

---

⁹⁶ During the restoration and repairs in 1997-9, Frank Gent discovered the original hole for the Ark before it was moved to its current location.
⁹⁷ *Jewish Chronicle*, 9 June 1854.
⁹⁸ Copy in the synagogue archives.

In 1905 the building underwent further repairs as it was in such 'a dilapidated condition'.[99] The renovations were completed by August 1905 and were largely due to the efforts of Mr Lionel Lawrence, formerly a native of Exeter, who raised funds from London. He contacted the descendants of Exeter's former minister Revd S Hoffnung,[100] and grandson Sidney Hoffnung-Goldsmid agreed to fund the restoration if a plaque was erected in his grandfather's memory. This was agreed by the Exeter congregation. The plaque's inscription read: 'this synagogue was renovated in memory of the Rev. S Hoffnung, minister 1840 to 1853, and of Sigmond Hoffnung, his elder son, August 1905.'

The re-opening ceremony took place in early October 1905, officiated by the minister Rev. Bregman. In his address he told the congregation: 'We are assembled in God's house, in honour of our friend Mr Hoffnung-Goldsmid who has been kind enough to contribute to the cost of the decoration of the synagogue, in memory of his late father and grandfather.' Bregman went on to offer sincere and humble thanks for the good work he had done 'in having the place of worship decorated so beautifully so as to render it suitable for service.'[101] In recognition of Hoffnung-Goldsmid's generosity, on behalf of the community, Charles Samuels presented him with a richly ornamented album containing an inscription and list of all the subscribers. Watercolours of the synagogue and local scenes by Devon artists appeared on twelve pages of the album. The album does not appear to have survived. Two watercolours of the synagogue in 1900 by Scottish born artist John White which show the exterior and interior of the building at this time may have originally been included in the album. Both paintings were at one time in the Royal Albert Memorial Museum in Exeter but disappeared in the 1990s. In his response Mr Hoffnung-Goldsmid expressed his thanks for their great kindness. 'The satisfaction he had received in being able to see the work carried out was the only recognition he desired as the memorial of a great man whose deeds endeared him to his contemporaries, and caused him to be greatly beloved in his own circle.'[102] On that occasion a prominent part was also played by Mr B. Salmen of the Board of Deputies in London, a representative for Exeter on the board as well as Trustee of the Exeter Jewish Burial Ground. He presented the synagogue with a Torah scroll and mantle in memory of his father Samuel Salmen.[103]

During the early half of the 20th century the community relied on outside donations to maintain its synagogue. Immediately after the 1905 renovations Mr Hoffnung-Goldsmid was able to send the community an anonymous donation of £25, as well as the sum of £10 10s. from Louisa Lady Goldsmid and £5 5s. from Mrs S Hoffnung.[104]

During the Second World War the city of Exeter, like Plymouth, was heavily blitzed by German bombers. Few parts of these cities escaped damage or civilian loss of life. The synagogue suffered partial damage when the first floor of the building was lost. The synagogue sanctuary itself was unaffected; however the flat above the porch where the minister once lived, and later the caretaker, was so badly damaged that it was demolished. The synagogue was rarely used afterwards, due to a combination of its poor condition and dwindling numbers. There were only a handful of Jews in Exeter, amongst them the Boam, Harris, Smith and Glynn families. The synagogue underwent another refurbishment in 1962 under the presidency of Mr Harris. This period saw some repairs carried out to the front of the building that had been damaged in the war and an application to the War Damage Commission for compensation. The work went out to tender. The lowest of four quotations for the work came from Messrs Herbert & Son at a total cost of £1,382.[105] Repairs to the slate roof the following year amounted to £110. However it was discovered in 1969 that the synagogue was suffering from rising damp, rot and wood beetle infestation due to the damp conditions. This situation more than any dwindling numbers in the community threatened the continued existence of the building. Work needed to be carried out to spray all timber surfaces, take out the *bimah* and remove the floor so that joists could be treated or replaced and rubble removed to improve ventilation. It may have been

A rare photograph of the synagogue after bomb damage in WW2

---

[99] *Jewish Chronicle*, 6 October 1905.
[100] *Jewish Chronicle*, 28 December 1906.
[101] *Jewish Chronicle*, 6 October 1905.

[102] Ibid.
[103] *Jewish Chronicle*, 13 October 1905.
[104] *Jewish Chronicle*, 27 October 1905.

The Ark, circa 1836. COURTESY EDDIE SINCLAIR

Presented in memory of Jack Posner.

during this period of structural work on the sanctuary that Rabbi Dr Bernard Susser happened to visit the synagogue and found Minute Books dating from the 1820s thrown in a skip outside. Fortunately he was able to rescue the books which are now part of the Susser Archive at the Devon Record Office.

During the 1970s the synagogue was used primarily for Friday night services by Jewish students from the University of Exeter.[106] Services for the few local Jews still resident in the city were held only for High Holy Days. However the building had deteriorated and was unsuitable for worship. It desperately needed rescuing for the future. Thanks to the efforts of Alfred Dunitz of London, a committee member of The Board of Deputies of British Jews, sufficient funds were raised to undertake the work. The synagogue was finally extensively restored in 1980 with replacement of the rear seating that had been damaged by damp and infestation. It also saw the reconstruction of the first floor which had been lost during the Second World War. A plaque commemorating the 1980 refurbishment hangs on the wall of the entrance lobby and reads:

This synagogue was built in 1763. It was restored and the Hillel extension added in 1980 through the efforts of A A Dunitz Esq J.P. and reconsecrated on the 19th of October 1980 (corresponding with the 9th of Marcheshvan 5741) by the Rev. Malcolm Wiseman M.A. oxon C.F. minister of smaller communities during the Presidency of Derrick Boam Esq.

In February 1988 the exterior of the synagogue was repainted. Inside, the downstairs room on the right as one enters was redecorated and named the A. A. Dunitz Room.

By the mid-1990s the synagogue was in desperate need of substantial repairs and restoration. The then President Sonia Fodor and Vice-President Frank Gent

---

[105] Copy of a letter dated May 1961 in the Synagogue Archives.
[106] *Jewish Chronicle*, 17 November 1978.

raised funding with Alfred Dunitz from English Heritage and the Heritage Lottery funding. This time the cost mounted to £150,000 and over 60% was awarded from these two heritage funds. The work needed to include the installation of a heating system to sort out problems of rising damp and rot, and installation of new toilets and plumbing; a necessity but not covered by the English Heritage grant. Sonia and Frank made known the historic nature of the synagogue to Exeter City Council who were forthcoming with a grant of £5,000. The Devon Historic Churches Trust undertook a sponsored walk and raised £500. Exeter Cathedral and three other churches also raised money in special collections for the synagogue. Donations were also received in memory of Derrick Nahum and Ann Lesh. It meant that all repairs could go ahead. The roof light was completely replaced with its new design by Stephen Emanuel and a cost of £11,000 which was funded by the Jewish Memorial Council. Newspaper coverage of the restoration appeal to Exeter churches brought in some financial support. During the two-year restoration all religious services were held in the downstairs A.A Dunitz Room.

Much of the two year work concentrated on the synagogue's interior, particularly on the Ark which was in a precarious state. The results of paint analysis carried out at this time by Eddie Sinclair during the course of conservation, revealed that the Ark retained in places no less than 29 different layers of paint, and at least four distinctive decorative schemes were identified. Her two special reports on the Polychromy of the synagogue and Ark are an invaluable record and provide an important insight into the extent of the renovations during this period. The following sections are based on her reports.[107]

After a meeting with English Heritage in December 1997 it was decided that Eddie Sinclair should carry out a more detailed investigation into some of the puzzling aspects of the upper parts of the Ark. In the first instance the Ark was carefully dismantled so that structural problems could be addressed. This was carried out by timber specialist Hugh Harrison and his conservation joiners. With the Ark separated into its many component parts, cleaning tests could be carried out alongside the necessary paint analysis. Certain elements were found to be coated with a thick black overpaint, applied to the Ark by 1910. One of the main decisions during the 1990s restoration was whether to remove this inappropriate black paint and if it could be done without damaging the paint beneath. This combination of analysis and cleaning tests provided information vital in helping understand the Ark's history. Sinclair comments that, 'What is of great significance is the realization that the Exeter Ark has had a far richer history than was hitherto realized.' In her initial description of the Ark, Sinclair wrote:

'It is constructed from wood and richly painted to look as though it were made with exotic marble. The plinth is

From the ladies' gallery

painted in imitation of a green marble, at present darkened by discoloured varnish, and in places a wash of black overpaint (which seems confined to the top of the plinth and the skirting). The sides and Attic storey at present appear as a yellow ochre/raw sienna marble, veined with black and streaked with green. The paint surface appears for the most part to be in good condition, apart from the central plinth where there is evidence of damp penetration. The brittle paint is lifting and losses have occurred, showing the red earth primer beneath. The varnish here has broken down and appears speckled and bloomy. Cleaning tests carried out in a variety of locations revealed startling results. The green marbling is extremely fresh and vivid, speckled with white and black/dark green. The yellow marbling is actually a pale buff colour, broken up by veins of a grassy green, with an underlying delicate deep blue streak, and in places what appears to be a crimson lake. The green revealed after cleaning was not one recognised as dating from the 18th century, and analysis of one paint sample revealed the green to be a mixture of chrome yellow and Prussian blue which indicates that what we see on the Ark today is a 19th century repaint (chrome yellow entered the artist's palette in the 1820s).'

During her study Sinclair took a total of 60 paint samples, mainly from the upper parts of the Ark. In her report she wrote: 'these have been studied in some detail

---

[107] Copyrighted information and extracts have been quoted in this chapter by kind permission of Eddie Sinclair.

at microscopic level, with particular emphasis on the examination and comparison of cross-sections. Samples are in places extraordinarily complex, with up to 29 layers of paint in evidence.' Sinclair emphasized the importance of the Ark and the fact that it is a feature of the original synagogue and as such should be at the centre of any restoration work:

> 'The Ark, as the focal point in the Synagogue and in itself a remarkable survival, must receive attention if it is to survive into the next century. As well as its symbolic function it is an important historic architectural feature. It represents a time when the present Synagogue first came into being, even though the exposed paint itself is not contemporary... As it stands the Ark is but a shadow of what it should be, as the imposing centre piece of the Synagogue.'[108]

Conservation of the paintwork of the Ark meant not only its cleaning and consolidation but the removal of inappropriate layers of paint where necessary that had been applied by successive generations over the years. The analysis had revealed several decorative paint schemes, each reflecting an important moment in the Ark's history. It was therefore not ethical to destroy more recent and intact schemes to uncover damaged earlier decoration, beyond the removal of harmful coatings such as bronze paint. Cleaning produced dramatic results and proved to be one of the most important exciting parts of the project, revealing the Ark to be a hidden gem. The cleaning phase involved removing the discoloured varnish which had been applied over the whole of the Ark, as well as the heavy black paint and bronze paint which had been latterly used instead of gold leaf. The rest of the Ark's paintwork was in good condition and apart from the doors which were re-grained, touching-up was confined to new fillings built up in places of loss. Elements with abraded gilding overlaid with cheap bronze paint were re-gilded with 23 and three-quarters carat gold leaf. After an extensive campaign of work, the Ark was reassembled with the vibrant late 19th century marbled scheme clearly visible, beneath which earlier decoration remains safely protected for future generations. Nineteen extensive months of microscopic examination and research had paid off. The Ark had once again become the crowning glory of the synagogue.

Another feature of the synagogue which needed Sinclair's attention were the synagogue's eight painted columns, five of which stood on their original plinths and were covered in black paint. The other three had been replaced in more modern times. Sinclair undertook an analysis of the paintwork on the column and again found it overlaid with a thickness of discoloured varnish. She reported:

> 'The columns are decorated with a painted stencil pattern, presumably from the 1830 restoration. The palette of buff, red, green, black and possibly brown appears to tie in with the colours found on the Ark. There is certainly evidence of an earlier scheme below the present decoration, visible through damaged areas of paint. The plinths, all painted black at present, bear many layers of paint beneath this top coating. There appears to be a crimson lying directly below the black which probably ties in with the 19th century scheme, though there is certainly earlier colour still. The columns are coated with a similar varnish to that found on the Ark, which cleans to reveal fresh bright colours below, with gilded mouldings at both head and base.'

Sinclair suggested the removal of the discoloured varnish from the eight columns around the Synagogue. Once cleaned they echoed the polychrome on the Ark.

When the roof lantern was replaced in 1997 an original oak timber was found. Today it rests in the synagogue office and has been carved into a sculpture by Marcus Vergette. In this room on the ground floor there is a large carved oak chair with seal of Solomon which

Bill Boam at the bimah

---

[108] Eddie Sinclair, 'Interim Polychromy Report. Exeter Synagogue: Ark Polychromy', 1998.

Invitation for Rededication Service, 1999

was given to the shul when the Torquay synagogue closed in the 1990s. Although it has no inscription it is probably a *sandek* chair used during a circumcision ceremony for a member of the family.[109] It dates to 1860-1880 in the West Country style and was on permanent loan to Torquay from Totnes Museum.[110] On the wall hangs a painting entitled *Yizkor* by artist Rikki Romain which commemorates the Holocaust.

The beautifully restored synagogue was rededicated in a special service on Sunday 11 July 1999, officiated by

Rededication Service, 11 July 1999

Rev Malcolm Wiseman. It was attended by 100 people, including civic and county dignitaries, congregants, descendants of former members, the Mayor of Exeter, local Christians and clergy, and the author herself. The then President Sonia Fodor said during the service:

> 'As a congregation we have grown of late and can boast a wide range of communal activities, amongst them a cheder {religious school}, a woman's group and adult Hebrew classes which are attended by two Christian clergymen. We also run a visitation service that covers hospital and prisons where Jews are inmates, and when required, officiate at weddings and funerals. The synagogue receives visits from around 2,000 school children a year.'

The synagogue is an extraordinary time-capsule and standing alone in the sanctuary one could easily be back in the eighteenth century. Its wall breath generations of prayer and dedication to God. And yet this jewel in the Anglo-Jewish crown is able to move with modern times and continues to provide a special place of prayer for the Jewish community of Exeter.

---

[109] Information provided by antique dealer Richard Halsey.
[110] Information provided by Frank Gent.

CHAPTER 5
THE BURIAL GROUNDS

THE EARLIEST EXTANT Jewish burial ground is in Magdalen Street adjoining Bull Meadow and dates to 1757. The nascent community found the need for its own burial ground even before a synagogue was built, to alleviate transporting bodies to London for burial. Surrounded by its original 18th century red brick wall the entrance through an archway and grilled iron gate allows a glimpse into a tranquil location outside the original city walls. The wall and arched entrance are now both Grade II listed.

Walking down the sloping path from the road to the cemetery's entrance one is conscious of the busy Exeter bypass, but entering the sheltered enclosed burial ground below road level there is a calm serenity where the oldest legible tombstone dates to 1807. Here are the graves of Moses Horvitz Levi (1754-1837), Minister of the congregation for twelve years and Solomon Aarons who died in 1864 at the great age of 102. Also another minister Rev. Abraham Rosenberg who died in 1913. Here too rests Hannah, daughter of Moses Vita Montefiore and relative of Sir Moses Montefiore. There are a number graves for members of the families of Gabrielson, Lazarus, Alexander, Levy, Aarons and Samuels; and the only Commonwealth War Grave of Pilot Officer H D Abrams, Air Observer of the Royal Canadian Air Force who died 3 August 1941 at the age of 24. Also buried in this burial ground is minor poet Barent [Isaac] Gompertz who died on 9 September 1824 and whose grave contains a line from the poem *Devon*. Although he had married out of the faith and baptized all his children, the Jewish community still permitted him to be buried in the cemetery. Today the old Jewish cemetery has just one burial plot remaining which has been reserved for a life-long member of the community. Other Jewish burials now take place in a special section at the Exwick Municipal Cemetery.

On 28 March 1757 Exeter City Council granted a lease to the Jewish inhabitants of the city for a burial ground to 'Abraham Ezekiel for a term of 99 years determinable on three lives in late Tanners plot in the parish of the Holy Trinity at the yearly rent of 10s. 6d.'[111]

Entrance to Jewish cemetery, Magdalen Street

One of the oldest surviving tombstones, now illegible

---
[111] Susser, *The Jews of South-West England*, p.128.

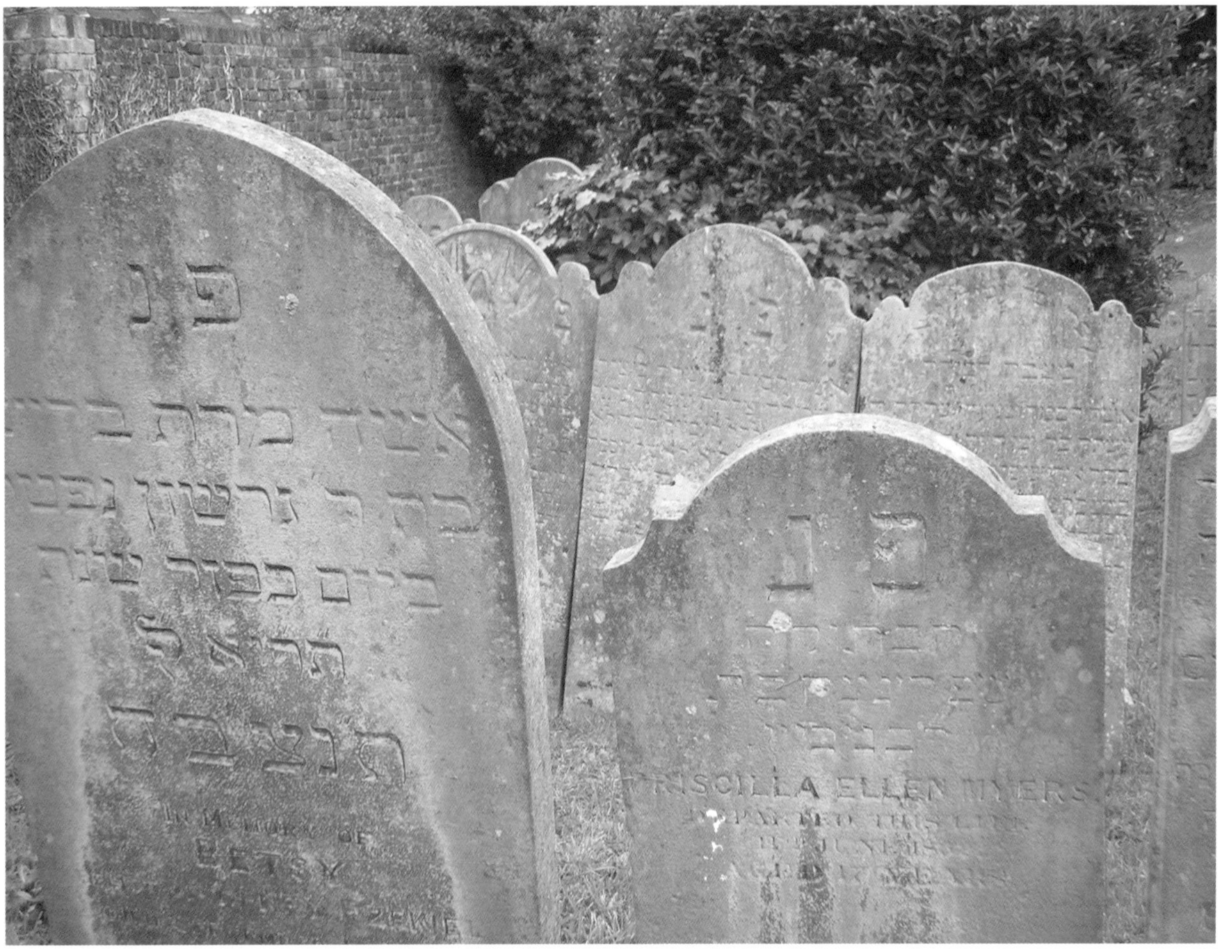
ELLEN MYERS

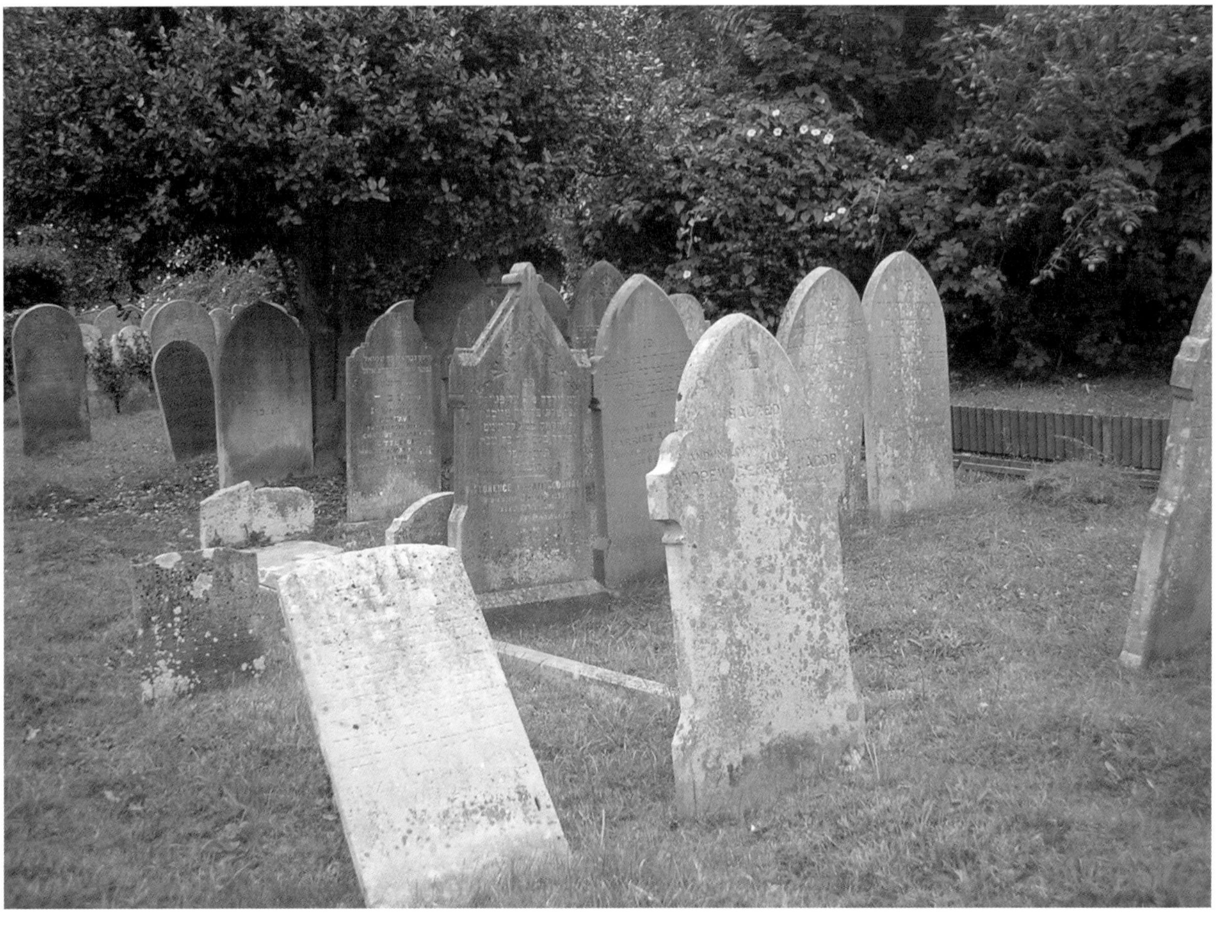

The original piece of ground was 20ft by 80ft and represents the oldest section of the cemetery. The actual lease was drawn up on 18 May 1757 and issued to one of the founding members of the community "Abraham Ezekiel of the parish of St Kerrian in the city of Exon, silversmith" by "the brothers and sisters of the house or hospital of lepers of Saint Mary Magdalen without the South Gate". It was given for 5 shillings and an annual rent of ten shillings and sixpence payable to the hospital, and the requirement to construct an 8ft high wall of brick, stone or cob, topped with coping. The three lives were Abraham Ezekiel (aged 31), his daughter Rose (aged 2) and Israel Henry (also aged 2), the son of Israel Henry.

On 7 January 1803 the lease was renewed for a further 5 shillings and double the rent to one pound and a shilling. It was issued to Moses Mordecai, silversmith, for the plot 'enclosed with a wall and now used by the congregation of Jews as their burial ground'. This time it was on the three lives of Solomon Ezekiel (aged 17, son of silversmith Ezekiel Benjamin Ezekiel of Newton Abbot),[112] Simon Levy (aged 12, son of silversmith Emanuel Levy) and Jonas Jonas (aged 12, son of silversmith Benjamin Jonas of Plymouth Dock). Five years later on 23 June 1807 Moses Mordecai took out another lease for a small piece of adjoining land to extend the burial ground to the south-east.

Extending the burial ground

A new lease of 24 September 1827 extended the ground to the north-east and was issued to four members of the Exeter Jewish community. The first was Henry Ezekiel, 'of the said city of Exeter, gentleman', the second Jacob Jacobs (pen manufacturer), and three silversmiths: Isaac Solomon, Simon Levy (of the parish of St Thomas) and Morris Jacobs. The lives were Solomon Ezekiel, silversmith and son of Ezekiel Benjamin Ezekiel of Newton Abbot; Simon Levy, Emanuel Levy and Jonas Jonas and son Benjamin Jonas of Plymouth Dock. The annual rent doubled again to two pounds and two shillings. The ground which was 'now in the possession of the Elders of the Jews Congregation of the city of Exeter', was 90ft long from north to south on the east side, and 70ft on the west side. At the south end it was 52ft and at the north 43ft.

By 1845 there was sufficient concern over the future of the cemetery for the community to write to the Chief Rabbi in London. In they letter they wrote that:

> 'Two out of the three lives have dropped and the third is very aged, which leaves us in a very precarious state. The trustees have offered to receive a piece of ground in lieu of it and to convey our present ground to us as freehold which will cost us £300. We have applied for subscriptions to the parties who have relatives lying there but have not succeeded.'[113]

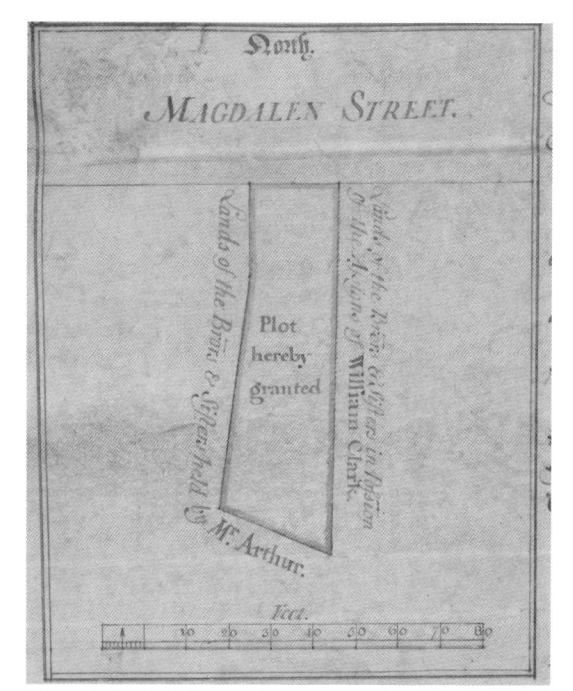

Plan of the burial ground, 1757. COURTESY OF THE TRUSTEES OF THE EXETER MUNICIPAL CHARITY

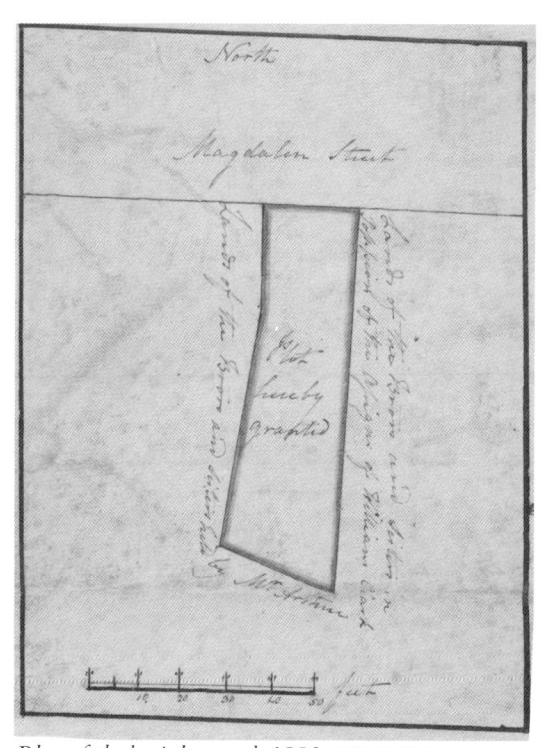

Plan of the burial ground, 1803. COURTESY OF THE TRUSTEES OF THE EXETER MUNICIPAL CHARITY

The concerns in the letter may have led to the 1851 agreement which was to be the final indenture granted to the community on the burial ground. Dated 25 May 1851, the new indenture doubled the size of the burial ground to the south and was negotiated for a period of a hundred years, taking the expiry date to 1951. It was issued to Moses Lazarus of Holloway Street (jeweller),

---

[112] Solomon Ezekiel is buried in the Penzance Jewish cemetery. See *The Lost Jews of Cornwall*.
[113] MSS 104, Chief Rabbinate Archives, p.37.

Joseph Marks of Fore Street Hill (clothier), Alexander Alexander of Fore Street (optician) and Emanuel Jacobs of Market Street (stationer). It was granted on the land already used for the burial ground and an extension to the west and south-west. The rent had increased to six pounds and six shillings to be paid in two installments annually. In addition, to mitigate against any possible arrears of rent in the future, the congregation paid a total fee of £200. The community was beginning to decline, and its leaders may have felt that by paying over an advance of fees at least the cemetery was secure for the future. Many members who had been prominent in the community for over 40 years had decided to leave the city, some in part due to ongoing squabbles. The cemetery was secure even if the future of the synagogue itself was shaky.

When former community member S. Lazarus visited Exeter again after twenty-five years he found, 'one particular thing struck me with delight, and that was the perfect order in which the little synagogue and burial ground were kept – in fact they may be quoted as a good example to any community.'[114] However, by the 1880s the burial ground had fallen into a deplorable state. The perimeter walls were in need of repair and the site was badly overgrown with brambles and weeds. Some of the earliest tombstones were already illegible. Emanuel Jacobs, whose name appeared on the 1851 indenture and had since moved to London, organized former members of the community to raise funds for the ground's renovation. The walls were restored, as well as restoration carried out on the tombstones and the ground made presentable. Throughout its history the community has been fortunate in the support of previous members for whom Exeter always held a special place for them.

In 1903 the last surviving trustee Emanuel Jacobs, listed on the 1851 indenture of the Jewish Burial Ground, died. One of the priorities under the presidency of Charles Samuels was to establish new trustees to oversee the cemetery. Exeter formed a new burial committee which consisted of Charles Samuels, Mr A. B. Salmen and Mr S. Jacobs. At the time of Emanuel Jacobs' death on 6 June 1903 he was no longer a resident of Exeter. It was his wish to be buried in the cemetery of his ancestors and his request which was readily granted by the Exeter Jewish community. He is in buried in plot 79. At the turn of the twentieth century the cemetery had largely fallen into disuse and was in a bad condition. The Board of Deputies in London expressed about the state of the burial ground and noted that the community was struggling to keep up with its commitments to pay the minister's salary and keep the synagogue building going. An appeal was launched during the latter part of the 1920s and families once connected to the community provided funds for the repairs that were desperately needed. The cemetery weathered the difficulties of upkeep during the twentieth century and saw many more burials in the next ninety years.

In 1951 the lease to the burial ground of 1851 expired without anyone in the Jewish community or the City Council noticing. Exeter City Council had become the successor of the St Mary Magdalen Hospital and now owned the Jewish burial site. During the 1950s and 60s the now tiny Jewish community had no reason to doubt

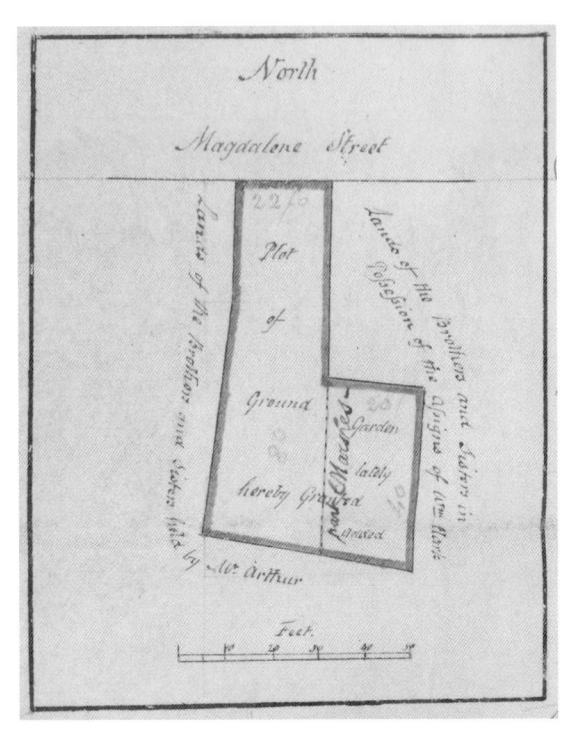

Burial ground, extended 1807. COURTESY OF THE TRUSTEES OF THE EXETER MUNICIPAL CHARITY

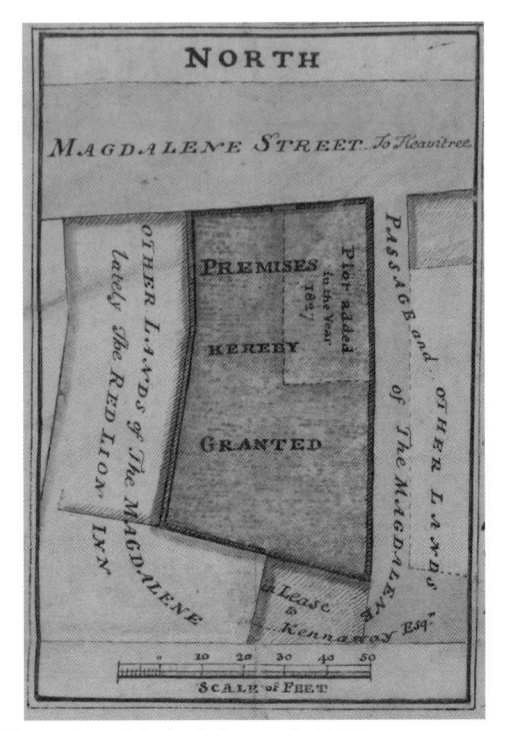

Expansion of the burial ground, 1827. COURTESY OF THE TRUSTEES OF THE EXETER MUNICIPAL CHARITY

---

[114] Letter to the *Jewish Chronicle* dated 28 August 1877, written by S Lazarus of London.

Old burial ground in the 1990s

that all was fine. Burials continued as normal during this period. The crisis came in the 1970s.

The risk of development

Far more serious for the future of the burial ground than the community's decline was the proposal in the early 1970s to construct an inner bypass through Bull Meadow that would involve the compulsory purchase of the cemetery and the exhumation of the graves. It was then that it came to the City Council's attention that the lease had actually expired. The future of the old Jewish cemetery seemed perilous. A struggle ensued to save the two hundred year old burial ground from urban development. The congregation was acutely aware that it did not actually own its own burial ground. Eventually the City Council abandoned its development scheme and the congregation was able to purchase the land outright. The freehold purchase was dated 18 December 1977 for the sum of £750, generously paid by two community members Kurt Wilhelm and Solomon Boam. The Land Certificate also granted ownership of the lane in front of the synagogue to the congregation. A further deed dated 31 May 1978 made clear that Wilhelm and Boam were acting on behalf of the congregation.

The ohel (chapel)

The 18th century wall and arched entrance to the ground is now Grade II listed. The tiny whitewashed interior chapel, used for prayers before burial, has tablets of the Ten Commandments in Hebrew on one wall. In Jewish tradition there is great emphasis on the sanctity of life, but also a requirement to observe dignity in death.

In the Jewish tradition, rituals surrounding death are in place to ensure that due respect is paid to the deceased. The Exeter Congregation Regulations of 1833 stipulated that two guards were to be employed to watch over the corpse until burial; with burial often taking place either

Entrance to cemetery chapel

The Ten Commandments in the cemetery chapel

the same day or the next. The regulations stipulated that the sum of one shilling was to be paid by each member towards the costs. The funeral of poor Jews was funded by the congregation. The corpse was washed and purified at the deceased's home rather than in the chapel (ohel), as is customary in some communities.

Clockwise from top left:

Samuel Levy, 1824

The only Commonwealth War Grave in the old cemetery, Pilot Officer H D Abrams

Moses Lazarus, 1811

Tomb of Barent Gompertz

In 1831 there was an outbreak of cholera in Sunderland which spread around the country and affected Exeter too. The following year on 22 August 1832 Nathan Harris of Exeter Jewish community died of the disease. Because of his poor circumstances the cost of his funeral was paid by the Exeter congregation. Only the previous month Exeter Council had passed an order on 20 July that anyone who died of cholera was to be buried in a separate area of a cemetery to prevent further spread of the disease which thrives in areas of poverty and poor sanitation. A small section of the Jewish burial ground was fenced off for such isolated burials but never used. Nathan Harris appears to have been the only Jewish death in Exeter from cholera. The Bishop of Exeter when asked for his opinion about burial arrangements during the cholera epidemic wisely responded, 'I have nothing to do with the Jews' burying ground and no control over it.'

In 1838 Exeter Hebrew Congregation wrote to Chief Rabbi Adler and asked whether they could recite *Kaddish* (the memorial prayer) for Mrs Jonas who had not been converted according to the Rabbinic Court, the Beth Din. It must have been favourable because husband and wife are both buried in a regular row in the cemetery.

In September 1874 the community defrays the costs for the burial of a Jew, Solomon Cappelle who originated from Groningen and whose body was found in woods at Broadclyst, Exeter.[115] The cause of death was unknown, although it was thought to be suicide. Aged about 35, he was found with various papers on him, a purse and Hebrew prayer book. Synagogue president Alexander took responsibility for the funeral arrangements. The itinerant pedlar was known to Alexander because Cappelle had already made contact with the community prior to his unfortunate demise. Cappelle had visited Falmouth and other Cornish places before returning to Exeter. His body was found wearing his prayer shawl and it was assumed he had been saying prayers: 'Mr Alexander has but little doubt the man is insane... after the inquest Mr Alexander took possession of the body and it was interred in the Jewish burying ground, Exeter.'[116] Today there is no record of the exact burial plot for Cappelle. It is likely that he was never given a headstone and, because of the possibility of suicide, his body may have been interred in a part of the cemetery away from the others.

The New Jewish Burial Ground

In October 1985 the congregation held an open meeting at the synagogue to discuss the lack of space remaining in the cemetery in Magdalen Street. Exeter City Council was approached but as of the following year had been unable to find a new burial ground. In April 1986, at the direction of Frank Gent, discussions focused on reviving the *Chevera Kadisha* (burial society). The Torquay synagogue's *Chavera Kadisha* offered space from its cemetery to the Exeter community. However the Exeter congregation eventually acquired a separate section in the Exwick Municipal Cemetery in Exeter. The first burial in it was of Rosemary Deborah Joseph who died on 21

---

[115] *Jewish Chronicle*, 11 September 1874.
[116] *Ibid.*

January 1992 at the age of 65. In January 1992 the Chevera Kadisha was finally re-established.

In September 1987 a headstone in the old cemetery was defaced with a swastika; a vivid reminder of the existence of the Far-Right in the region. At the end of 1987 repairs to the old cemetery commenced with labour costs estimated at £5,000 which were met by Exeter City Council MSC Community Programme Scheme. The cost of £2,000 for materials was covered by the congregation. With Jewish funerals again taking place Frank arranged for the chapel to be rebuilt and the walls repaired. The work was completed in May 1998.

Moses Alexander, aged 8 months

Secure for the Future

No burial register survives for the old Jewish Burial Ground and therefore details for the earliest burials are lost. Information which survives today is taken from the first list to be made of extant headstones which was compiled by Michael Adler in 1940. When Alder carried out his survey, the earliest legible tombstone was 1807. There is therefore no proper record of persons buried between the opening of the ground in 1757 and 1807. Adler's original list has become the most important source for burials up to the 1940s and many of these old tombstones are illegible seventy years later. Annotated notes were made to Adler's list by Rabbi Dr Bernard Susser in 1963 but he did not record burials after 1940. A survey of the site in 2012 by the author has enabled the original list to be substantially updated and an appendix of known burials in the cemetery is included at the end of this book. In the early 1990s the author also photographed every extant headstone in the cemetery which proved valuable because over twenty years later many are now illegible.

The main challenge for the congregation today remains the same as 250 years ago – to consistently maintain the old burial ground in a good state against the ever-encroaching brambles, ivy and weeds. Nothing can be done to save the oldest tombstones from the elements but at least many inscriptions have been recorded for posterity. The cemetery is a memorial to the community's members and its life over the last three centuries. It also provides an important record and a window onto the community's long history and, through the people buried there, its contribution to the life of the city.

Julia Lazarus, 1836

Three children of Myers and Deborah Solomon

View of old burial ground

CHAPTER 6
THE COMMUNITY 1800-1880

ECONOMIC OPPORTUNITIES brought Jews to the South-West of England in the 1800s. By 1820 the Exeter Jewish congregation numbered fifty-two members. In a statistical survey of the Jews of England in 1847 it was reported that the Exeter Jewish community had around 175 individuals. Those members who had arrived from the 1740s settled and had families such that the generation consisted of indigenous Jews who had been born in the city. The census returns from 1841 reveal much about the lifestyle of Exeter's Jews. All were in business and many were successful such that they had a comfortable middle class or upper-middle class lifestyle. The census returns from 1841 onwards show that many of these families employed one or more servants.

By 1815 four Moroccan (Sephardi) Jews had a shop in the city for at least five years. Two other Sephardi Jews are known to have been living in the area because they are buried in the old cemetery. They were Aaron Amzalek who died in 1838 and Hannah Montefiore who died in 1839. Hannah was the daughter of Moses Vita Montefiore and first cousin of one of Anglo-Jewry's most famous figures, Sir Moses Montefiore. David Joel settled in Exeter circa 1825, while members like Jacob Abraham, an optician of Fore Street, Exeter took himself off to Bath in 1800. Abraham had been trading in the city in the late 1700s in premises opposite St John's Church and advertised his services in a local newspaper in 1799.[117] This was also the period in which Sir Menasseh Masseh Lopes became Sheriff of Devon in 1810 and MP for Romney in 1802. In the city from the 1830s was Polish-born Solomon Aarons and his wife Caroline who had moved from Barnstaple, North Devon where they had been resident in the 1820s and where their two first two children Aaron and Harriet had been born. A third child Fanny was born in Exeter in 1833.

Isaac Woolf (born circa 1774) arrived in Exeter from Poland around 1790. He settled in the city and married

Jacob Solomon (1782-1857), COURTESY OF JEWISH MUSEUM LONDON

Leah [surname unknown] of Barnstaple in 1809. They had several children: William (1810),[118] Myers (1812),[119] Henry (1819), Ezekiel (1821),[120] Michael (1825),[121] Rachel (b. Plymouth, 1829)[122] and Priscilla (1833).[123] Isaac died in Exeter on 28 January 1850 and may be buried in the old Jewish cemetery, although no record or headstone has survived.

Others in the city by the mid-1800s included Aaron Israel, a jeweller, also Caroline Dimond and Caroline Aarons, both jewellers, and Israel Silverstone and Joseph Marks, both watchmakers. There was the unfortunate

---

[117] *Trewman's Flying Post*, 17 January 1799.
[118] William Woolf (shopkeeper) married Ann Levi in 46 Chapel Street, Plymouth on 1 August 1838 under the auspices of the Plymouth Hebrew Congregation. The marriage was performed by Rabbi Myer Stadhagen.
[119] Myers Woolf (optician) married Phoebe Abrahams, daughter of Solomon Abrahams, at 64 Cambridge Street, Plymouth under the auspices of the Plymouth Hebrew Congregation on 31 December 1845.
[120] Ezekiel Woolf married out of the Jewish faith when he wedded Elizabeth Peyman in Abingdon on 30 March 1846. By the 1861 Census Ezekiel (general dealer) was living with his family in Birmingham.
[121] Michael Woolf married Mary Ann Crocombe on 2 February 1854.
[122] Rachel Woolf married Isaac Moss in Whitechapel in 1851.
[123] Priscilla Woolf married Samuel Romaine at Houndsditch on 10 March 1857.

case of Uriah Moses who was tried at the Old Bailey on 10 January 1798 for breaking into a draper's shop and given the death penalty. This was subsequently reduced to transportation to Australia in 1800. In 1827 Solomon Levy was trading as a jeweller. In 1828 draper and tailor Morris Jacobs of 169 Fore Street advertised for an apprenticeship vacancy in the local newspaper.[124] Another trader in the city was Mr Levi who advertised in 1848 for 'a young man, experienced in fancy hardware, also a respectable youth and son apprentice.'[125] Many of the local Jewesses stayed at home and raised their family. Some were in business, like the case of Mrs E Berstein, manufacturer of Honiton Lace. It is likely that she employed three of Israel Silverstone's daughters, Bella, Sarah and Rosina whose occupations on the 1851 census are given as Honiton Lace Manufacturer. By 1857 Mrs Berstein had moved to London and set up a business making wedding clothes at 22 Jewry Street, Algate.[126] At the end of June 1871 an advertisement appeared in the *Jewish Chronicle* about the sale of the rag and metal merchant business of R & H. Hynes at Quay Stones, Exeter due to the death of the junior partner Henry Hynes the previous month.[127] Hynes is buried in the old Jewish cemetery.

A son of Betsy Levy of Totnes

Asher Barnard came to Exeter during the 1850s and settled in the city, trading as a general dealer. He was born in 1825 in Rochester, Kent to Berman Issachar Barnard and Hannah Tobias and married Rebecca Nathan. They lived for a time in Ipswich before moving to Exeter. They had eleven children, seven of whom were born in Exeter: Julia (1855), Hannah (1857), Joseph (1858), Solomon (1860), Samuel (1862), Henry (1863) and Katie (1867).

Since its inception in the 1720s Exeter's Jewish community has consisted mainly of skilled and educated tradesmen who swiftly established a middle class or upper middle class standard of living. It is true too that during the 1800s the city saw its fair share of pedlars passing through and the Jewish community aided them wherever possible. A number applied for licences from Exeter and their names are included in an appendix at the end of the book.

In 1853 there was an unfortunate incident whereby pedlar Tobias Tobias, a German immigrant, was brutally assaulted near Exeter. He was beaten up by an unidentified person, lost the sight of an eye and damage to an ear. He was robbed of his wares and had to spend nearly four months in Exeter hospital. The city's Jewish community raised £22 to enable him to buy new goods and work again.[128]

Lazarus Family

The first Lazarus settlers in Exeter appear to be Moses and Nancy Lazarus who had three sons: Eleazer and David who lived in Exeter, and Lyon who resided in Plymouth. Moses Lazarus died in 1811, predeceased the previous year by his wife Nancy. Both are buried in the old Jewish cemetery in Exeter. Their son David Lazarus (b.1793), a quill and pen manufacturer, married Betsy (maiden name unknown) and they had eight known children: Ann, Moses, Esther, Caroline, Fanny, Eleazar, Julia and Henry. David died in 1862 and is buried in the old Exeter cemetery along with his wife who had died several years earlier in July 1848 at the age of 44. Their daughter Ann was a general dealer who married Abraham Levy in 1851. Another daughter Esther married Maurice Dyte, a herbalist in Exeter, in 1862, and Julia Lazaraus married Aaron Aarons in Exeter in 1867.

Another of Moses and Nancy Lazarus' sons Eleazar was the Yiddish/English translator for the Exeter congregation. A jeweller and stationer by profession he married Julia Solomon and they are known to have had the following children, all born in Exeter: Moses, Caroline, Isaac, Nancy, David, Samuel Joyful, Nathan, Deborah and Solomon. Julia died in 1836 is buried in the

---

[124] *Trewman's Flying Post*, 30 October 1828.
[125] *Jewish Chronicle*, 21 April 1848.
[126] *Jewish Chronicle*, 23 January 1857.
[127] *Jewish Chronicle*, 30 June 1871.
[128] *Jewish Chronicle*, 27 May 1853, 22 July 1853 and 11 November 1853.

David Lazarus (1822-1895), standing behind his daughter Caroline and her husband John Hyman and their two eldest children, Catherine and Deborah

old Jewish cemetery. Four years later on 6 September 1840 Eleazar remarried under the auspices of the synagogue at a ceremony in North Street and wedded 50-year old Esther Jacobs. The marriage of Moses Lazarus (second son of Eleazar and Julia) to Rebecca Schultz on 10 January 1838 was the first to be entered into the synagogue's Marriage Register after a law was passed that all civil and religious marriages be officially registered. Rebecca Schultz originated from Poland, the daughter of Lewis and Caroline Schultz. Moses and Rebecca had ten children: the eldest Baruch/Barnet was born in Exmouth, the others in Exeter: Julia, Joseph, Samuel, Eleazar/Edward, Nathan, Rachel Kate, Gertrude, Edith and Lionel. Moses was a watchmaker and jeweller who, by the 1851 census, was living with his family at 5 Lansdowne Terrace, Exeter. About 1860 Moses and Rebecca moved from Exeter to London where Barnett became a primary mover in the foundation of, and briefly Captain in Command of, the first Jewish military unit in Britain. He ultimately settled in Toronto, Canada under the surname Laurance where he had an optical company. Barnett's brothers Nathan and Lionel also became opticians. Nathan Lazarus went to India to practice, and Lionel Laurance became an influential professor of optics in London. Edward Laurance also immigrated to Canada where he had a varied career as a dental surgeon, journalist, then working for Barnett's optical company.

Of Eleazer and Julia Lazarus' other children: daughter Caroline married Rev. Abraham Barnett (minister of the New Synagogue, Great St. Helens, London) in the Exeter Synagogue in 1838. Isaac, a watchmaker and jeweller, married Eliza Jacobs of Falmouth and settled in Northernhay, Exeter. They had five children: Julia, Lewis, Edward, Montague and Sophia, and moved to Birmingham in about 1855. Eleazar and Julia Lazarus' son David (b. circa 1820) left Exeter for Melbourne, Australia during the period of the gold rush of the early 1850s and set up as a jeweller and watchmaker. Their daughter Nancy married Joseph Marks of Poland (jeweller and Hebrew teacher) in London in 1856. Nathan Lawrence (optician) married a Plymouth cousin: Lippa Lazarus' daughter Fanny. They spent a number of years in Canada and Hartford, Connecticut, before settling in London. Samuel Joyful (wholesale optician) married Fanny's sister Nancy in Exeter in 1846. By 1851 they were living in London's East End. Deborah, a dressmaker, married Meyers Solomon of Prussia (the son of Nathan and Fogel) in Exeter in 1849. Deborah and Meyers had eleven children, the youngest only about three years old when Meyers died in 1874. By 1881 Deborah was an ostrich feather merchant living in Islington, London. Solomon appears in the 1851 census as an optician with his cousin Moses (son of Eleazer's brother David) in Neath, Wales, where they are presumably travelling.

Alexander Alexander

From the mid-1820s one of the most prominent and active members of the Jewish community was Alexander Alexander who served the community for over 40 years. At various times he held the position of treasurer, President and trustee of the Burial Ground. He became a well-respected figure in the wider society. Politically he was a staunch Liberal and held the position of Vice-President of the Exeter Liberal Association and Chairman of the St Paul's Ward Liberal Association.

Born in Sheerness in 1805 Alexander Alexander arrived in Exeter in 1826. Four years later on 20 October 1830 he married Tryphenia Johnson, the daughter of Moses Johnson.[129] They were married under the auspices of the Exeter Hebrew Congregation in the Exeter Assembly Rooms. They had eight children: Fanny, Moses, Eliza, Lawrence, Jacob, Miriam, Fanny and Alfred. On 31 August 1864 their son Jacob Alexander married Lizzie Jessel, daughter of Michael Jessel of Bristol, at the bride's home and officiated by Revd. Jacobs. Jacob and Lizzie Alexander eventually emigrated to Melbourne, Australia where he is known to have died on 14 July 1891 at the age of 52.

Alexander Alexander and his brother John Alexander were both opticians by profession with business premises at 6 High Street. Two brothers married two sisters: Alexander Alexanders's wife Tryphenia had a sister Isabella Johnson who became the wife of John Alexander. In 1833 Alexander Alexander was appointed to the prestigious position of Royal Optician to King William IV. It was an appointment which extended to the young Princess Victoria (later Queen Victoria) and the Duchess of Kent. That same year he wrote *A Treatise on the Nature of Vision, Formation of the Eye and the Causes of Imperfect*

---

[129] Referenced in his obituary in the *Trewman's Flying Post*, 23 February 1887.

Vision which he dedicated to William IV and published in Exeter. The publication was supported by 200 subscribers, including local MPs and 70 surgeons. In 1837 another of his books was published in Exeter, *Observations on the Preservation of Sight and Hints to Spectacle Wearers*. He was quite inventive and devised a ventilating eye shield for his patient, the Earl of Carnarvon. He also invented a Graphic Mirror.[130] It was from 1837 to 1840 that Alexander became optician to the new Queen Victoria. On Queen Victoria's visit to Exeter in the summer of 1845 he sent a special address to the Queen in which he wrote:

> 'May it please Your Majesty, to receive this my humble address, on the occasion of your Majesty passing through this ancient city... your Majesty's philanthropy, particularly towards my Jewish brethren, calls forth from me the highest meed of thanks possible to be conveyed to your Majesty. May the God of Israel in his infinite mercy, grant your Majesty many, many years of health and happiness, to live in the hearts of the British people, *is the sincere and heartfelt prayer of your Majesty's most grateful, humble and obedient servant, Alexander Alexander, 6th August 1945.'*

The address was passed to Queen Victoria on her arrival at the hotel. A reply from her chamberlain Earl Howe was duly sent to Alexander and read:

> *'Mr Alexander, your address has been presented to her Majesty and was most graciously received; and I am directed to state that her Majesty will at all times be most happy to render any service in her power to the members of that community to which you belong.'*[131]

Alexander Alexander's name appears frequently in the congregation's Minute Books. It was largely due to him that the synagogue was enlarged in 1836 and overhauled again in 1853. At the consecration service of 1853 Alexander gave a key note address to those in attendance.[132] On 11 August 1850, on Alexander's suggestion, the community voted to form The Exeter Jewish Literary Society.[133] Alexander was voted in as Chair, proposed by Moss Lazarus and seconded by Emanuel Jacobs. Thirty people present at the meeting enrolled as members for a subscription of 2p a week. Collectors were Barnett Lazarus and Lewis Alexander. Emanuel Jacobs was elected treasurer and D Lazarus jnr as honorary secretary. On the committee were Alexander Alexander, M Davis, Moss Lazarus, Myers Solomon and Emanuel Jacobs.[134] The latter also served as treasurer of the synagogue during Myer Solomon's presidency of the community.

During the Chief Rabbi Dr Adler's special visit to the community on 20 August 1854 the Vice-President Moses Lazarus gave a glowing summary of Alexander's contribution to the community. The Chief Rabbi himself spoke about Alexander's energy through whom the synagogue 'had been repaired and beautified.' However community relations were not always harmonious and smooth. On numerous occasions elusions to, or explicit remarks about, tensions in the Exeter community were made in the Jewish press. Alexander was often at the centre of them, possibly because of his central role as president in the community. On one occasion it was reported:

> 'We are sorry that the state of the Exeter Congregation is becoming much reduced in number. Forty years ago it was an important congregation consisting of more than seventy families. Today it has dwindled to three or four families, owing to numerous removals from the ancient city of the west. An unseemly fracas took place during Tabernacles in the synagogue. We earnestly hope some

Headstone of Emanuel Jacobs, 1903

---

[130] *Trewman's Flying Post*, 30 January 1834.
[131] Reproduced in *Jewish Chronicle*, 19 September 1845.
[132] See chapter 3 on The Synagogue.
[133] *Jewish Chronicle*, 16 August 1850.
[134] Emanuel Jacobs was married to Sarah Jacobs who died on 10 October 1899.

moderating influences will be brought to bear on small provincial communities.'[135]

This was not the end of friction. In 1877, acting then in his capacity as treasurer of the synagogue, Alexander brought a court case against fellow congregant Albert Myers for non payment of £3 13s.6d for half yearly seat rental and 2s.6d half yearly maintenance towards the burial ground. Myers who originated from Poland was also an optician in the city. The judge told them the matter should have been settled out of court less they bring ridicule on their community from the Gentile world.[136]

Alexander contributed in no small measure to the civic life of the city. In 1864 he and Solomon Elsner were elected by the Town Council of Exeter to be part of the deputation to present an address to General Garibaldi.[137] A measure of the respect in which he was held locally was shown in his inclusion in a Reception Committee to receive Mr Gladstone on his visit to Exeter in July 1877: 'we learn that the right honourable gentleman in conversation with a coreligionist at Exeter expressed his intention to advocate the cause of the Jews in Servia (*sic*) and Roumania (*sic*), should the subject of their condition ever be brought generally to the House of Commons.'[138] That same year Alexander had been elected a Guardian of the Exeter Poor Corporation, a position which he held until his death in 1887.

A positive relationship between the synagogue and the Bishop of Exeter and Cathedral were shown through a measure of cooperation during Alexander's presidency. In 1870 the University Tests Abolition Bill was being given a second reading in The House of Lords. It sought to remove prejudices against Jews holding office in the Universities of Oxford, Cambridge and Durham and their colleges. At Alexander Alexander's request, the Bishop of Exeter consented to present a petition to The House of Lords on behalf of the Exeter Jewish congregation in favour of the University Tests Abolition Bill. It was testament to good relations and mutual respect between Exeter's Jews and its Christian neighbours.

On 20 October 1880 Alexander and Tryphenia celebrated their golden wedding. The local newspaper reported:

'They were married in the first year of the reign of King William IV and have ever since occupied the same house from which Mrs Alexander went forth a bride fifty years ago. The nuptials of the pair were celebrated according to the Jewish rites in Exeter Assembly Rooms, and the ceremony, which was attended by hundreds of persons, was noticed in public journals at the time. They are both hale and hearty after half a century of wedded life.'[139]

Headstone of Alexander Alexander

It had been mooted in wider Jewish circles that Alexander acted as honorary Reader for the High Holy Day Festivals in Plymouth because the Exeter community was in decline. However this was not the real reason he moved his allegiance to Plymouth. It had to do with divisions within his own community in Exeter. It was reported in the *Jewish Chronicle* that, 'in recent years, owing to the difficulties of a local character [unnamed], Alexander read at Plymouth synagogue.'[140] Divisions within the community are also borne out in the Exeter Minute Books which have survived. The rumblings seemed to begin in the 1850s. Alexander often found himself at the heart of the disputes. In 1854 he was elected President, with Myer Solomon as treasurer and Israel Silverstone in the office of warden.[141] In spite of the community disputes the Exeter Hebrew Congregation could still be praised for 'pursuing an honest livelihood, yet supporting a neat and appropriate building, maintaining their own poor, and sustaining a clergyman in respectability, all out of their own personal contributions.'[142]

---

[135] *Jewish Chronicle*, 17 October 1873.
[136] *Devon Weekly Times*, 30 November 1877.
[137] *Jewish Chronicle*, 6 May 1864.
[138] *Jewish Chronicle*, 20 July 1877.
[139] *Exeter Gazette*, 21 October 1880.
[140] *Jewish Chronicle*, 16 August 1850.
[141] *Jewish Chronicle*, 20 October 1854.
[142] *Jewish Chronicle*, 10 June 1853.

Twenty years later the situation for Alexander Alexander came to a head and in 1877 he was barred from reading from the scroll of the Torah in Exeter synagogue. A former member who identifies himself only as SJL [probably S Lazarus] wrote to the *Jewish Chronicle* of the disgrace which he encountered when he re-visited the community:

'Five and twenty years ago myself, my brothers and several friends left Exeter entirely for the simple reason because constant disagreements and quarrels among the members of the community reigned in such a manner as to make life most disagreeable... my joy was soon marred when I found that the few members now remaining, namely out of which four were considerably over 70 years of age each, were still living in the same quarrelsome way as they did twenty five years ago, which will easily account for the fate Mr Alexander had lately to experience.'[143]

In spite of disagreements with the synagogue committee Alexander remained a pivotal figure in relations with Christian neighbours and promoting Jewish causes. On the centenary of Sir Moses Montefiore in October 1884, Alexander forwarded material to be read in local churches:

'In many of the churches in Exeter the centenary of Sir Moses Montefiore was referred to in the discourses of the day, and in some of them suitable portions of the order of service, issued by the Chief Rabbi and forwarded to the respective clergymen by Mr A Alexander, were read in an impressive manner.'[144]

Alexander Alexander died on 22 February 1887 at the age of 83 and is buried in the old Jewish cemetery. Tributes appeared in the Jewish press and local newspaper in which he was described as 'a venerable citizen of Exeter,' whose, 'patriarchal face and genial countenance will be much missed.'[145] His wife died in Kilburn, London in 1898 at the age of 88.[146]

John Alexander

By the late-1860s Alexander Alexander's brother John Alexander had left Exeter for Birmingham. His son married in the city in 1868 and in the newspaper announcement of the marriage, John is listed as living at 125 Vyse Street, Birmingham and 'formerly of Exeter'.[147] By 1879 John Alexander had emigrated to Cape Town, South Africa. It seems likely that he emigrated there to be nearer his third son after the death of his own wife in January 1879. On 5 September 1876 John Alexander's nephew Jacob (the third son of Alexander Alexander) married Rachel Levy (daughter of the late Asher Levy of London) in the Cape Town synagogue. Jacob Alexander's first wife Lizzie Jessel of Bristol died in childbirth in August 1865, just a year after their marriage. Jacob and his second wife Rachel had a daughter born to them in 1879 and a son in 1880. John Alexander's son Eustace remained in Exeter for his studies and became the first Jewish pupil at the Exeter Grammar School. In 1879 Eustace Alexander gained the Latin prize which was presented by the Bishop of Exeter.[148] That same year his sister Isabella Frances Alexander married Edward Henry in London at 24 St Paul's Place, Canonbury. John Alexander junior, the third son John Alexander, married Bertha Lyons in Cape Town synagogue in July 1877.

Solomon Family

Several members of the Solomon families have resided in Exeter and are shown on various census returns. Finding a genealogical link between them is not easy. However Jacob Solomon (1782-1857) was known to be trading in Exeter by the late 1820s. He married Sarah Phillips (1789-1875) of Plymouth synagogue and they had twelve children. According to family tradition Jacob acted as cantor for synagogue services and kosher slaughterer for the community. Two oil portraits on canvas of Jacob and Sarah Solomon survive in the Jewish Museum in London.[149] The portraits show an elegant, prosperous upper middle-class couple. Jacob is wearing a jacket, smart waistcoat and cravat, and has a thick gold ring on his right hand. His facial expression is that of a gentleman who is pleased with his lot in life. Jacob initially traded as a jeweller but in 1830 he and his wife left Exeter for London where Jacob extended his trade and became a quill dresser and cutter. He established a hardware business in quills, silverware, watches and clocks but maintained his connections with the South-West. He continued to trade with Exeter as well as the port cities of Plymouth and Portsmouth.

In August 1844 S. Solomon & Co of 193 High Street advertised for 'one of two young men as salesmen in a tailoring and outfitting establishment to whom liberal salaries will be given.'[150] Another advert appeared the following year for two tailors' and Woollen drapers' assistants: 'None need apply but those who have a thorough knowledge of the trade and can furnish

---

[143] Letter to the *Jewish Chronicle*, 28 July 1877.
[144] *Jewish Chronicle*, 31 October 1884.
[145] *Jewish Chronicle*, 25 February 1887.
[146] *Jewish Chronicle*, 12 August 1898.
[147] Lewis Alexander married Rebecca Lyons, eldest daughter of Dr Lyons on 2 August 1868 at the Shrubberies, Mosely, Birmingham.
[148] *Jewish Chronicle*, 8 August 1879.
[149] The artist is unknown.
[150] *Jewish Chronicle*, 16 August 1844.

Sarah Solomon (1789-1875), COURTESY OF JEWISH MUSEUM LONDON

unexceptionable references.'[151] The previous year an advert had appeared in the *Flying Post*, for John Solomon's business making bespoke clothes.[152]

The 1841 census lists jeweller Nathan Solomon and his wife Fanny, both aged 55 and born in Prussia. Another was Isaac Solomon, also born in Prussia and a jeweller, aged 65 and living with his wife Rosetta and daughter Caroline at Bartholomew Street. Caroline Solomon married David Kauffman on 13 August 1851, by which time Isaac Solomon had retired and was living at 125 Fore Street. Isaac Solomon and Nathan Solomon may well have been brothers but such details are difficult to confirm prior to 1838 because records are scant. Isaac Solomon died at the age of 82 in 1854 and is buried in the old Jewish cemetery.

Myers Solomon

Another optician and jeweller in the city was Myers Solomon. He also hailed originally from Prussia and became an active and loyal member of the Exeter community for over 40 years. At various times he served as President of the synagogue. He is not listed on the 1841 census for Exeter, so either he had not yet arrived in England or maybe he was living somewhere like the Jewish East End of London. On 8 August 1849 he married Exeter-born Deborah Lazarus at 14 Higher Bartholomew Street.[153] Myers and Deborah had ten surviving children, all born in Exeter: Julia, Elezer, Sarah, Esther, Samuel, Nathan, Fanny, Ruth, Catherine and Eve. On the 1861 census they were registered as living at 60 High Street where Myers then traded as an optician.

It is known that Myers and Deborah Solomon lost at least five children before adulthood, all of whom are buried in the old Jewish cemetery. Fogol died at only three weeks old in May 1859, possibly named after [his grandfather?] Fogol Solomon who died in 1857 and is buried in the plot next to him. Fanny Solomon died in 1871 at the age of 11, and a tombstone with a simple inscription marks the spot behind which three unnamed children of Myers and Deborah Solomon are buried.

Myers Solomon became a respected person locally and was described as a 'conscientious member of the Hebrew persuasion'.[154] He was so concerned over the disagreements within the community during the 1850s and 1860s that the *Jewish Chronicle* reported, 'Mr Myers Solomon, a correspondent from Exeter, complains of grievances in his congregation, most of which are not of public interest... It seems bad management has caused the decay of the Exeter congregation. There is some sense in Mr Solomon's observations, and the time has arrived for concerted action on the part of intelligent members of country congregations to prevent abuses and establish a satisfactory system.'[155] In 1874 Solomon and his wife left Exeter for London where they hoped his business abilities and personal respectability would 'secure him with prosperity.' He died two months later on 24 November 1874 and was buried in the West Ham Jewish Cemetery.

Joseph Marks

Joseph Marks, who was born in Portsea circa 1806, settled in the city and married Julia Solomon of Exeter in the 1830s. Julia was the daughter of Isaac Solomon originally of Prussia and Rosetta Solomon of Rochester in Kent. Joseph and Julia had thirteen children, ten of whom had been born by the 1851 census: Isaac, Sarah, Charles, Josiah, Ellen, Rose, Isabella, Henry, Alexander and Kate. The Marks family joined Exeter Hebrew Congregation in 1832 and by 1838 Joseph was running a shop in Fore Street, probably 113 Fore Street because he is registered at that address on the Voters' Register in 1843 and 1849. Six years later he had opened a shop in King Street where his occupation is described as a clothier. He served as President and Treasurer of the Exeter Congregation and left the city in 1853 after twenty years of service to the community. At a committee

---

[151] The Voice of Jacob, 28 February 1845.
[152] *Trewman's Flying Post*, 8 August 1844.
[153] *Trewman's Flying Post* 30 August 1849.
[154] *Jewish World*, 18 September 1874, quoting from the Western Times.
[155] *Jewish Chronicle*, 24 October 1873.

meeting on 5 July 1853 the Board members recorded a resolution of thanks to Joseph Marks: 'that we sincerely regret losing Mr Marks as a member of this Board, he having during a term of twenty years sat amongst us, filled the various offices of President, Treasurer, etc with honour to himself, and at all times evincing a deep interest for the religious and political prosperity of the congregation.'[156]

The family left Exeter for Australia where they became involved in the Melbourne Hebrew Congregation. Their son Solomon who had been born in 1837, died shortly after arrival in Australia. Another son Samuel Marks died in 1870 and was buried in the old Jewish cemetery in Exeter, having probably never emigrated to Australia with his family.

Moses Hart

Early Exeter Jewish clockmakers included H. Cohen in 1835 and Moses Hart. Moses Hart (b. Plymouth c.1782) appears to be the son of goldsmith Moses Mordecai Hart who arrived in Exeter from Plymouth and registered his mark at the Exeter Assay Office in 1788. Moses Hart junior, was married to Esther who originated from Amsterdam. They had a least four children: Mordecai [Morris], Grace, Saul and Leah listed on the 1841 census. Moses Hart junior ran a business in Fore Street, trading as a watchmaker and general dealer until he left for Liverpool just prior to the 1850s.[157] His son Morris also became a silversmith and took over his father's business premises in Fore Street after his father left Exeter. In 1874 Morris Hart was entrusted with providing a silver plate presented to Sir Edward Watkins MP, by the Liberals of Exeter.[158] Four years later he was elected Guardian of the Poor and in 1879 became the first Jewish member of the Exeter Town Council for the St Petrock Ward.[159] In 1875 he was elected President of the Exeter Synagogue when Barrow Jonas served as Treasurer.[160] These two figures effectively ran the community business and tried to keep the community going during a difficult period of decline. During the 1880s Morris Hart and his wife moved to Cheltenham. On 4 December 1884 their only son Joseph died in a hunting accident.[161]

Mention has already been made of Emanuel Jacobs who was active in the community as treasurer and a trustee of the Jewish Burial Ground. On his death at the age of 83 on 6 June 1903, the *Jewish Chronicle* reported that, 'he was as much respected and esteemed by members of the Christian community as by those of his own creed. No deserving cause ever went unheeded by him.'[162]

Exeter Jews prospered during the early 1800s and were held in high regard by the Gentiles around them. When Abraham Solomon Palmer, a General Dealer of 43 Southernhay, Exeter, died at the age of 85 on 15 March 1879 he was described as 'a great friend to the cause of Judaism.' He bequeathed his whole estate for charitable purposes. This included a bequest of £1,000 to fund a scholarship at Jews' College in London and the interest on a £1,000 to form a marriage portion annually for a Jewish girl.[163] His executors were Hermann Adler of London and two members of the Exeter synagogue, Samuel Platnauer and Henry Solomon.[164] Palmer is buried in the old Jewish cemetery.

Silverstone Family

Israel Silverstone came to Exeter from Poland in about 1830 and opened a jewellery shop first at 95 Fore Street in 1831 and then 107 Fore Street from 1833.[165] He and his wife Paulina had eleven children, all of whom were born in Exeter: Rosina, Bella, Sarah, Rebecca, Isaac, Clara, Maurice, John/Jacob, Selina, Abraham and Fanny. Their eldest son Isaac married Henrietta Blankensee and later settled in Birmingham. Two of Israel Silverstone's daughters married ministers of Exeter synagogue. In August 1854 Bella married Rev. Berthold Albu and four years later her sister Rebecca married Rev. Myer Mendlesohn. Bella and Rosina were Honiton Lace Manufacturers based in the early 1850s at Cathedral Yard

Isaac Silverstone and family

---

[156] *Jewish Chronicle*, 5 July 1853.
[157] On the 1851 Census Moses Hart was residing with his family at 134 Park Lane, Liverpool.
[158] *Jewish Chronicle*, 11 December 1874.
[159] *Jewish World*, 22 March 1878 and *Jewish Chronicle*, 21 February 1879.
[160] *Jewish Chronicle*, 29 October 1875.
[161] *Jewish Chronicle*, 14 December 1884.
[162] *Jewish Chronicle*, 12 June 1906.
[163] *Jewish Chronicle*, 21 March 1879.
[164] *Jewish Chronicle*, 13 June 1879.
[165] *Exeter Pocket Journal*, 1831 and 1833.

in Exeter. Ten years later their sister Sarah was a Lace Manufacturer at 27 High St, an address described on the 1861 Census as 'Lace Premises'. Rosina who married Solomon Elsner died in 1863 (see below), but the other sisters who had worked as Honiton Lace makers moved to Birmingham in 1864 at the same time as Israel and Paulina Silverstone.[166] Israel took up occupation as a pawnbroker there and for a time was in business with his son John until they parted company as business partners.

Elsner Family

Prominent in the community during the 1850 and 1860s was Solomon Elsner who originated from Prussia. On the 1851 census he was listed as a general dealer with a shop at 230 High Street, Exeter. Two years later on 28 September 1853 he married local-born Jewess and lace manufacturer Rosina Silverstone, a daughter of local silversmith Israel Silverstone. By then Elsner's occupation was given on the marriage certificate as optician of 5 North Street. The ceremony was described in the Western Times and attended by the mayor:

> 'The usual afternoon service was read; after which a canopy was erected before the Ark under which the marriage ceremony was celebrated. The Synagogue was brilliantly lit, although broad daylight prevailed. Four Jewish youths held the post which supported the canopy, the reader (or priest) standing in front of the awning awaited the bridegroom's coming; the happy man soon appeared leaning on the arms of two friends, and after a prayer and psalm in Hebrew had been said and sung, the veiled bride was led in by matrons, followed by a bevy of Hebrew maidens, chastely attired and bearing beautiful bouquets in their hands, followed by female friends and relatives of the bride who surrounded her under the canopy. The remainder of the service was then celebrated, the ring encircled the finger of the bride, the marriage cup was partaken of by bride and bridegroom, and a glass vessel laid on the floor near them was crushed by the bridegroom's heel to typify the brittleness of life;[167] every religious ceremony of the Jew has an emblem suited to teach the truth, and the sunniest moment of his life in not exempted. The blessing closed the ceremony, the bridegroom leading off his bride from the weeping maidens, some of them apparently sisters of the bride. There were many Gentile spectators, amongst whom we noticed our worthy Mayor and his worshipful lady, Mrs Cornish. The bride was the fair Miss Silverstone and she illustrates in person the beauty of the Hebrew maiden.'

Breastplate donated in memory of Rosina Elsner

The couple lived at Stoke Cottage and had three surviving children, Dora, Jacob and Pauline (died 5 May 1880). Two sons, Albert and Arthur died in infancy. Of the surviving children, Jacob Elsner (1860-1912) emigrated to Australia and married Sophia Solomon (1865-1927) on 5 August 1890. They had two children, Arthur (1891-1945) and Hubert (1893-1978). Solomon Elsner's name is inscribed in the front of the Exeter Memor Book (1857) which survives today in the Jewish Museum, London.

Rosina Elsner died at their home near Exeter on 25 December 1863 at the age of 31 and is buried in the old Jewish cemetery. Solomon donated a mantle for one of the synagogue's Torah scrolls and a silver breastplate in memory of his wife. Business appeared to decline after his wife's death and an advertisement about the insolvency of his business appeared in the Exeter *Flying Post* on 1 February 1855:

> 'INSOLVENT DEBTORS – Solomon Elsner, late of 11 Castle St in the City of Exeter, previously of 9 Cowick St, St Thomas the Apostle, Devonshire, Optician & Jeweller.'

---

[166] *Jewish Chronicle*, 17 June 1864.
[167] Crushing a glass at the wedding ceremony represents the destruction of Jerusalem at the time of the Second Temple. Another tradition suggests that anyone who can put the glass together from the shards has the right to dissolve the marriage just solemnized.

The business was formally dissolved at Exeter County Court later that month.[168] Elsner remained active in synagogue affairs after his wife's death and is mentioned in the Minute Books (1860-1897) from the earliest entry in 1860. During the 1860s he served as an efficient and respected treasurer to the synagogue. It was not without its stresses during this period when Exeter County Court heard evidence of a dispute between Elsner and Moses Lazarus who had been 'brawling in the synagogue' regarding the payment of £10 16s. 9d. In 1862 the two were involved in a dispute with a hawker who tried to sell goods in the synagogue, just before Sabbath – on this occasion, the hawker was admonished for making a 'market-place of the house of prayer of any persuasion' and told to pay costs. By the 1870s Moses Lazarus, who had once faithfully served the synagogue committee, had moved to London possibly as a result of the 1862 dispute where he died after a short illness on 1 October 1873 at the age of 61.[169] Of Solomon Elsner, the Minutes (1860-1897) record that he stood down as treasurer at a special meeting on 26th September 5627 (1867) and left the congregation the following day. The minutes record a vote of thanks for the 'great exertions he has at all times used to advance the funds of the Congregation' and wished him 'years of health and happiness ...to rear his children with the blessings of providence...'

Solomon married a second time to Rachel Cohen on 8 February 1865 in London. They had two children, Albert Elsner (1866-1921) who married Eleanor Byers, and Eliza Leily Elsner (1867-1920 who married Max Nathan Bingen. Solomon Elsner died on 12 November 1876 at the age of 46.

The Levander family

James Levander is first listed in the congregational ledger for 1827. He had a dental practice at 23 Southernhay Place and in 1835 advertised for an apprentice in the local newspaper.[170] He married Julia Jones on 17th February 1825, possibly in London where both originated. What is known is that they had six children: three boys and three girls. They are listed on the 1841 census as living at Bicton Place in Exmouth. Their youngest son Frederic was born in Exmouth on 29 April 1839 and left a memoir which provides some scant family details.[171] Frederic attended Barnfield School which was headed at that time by Miss Knox. The education that he received was of such a high standard that he was successfully admitted to Exeter Grammar School at Easter 1850. He wrote in his unpublished memoirs:

> 'Here my greatest friend for some time was a boy of the name of Huish, who afterwards (for no reason) turned against me and became the ringleader of a set of bullies who made my life almost unbearable. My home life was, like that of most schoolboys of the time, spent chiefly in work - 3 schools a day and a lot of preparation. My chief solace, when I had any spare time, was reading the very few books to which I had access. Those I liked best were Robinson Crusoe (in Latin) and Anton's Voyages - and watching my brother Edward, who was very fond of drawing and making models... Especially my younger sister Louisa and myself were always wishful to learn about father's and mother's families. Who was the "Grandfather" whose portrait used to hang in the dining room?'

At some point prior to 1850 James Levander converted to Christianity to enable Frederic to advance his education in a society that barred Jews from entering university. Frederic was a brilliant pupil who received a number of academic awards and became Head boy. He was set to go to Oxford University but Headmaster Rev. H. Newport changed allegiance in favour of another pupil and Frederic was unable to go. James Levander's decision to convert was fated because the family was never completely accepted by English Christian society.

---

[168] *Exeter Flying Post*, 22 February 1855.
[169] *Jewish Chronicle*, 10 October 1873.
[170] *Trewman's Flying Post*, 17 December 1835.
[171] Frank Gent has included the Levander memoir on the website of synagogue archives.

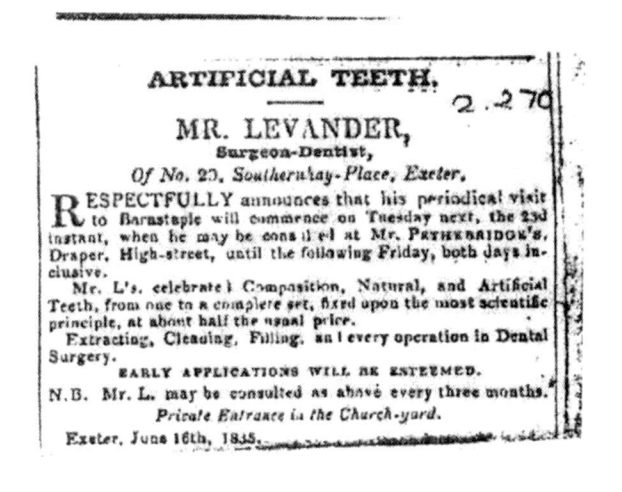

> **ARTIFICIAL TEETH.**
>
> **MR. LEVANDER,**
> Surgeon-Dentist,
> *Of No. 23, Southernhay-Place, Exeter,*
>
> RESPECTFULLY announces that his periodical visit to Barnstaple will commence on Tuesday next, the 23d instant, when he may be consulted at Mr. PETHERBRIDGE'S, Draper, High-street, until the following Friday, both days inclusive.
> Mr. L's celebrated Composition, Natural, and Artificial Teeth, from one to a complete set, fixed upon the most scientific principle, at about half the usual price.
> Extracting, Cleaning, Filling, and every operation in Dental Surgery.
> EARLY APPLICATIONS WILL BE ESTEEMED.
> N.B. Mr. L. may be consulted as above every three months.
> *Private Entrance in the Church-yard.*
> Exeter, June 16th, 1835.

> **POSTPONEMENT.**
> **MR. LEVANDER,**
> SURGEON DENTIST,
> Of No. 20, SOUTHERNHAY PLACE, EXETER,
> BEGS to inform his Friends that Particular Engagements will prevent his having the honour of seeing them at NORTHAMPTON, for a short period.
> Exeter, September 2d, 1835.
> Prepared only by Mr. LEVANDER, and sold at The Mercury

By the 1850s Levander's dental practice was in decline due to younger, cheaper competitors in the city. It was also a tragic period for the family with the deaths of three children within four years. The eldest child Esther died of TB in 1852, a second son in 1854 and Charlotte in 1857. Just prior to the son's death the family had to move from 23 Southernhay to 2 Southernhay. Finally, due to further financial constraints, they were forced to move into lodgings in Longbrook Street and then take up consulting rooms at the premises of Mr Ross, a watchmaker in High Street.

James Levander died in 1857, followed by the death of another daughter Louisa (Lily) in 1860. Five years later James' wife Julia died in Winchester. None of the Levanders appear to have been buried in the Exeter Jewish cemetery, unless their tombstones have not survived and that cannot be known because no burial register exists for the community.

David Franklin

Little is known about David Franklin which is surprising given that he was involved in the Jewish community for forty years. From the 1841 census he appears to have originated from Poland and his original Polish surname is not given. At a quarterly meeting in the synagogue chambers on 17th December 1866 under the presidency of B Myers, Alexander Alexander proposed the following vote of thanks on the announcement of the imminent departure of David Franklin: 'the members of the Board take into consideration the great usefulness he has always been during a residence among us for the past forty years, cannot allow him to leave their midst without their hearty good wishes for his health and long life, and should it be his desire to be interred in our ground, that we allow him that privilege.' The motion was carried. Present also at the meeting were J Levy, B Jonas and A Aarons.

A Case of Food Poisoning

In June 1860 Mrs Jacobs of 'the Hebrew persuasion', whose first name is not given, found herself embroiled in a coroner's case because of the sudden death of her neighbour under peculiar circumstances:

> *'Mr Samuel Hookway, coppersmith of St David's Hill {Exeter}. On Whit-Monday Mrs Jacobs gave a small portion of fried gurnet to Mrs Hookway for her daughter who was ill. The daughter was unable to eat any of the fish, but the deceased, his wife and a grandchild partook of it. On the following morning Mrs Hookway was taken ill and the deceased fetched the surgeon who immediately attended upon her. Shortly after Dr Webb had left, the deceased himself complained of illness ... the symptoms became so alarming that the family of the deceased consulted Dr Budd. All efforts, however, to restore the deceased were unavailing and he died on Sunday afternoon.'*[172]

A post mortem found no trace of poison in his system and therefore the cause of death was not considered suspicious by the Coroner, but mysterious. However it was not an isolated incident of food-poisoning. Mrs Jacobs had also purchased the same day approximately 10lbs of beef and veal and given some of it to her underprivileged neighbour Mrs Maunders. Mrs Maunders and her daughter ate a small portion of it and became ill in the same way as Samuel Hookway. A judge and jury heard evidence that the fish had been fried in oil and egg but had no statement on the state of the fish itself. The court passed a verdict on Hookway's death which stated that it was not an attempt by Mrs Jacobs to poison him and 'the deceased died from the effects of eating fish fried while in a partial state of decay, and therefore poisonous.'[173]

David Parish

David Parish was a local Jewish doctor who practiced from 10 Bartholomew Street. He worked long hours and advertised himself as available for consultancy between the hours of eight in the morning and two o'clock in the night. An extract about his professional services appeared in the *Exeter Flying Post*:

---

[172] *Jewish Chronicle*, 15 June 1860.
[173] Ibid.

Lewis Schultz, portrait by Isaac Bird of Exeter.
COURTESY OF AUDREY VAUGHAN

'His extensive practice has rendered him the depository of many distressing secrets, which are kept with unblemished faith and honour. To persons so afflicted it is highly necessary to observe that an early application is of the greatest importance, and that with such a practitioner any hesitation in disclosing their disorders, must amount to a delicacy as destructive as is false and unnecessary. - A Private Entrance first door up the Passage.'[174]

Parish's name appears in several of the community's documents. He is listed in the Congregational Ledger for 1827 and in the Account Books for the Hebrew years 5595 and 5596 [1834-6] as a full paying seatholder.

Around 1838 he and his wife resigned their seats in the synagogue, although no explanation of why has survived in any of the community's archives. During the 1830s they had been regular purchasers of kosher meat on a weekly basis as attested in the Meat Ledger. Their purchases are recorded from 8 June 1830 to the end of the ledger on 18 September 1832.

The Exeter Jewish community was never large. In 1842 there were around thirty families, i.e. some 175 individuals. From the mid-1850s the community began to decline as some families moved elsewhere: to London or emigrated to South Africa, America or Australia. In 1855 there were only twenty families contributing to the

---

[174] *Exeter Flying Post*, 1 December 1831.

life of the synagogue. By 1878 it had fallen to less than ten. The 1851 census shows around 135 names of Jews resident in Exeter. By the next census in 1861 this had fallen to around 88. Ten years later in the 1871 census it had declined to 65. Families which had formed the main stay of the community began to move away. By 1871 the Elsner family had gone to London, Hyman Davis was living at 61 Colston Street, Bristol and the Silverstone family had moved to Plymouth. Jonas Levy (b. Exeter c.1801) had moved to Penzance. Aaron Israel had moved to 6 Tavistock Place in Plymouth with daughters Fanny and Rachel, and by 1891 Julia Aarons and her family were listed as living in Stepney in London's East End.

In 1870 the community could still muster a good attendance at the High Holy Day services which were led by Alexander Alexander and the newly appointed reader Rev David Shapiro. The *Jewish Chronicle* reported, 'there was no abbreviation of the ritual. The synagogue was full, but not inconveniently crowded on the first day.'[175] However within just two years the situation had changed. A letter from Alexander Alexander to the newspaper in 1872 portrayed a community that was in decline and yet was still acutely conscious and proud of its unique heritage:

'I regret that our numbers are considerably reduced, for very many of our congregants and supporters have left the queen city of the west... In the ark of our ancient and beautiful synagogue is deposited a Sepher {Torah scroll} written on goat's skin, said to be the work of Ezra the scribe; and our cemetery which bears dates on some of its tombstones of more than a hundred and fifty years back, should not be forgotten.'[176]

In his book *The Jews of South-West England* Bernard Susser attributes the decline of Exeter Jewry from the late 1870s to the expansion of the railways. Local people and farmers no longer relied on Jewish commercial travellers and hawkers to supply goods. The population was upwardly mobile and could acquire wares more easily themselves. This may not however account for the demise of Jewish businesses in the city.

It was rumoured that by 1880 the congregation had formally disbanded and the synagogue maintained by a caretaker. However a letter written by community member L. Kahen of 1 Castle Terrace, Exeter to the *Jewish Chronicle* in July 1881 paints a different picture. It reveals that services were still being held. In his letter Kahen refers to the few members who: 'by great exertions and considerable have re-opened this ancient synagogue. The synagogue has not been closed for nearly two years, we having had the services of a minister up to nearly twelve months since. We are much indebted to non-resident members for their assistance, and more particularly to Mr Isaac Lazarus of London who has liberally helped us for some years past.'[177] With no shochet it was difficult for the community to obtain kosher meat, except by arranging for it to be sent the long distance from London.

By 1885, for the first time in its long history the community could not gather enough men for a minyan, [the ten males required for a full service] for the High Holy Days. Former member Mr M. L. Dight who had moved to Birmingham wrote a letter to the *Jewish Chronicle* informing readers that the Exeter community had been one male short of a minyan. He laid the blame with former President Alexander Alexander who was participating as a reader at services in Plymouth instead. Dight expressed the hope that by the next year's High Holy Days, 'an amicable arrangement should be made for a full attendance of worshippers.'[178]

Two weeks later the then minister A. Muller responded with a letter to the editor of the *Jewish Chronicle* that the lack of a minyan for the recent High Holy Days did not 'make any difference to our congregational affairs, which will, we hope be kept up for many years to come.'[179] He also assured readers that visitors to the community would be able to obtain supplies of kosher meat and poultry locally.

The community struggled on and by the mid-1880s it reached its lowest ebb with the abandonment of regular services. It would be almost a decade before the community witnessed another revival.

---

[175] Jewish Chronicle, 7 October 1870.
[176] Letter dated May 1872 from Alexander Alexander to The Jewish Chronicle.
[177] *Jewish Chronicle*, 22 July 1881.
[178] *Jewish Chronicle*, 2 October 1885.
[179] *Jewish Chronicle*, 16 October 1885.

CHAPTER 7
DECLINE AND REVIVAL: THE 1890s AND 20TH CENTURY

IN THE LATTER half of the nineteenth century pogroms and persecution in Poland and Russia led to a new influx of Jewish refugees into Britain. Some made their way to the South-West and joined the existing communities of Exeter and Plymouth. For Exeter the arrival of two émigrés led to a revival of Jewish life in the city. They were Samuel Gittleson who hailed from Riga in Latvia around 1885 and Solomon Glinternick from Moscow, both of whom anglicized their names to integrate into English society. Samuel Gittleson became Charles Samuels and Solomon Glinternick became Saul Glynn. Charles Samuels was instrumental in holding the Exeter Jewish community together from the 1890s until his death nearly sixty years later. Others in the city in the 1890s included Joseph Hart, hardwareman, with his wife Flora and son Moses; also Frederick Woolf, a 27-year old draper who had been born in Redruth, his wife Jennie from Devonport and their son Havelock (b. Plymouth). Other Woolfs in Exeter included Michael and Anna Woolf with their five children, all born in Exeter: Rose, William, Charles, Leah and Alfred. There appears to be no familial connection to Frederick Woolf and his family.

In March 1894 Chief Rabbi Adler visited Plymouth synagogue and on his return to London stopped at Exeter to conduct the first service there since the 1880s. Afterward the service Chief Rabbi and Mrs Adler took tea at the home of Mr and Mrs Samuel Fredman. 'Their departure from St David's station was witnessed by several prominent citizens.'[180] At the end of July 1895 he made a further brief visit to the synagogue. That September the

Charlotte and Charles Samuels with their sons Isidor, Jack, Arnold, Julius and Edgar; and daughters Dolly, Ida, Marjory, Eileen, Phylis and Constance, circa 1909

---

[180] *Jewish Chronicle*, 23 March 1894.

DECLINE AND REVIVAL: THE 1890S AND 20TH CENTURY

Charles Samuels

Arnold Samuels

Charles Samuels' first car in Exeter.
COURTESY OF JUDITH HORNUNG

synagogue was open for High Holy Day services, again the first such services for several years.[181] At the annual meeting in April 1898 Charles Samuels was re-elected President and Sam Fredman as treasurer and honorary secretary. That same year the community decided to support Dr Theodore Herzl's new Zionist movement for the foundation of a Jewish state. They formed a local branch in Exeter called the Bnai Zion Association and sent £5 5s. to support Herzl's National Fund. Elected to the local committee were Mr R. Cohen as Commander, Mr Samuel Fredman as Vice-Commander, Treasurer Mr A Hyams, Hon. Secretary Mr A Schneider, Delegates: Charles Samuels and Mr A Salmon (of London).[182]

The High Holy Day services in October 1906 were conducted by Rev Daniel Caplan and Mr E Ellis of Plymouth.[183] Rev. Caplan appears to have moved from Plymouth to serve as Exeter's minister for a short time until 1908.

By 1910 community membership had increased and new members were actively involved in the religious life of the community. At the annual meeting in May 1910 Charles Samuels was re-elected President. The treasurer was Samuel Roseman, J. L. Sager was elected honorary secretary and E. Rubinstein as representative to the Board of Deputies.[184]

At the beginning of January 1915 another Jewish figure arrived in Exeter. Leon Simon of London took up residence in Exeter after his appointment as Post Office Surveyor in Devon and Cornwall. He was noted as being a staunch supporter of the study of Hebrew in the Jewish communities and an editor of the newspaper *Zionist*.[185]

---

[181] *Jewish Chronicle*, 13 September 1895.
[182] *Jewish Chronicle*, 11 February 1898.
[183] *Jewish Chronicle*, 5 October 1906.
[184] *Jewish Chronicle*, 3 June 1910.
[185] *Jewish Chronicle*, 17 January 1915.

Ida Samuels on her wedding day with mother Charlotte, 1918

Marriages: 1902-1938

The Jewish weddings which took place in Exeter over the first three decades of the 20th century were members of the Samuels or Gabrielson families. In 1902 the community witnessed its first Jewish wedding for thirty years. The marriage between Solomon Glinternick (Saul Glynn) and Everetta Gabrielson Zeitung took place on 24 September at the Cedars, St Leonards, home of synagogue president Charles Samuels. Five years later on 4 September 1907 Everetta's sister Miriam married David Jacobson of Bristol, also at the Cedars. Afterwards the couple settled in Bristol.

On 10 February 1909 another wedding took place at the Cedars between Max Dymond and Anna Dinah Gittleson, daughter of Joseph Gittleson (distiller) and sister of the synagogue president Charles Samuels. Max Dymond was a draper from New Tredegar in Wales and son of the late Lazarus Solomon, a merchant of Plymouth. Anna Gittleson's address at the time of marriage was given as the cottage in the grounds of the Cedars and her occupation as a milliner. Synagogue secretary Judah Sage officiated. Sage officiated again at the next wedding six months later on 1 September 1909 when Sara Gittleson married Harris Hamburg, a widower residing at 49 de Burgh Street in Cardiff. Harris Hamburg was Reader at a synagogue in Cardiff and son of merchant Moses Aaron Hamburg. The marriage took place in Exeter synagogue and was witnessed by Charles Samuels [Gittleson] and Samuel Roseman. It would be another nine years before the community witnessed another Jewish wedding when one of Charles Samuels' daughters married on 27 February 1918. Twenty-two year old Ida Samuels married twenty-six year old Herschell Lazarus of Plymouth. The wedding received coverage in Lady Magazine and perhaps illustrates the status which the Samuels family had acquired by now:

> '{The bride wore} a gown of ivory Georgette and silver lace, with a full Court train of silver tissue, lined with pale pink ninon bordered with silver leaves and draped with beautiful old Limerick lace.'[186]

It was still wartime and Rev. Solomon Lipson, Chaplain to the Home Forces, officiated at the ceremony which took place in the synagogue with the assistance of the local minister Rev. Shinerock. The legal witnesses to the marriage were Lipson and Moses Montefiore Cohen. Britain had entered the final year of the First World War and therefore three of Ida Samuels' brothers, Lieut. Isidore Samuels, Lieut. L. Samuels and Rifleman E. Samuels, were unable to attend because they were still on active service. The groom's brother, Gunner S Lazarus of the Tank Corps, was also on active duty abroad. A reception was held afterwards at the Cedars, home of the bride's parents.

It was almost another decade before a wedding took place again in the community. On 8 June 1927

Wedding of Constance Samuels, 1927

---

[186] *Lady* Magazine, 23 March 1918.

Constance, another daughter of Charles Samuels, married Solomon Zeidman, a master draper from Cardiff. The Exeter synagogue was beautifully decorated for the occasion and the day received extensive coverage in the local newspaper:

> 'The wedding party and guests filled to overflowing the little synagogue which had been brightly decorated with garlands of white and blue lupins, yellow genista, white and red and pink roses, myrtle, purple iris and green foliage, masking the slender pillars supporting the gallery and hanging in festoons in front of the gallery paneling.'[187]

The Ark curtain used on the occasion was described as of 'ivory brocade embroidered with the entwined triangles, emblem of eternity, in gold thread and there was a similar decoration centring the ivory brocade of the canopy under which the bride and bridegroom stood.' The ceremony was conducted by Rev. Wykansky and Rev. Zeffert. Afterwards a reception for 150 guests was held at the Cedars, which by now had witnessed several family weddings.

A third daughter of Charles and Charlotte Samuels married in the synagogue on 1 April 1936. It was 36-year old Phyllis Samuels who married 28-year old bachelor Samuel Wolfe Hirschman, a doctor. From the 1930s Charles and Charlotte Samuels' eldest son Julius became Secretary for Marriages and afterwards officiated at eight weddings held under the auspices of the Exeter Hebrew Congregation. The final wedding to take place before the outbreak of the Second World War was that of Charles and Charlotte Samuels' youngest daughter Eileen to Louis Roseman who married on 11 September 1938 in the newly refurbished synagogue. The ceremony was conducted by Rev W. Wolfson and Rev M. Goodman. It was reported that 'rich crimson carpeting of the whole synagogue is one of the features of its restoration and this formed an effective colour setting for the beautiful floral decorations (gold and red begonias) and for the dignified Jewish marriage ceremony.'[188] Eileen Samuels wore an 'exquisitely dainty gown of white chantilly lace with the widely flaring skirt inset from the waist with panels of fine silk net.'

Constance Samuels' ketubah (wedding certificate)

---

[187] *Express and Echo*, June 1927.
[188] *Express and Echo*, 8 September 1938.

Eileen Samuels' wedding, 1938

The Samuels family

One of the key members who contributed to Exeter's revival from the 1890s was Samuel Gittleson. Born in Riga, Latvia in 1862 he came to England in the mid-1880s and first settled in Plymouth. Once settled and established, he brought over his brother Conrad, sisters and father from Latvia. The only exception was sister Freda who remained in Latvia and later perished in the Holocaust. Samuel Gittleson was keen to assimilate into English society, to make a name for himself in business and become a true 'English gent'. In that he succeeded and by the middle of his life it was not possible to tell he had once been an immigrant from Eastern Europe. The first step in the process of assimilation came when he anglicized the family name from Gittleson to Samuels at some point between the census returns of 1891 and 1901,[189] and thus Samuel Gittleson became Charles Samuels.

During his brief time in Plymouth he met Charlotte Gabrielson (b.1866, London) who was resident in the city.

Charlotte and Charles Samuels with sons Julius and Arnold, and staff

Charlotte was a daughter of Austrian-born Morris Zeitung and Harriet Zeitung (neé Prager from Cracow). The family had already anglicized their surname from

---

[189] It took a while to use his new surname because interestingly on his sister's marriage certificate in 1909 he signed as Charles Samuel Gittleson.

79

Constance Samuels *Charlotte Samuels*

Zeitung to Gabrielson by the time of Charlotte's wedding.[190] Charles and Charlotte married in Plymouth synagogue in October 1886 and afterwards settled in Exeter. Charles opened a business in Fore Street and became a highly successful picture framer. Against the back wall of the shop piles of wood were stacked for framing which had been imported from Latvia. Later Charles Samuels undertook picture restoration and became an eminent art dealer. He was well-known in the South-West as an art connoisseur and was instrumental in bringing Devon artists to the public attention. He also undertook restoration of oil paintings hanging in the boardroom of the Devon and Exeter Hospital.

The Samuels first lived at 2 Haldon Road, Exeter and it was here that their son Gustave died at the age of eight months on 24 August 1893. He is buried in the old Jewish cemetery under the original family surname Gittleson.

Success in business meant that Charles Samuels was soon able to purchase an idyllic English house in which to raise his growing family. Cedars was a smart three-storey town house in the St Leonards district of Exeter with large grounds. Steps to the house were flanked by two lions. The house itself had an extensive basement with several pantries (a china pantry and food pantry). There was also a large glass atrium with exotic flowers grown in pots.

Constance Samuels

---

[190] Charlotte's parents Morris Zeitung and Harriet Prarger had been married in London's Great Synagogue in St Duke's Place on 21 January 1863 by the Chief Rabbi.

Although the house had only one bathroom there were washbasins in every bedroom. The house survives today and is a Grade II Listed building. At Cedars Charles and Charlotte brought up their eleven surviving children: Julius (1887), Arnold (1888), Isidor (1890), Louis (1891), Theresea (1894), Ida (1895), Edgar (1897), Phyllis (1900), Constance (b.1903), Marjorie (b.1906) and Eileen (1907). Two children did not survive infancy: Gustave, born in 1893 and Bertrand born in 1904. There is no tombstone for Bertrand, so it is unclear what happened to his body after death. He may be in a plot in which the tombstone has not survived, or buried with no marker at all.

The Samuels family kept a traditional Jewish household with kosher meat sent weekly by train from London. Charles's brother Conrad Samuels worked in the framing business too and Charles' daughter Theresea worked as their secretary. Later after the death of her father and uncle Theresea ran the business in Exeter. The Samuels were by all accounts a close-knit family and actively kept the synagogue running with Charles Samuels serving as its president for 58 years until his death in 1944. His pastoral work extended to visits of any Jewish inmates of Exeter prison. When necessary the prison warden rang Charles for practical advice about observant Jews in the jail; for example if someone needed to keep Passover while in prison. Charles ran an open house for visitors. 'His home was ever open to the poor and needy of all creeds... His hospitality and kindness to strangers were unbounded,' ran an obituary after his death.[191] His granddaughter Judith Hornung recalls:

> 'One Passover when I was staying with my grandparents I remember grandfather coming into the room where the table was laid with matzas and fried fish balls. He was about to reach to take some fish balls for a prisoner when my grandmother Constance objected and said, "he might have murdered someone. He's not having my fish balls!" He ended up going to the prison with just the matzas.'

In May 1933 Charlotte Samuels wrote to her daughter Ida in Australia where Ida had emigrated with husband Herschell Lazarus. Charlotte told her, 'we had fifteen to Seder [Passover meal] this year which was rather a crowd for us as we have not had so many of late years.'[192] Later that same year on 16 September Charlotte died at the age of 67 and is buried in the Samuels family area of the old Jewish cemetery. Her husband Charles was a widower for eleven years and remained a pivotal figure in the Exeter Hebrew Congregation until his death. On 20 November 1944 Charles Samuels died at the age of 82. His funeral took place in the old Jewish cemetery and was conducted by Rev. Sussman of Plymouth Synagogue. His grave is situated in an area reserved for the Samuels family. An obituary in the *Jewish Chronicle* reported that during his lifetime Charles Samuels 'earned high respect amongst

Charles Samuels

Plaque to Charles Samuels in Exeter synagogue

Charles Samuels' tombstone in the old cemetery, Exeter

---
[191] *Jewish Chronicle*, 8 December 1944.
[192] Letter lent to the author by Judith Hornung.

Phyllis Samuels

the citizens of Exeter'.[193] He was a generous benefactor and member of "Semper Fidelis" Lodge of Freemasons. A plaque commemorating his long service to the community survives in the synagogue today and reads:

> 'Charles Samuels was president of the Exeter Hebrew Congregation for a total of 58 years from 1886 until his death in 1944. He is buried in the old cemetery in a section where many of his family members have been laid to rest.'

The Samuels Children

Julius Samuels worked in his father's framing business and married Josephine Woolf of London. They raised two daughters in Exeter, Barbara and Pamela, both educated at The Maynard School. Arnold Samuels was the artist of the family who studied at the Slade School of Art in London. He had aspirations to be the next great Picasso and made a decision to live in the South of France prior to the 1930s. Making a living as an artist was difficult and his father supported him with an annuity of £2 a month from a bank in Exeter. After the outbreak of the Second World War Arnold Samuels managed to escape Vichy France on the same ship with notable author Somerset Maugham. Arnold returned to England and settled for a time at 1 Brookdale Villa in the seaside town of Ilfracombe, North Devon. In 1952 he was tragically killed when hit by a car whilst crossing the road. Arnold always remained single and never married.

Ida Samuels who had married Herschell Lazarus, a master house furnisher originally of 64 Union Street, Plymouth, had two children Desmond (b.1920) and Joan (b. 1922). Marjorie Samuels became a schoolteacher and married in London in 1947. Phyllis became a nurse and later matron at the London Jewish Hospital. She met Jewish doctor Samuel Hirschman who had a practice in Hampstead Garden Suburb in North-West London and they became members of Norrice Lea Synagogue.

Louis Samuels went into the furniture business. Isidor and Edgar Samuels had a dental practice together in Exeter. Isidor married Mae Hereford-Levy and they had two daughters Jane and Susan. After finishing her education Constance Samuels managed the household at Cedars with her mother. After marrying Solomon Zeidman in June 1927 she settled in Cardiff where they raised a family of three children: Joseph (1934-1973), Judith (b.1931) and Michael (1928-1929). Constance died in South Wales on 25 April 1954 and her husband Solomon on 2 May 1965.

Samuels family at Cedars, Exeter

[193] *Jewish Chronicle*, 8 December 1944.

Harriet Gabrielson

The Gabrielson family

Morris Gabrielson and wife Harriet [Hetty] were living at 16 Oxford Road in Exeter by the time of the 1901 census. Both originated from Poland: Morris from Warsaw and Harriet from Cracow. They came first to London where they married and their first three daughters Charlotte, Amelia, Everetta were born. They settled for a time in Plymouth where youngest daughters Madge and Laura were born. Morris's occupation was commission agent, a flexible job which meant that he travelled at times. It was in Plymouth that his eldest daughter Charlotte married Charles Samuels (Samuel Gittleson). The Gabrielsons moved to Exeter once Charles and Charlotte had settled in the city. By 1901, lodging with them was another new comer to Exeter Saul Glynn [Solomon Glinternick] who originated from Moscow and eventually married one of the Gabrielson daughters.

On 5 January 1905 Morris Gabrielson died at the age of 60; his wife Harriet survived him for another twenty-four years and died February in 1924 at the age of 78. Both are buried in the old Jewish cemetery. Their unmarried daughter Laura died on 12 March 1937 at the age of 55 and is also buried near them.

Glynn family

Solomon Glinternick was born in Moscow in 1873 and had emigrated to England by the turn of the century. In the 1901 census he is listed under his new name Saul Glynn, lodging with the Gabrielson family at 16 Oxford Road and this is how he met his future wife. The following year on 24 September 1902 he married Everetta Gabrielson Zeitung at the Cedars. The marriage certificate was written under his original name of Solomon Glinternick. The surname was formally changed to Glynn at some point soon afterwards. Saul and Everetta had three children: Gerald (b. 1904), Maurice (b. 1905) and Queenie/Muriel (b. 1908). Everetta died at their home in West Grove Road, Exeter on 14 March 1910 at the age of only 34 and is buried in the old Jewish cemetery. Saul married again. His second wife Selina Bergman originated from Minsk (b. 1885) and they had six children: Leonard/Lennie (b. 1914), David (b. 1916), Thelma (b. 1918), Stella (b. 1919), Bertha (b. 1923) and Sarah (b. 1930); all raised at 16 Oxford Road, Exeter. Saul worked as a travelling salesman and sold textiles, bedding and clothes as many Jewish immigrants did at this time. During the 1930s he progressed to having three 'lock-up' units in the markets at Tiverton, Newton Abbot and Okehampton. As he became more successful he took over a general drapers and outfitters shop in Fore Street, Exeter and then opened larger premises in Sidwell Street,

Saul Glynn's shop, Exeter

Saul and Selina Glynn

Lenny, Bertha, Thelma, Stella, David Glynn

'One Passover there was a Seder meal and celebration for all the Jewish community which took place over our store in Sidwell Street. There were several local Jewish families there, including the Samuels, the Boams, the Smiths and Golda Weinberg. Golda was a widow who ran a fabric shop also in Sidwell Street near the Odeon. Her only son went on to become a Professor at University in America and died young.'

opposite the Methodist Church. The family lived above and behind the store in Sidwell Street until it was badly damaged in the Blitz and they relocated to another store in Queen Street.

Selina Glynn was more religious than her husband and kept an observant home, eating only kosher meat, separating meat and milk, and changing all the crockery at Passover time. On Friday nights she lit the Sabbath candles and always fasted at Yom Kippur. Although the Glynn children grew up in a Jewish home they rarely went to synagogue services, probably because, as they recall, it was only open for High Holy Days once a year during the Second World War. They remember that the few services that did take place were packed with American-Jewish soldiers and Jewish evacuees. The Glynn sisters recall:

The three sisters Stella, Bertha and Sarah attended the Bishop Blackall Grammar School in Exeter. Afterwards Stella opened her own dance studio above the family-owned store in Sidwell Street. Stella trained at the Coleridge School of Dancing and then went to London to learn ballet and tap at the Royal Academy of Dance. She also became a member of the Imperial Society for Teachers of Dance. Sarah moved to London to train as a teacher and taught in a Jewish school in London. Bertha took up a retail apprenticeship in Bobbie's department store in Exeter. When the family's drapers and outfitters store moved to Queen Street after the Blitz, Bertha and her older brother Lennie Glynn managed the business. Lennie married in 1944 and moved to London.

In 1949 Saul and Selina Glynn left Exeter for London and settled in Barnhill in Wembley Park with their children Stella, Sarah and David. Saul died in London at the age of 79 years and Selina at the age of 87. Both are both buried in Bushey Jewish Cemetery.

After serving in the Royal Navy, Gerald Glynn (by Saul's first marriage) moved to London. His sister Queenie looked after her four half-sisters in Exeter and

Dorrie Boam with Glynn sisters

then met a German man, married and moved to Canada. Maurice Glynn married and lived in Roseberry Road in Exeter with his wife and then moved to Manchester with their son. Thelma Glynn married Solly Solomon and they moved from Catherine Street in Exeter to set up a business in Plymouth. In 1955 Sarah Glynn moved to Spain after marrying a Czech man, Vladimar Bleier, whom she had met on holiday in Majorca. They had five children and remained in Barcelona for eighteen years. In 1973 they returned to Plymouth because Vladimar was to work with Thelma's husband Solly Solomon. Sarah is now widowed and lives in Plymouth near her sisters Bertha and Stella who both live together.

Religious Life of the Community

Little is really known of any detail about the religious life of the community during the first half of the twentieth century. No Minute Books or records survive for the congregation for that period. Names of those involved in the community are gleaned from scant sources, like the seatholder ledger for example, which has numerous references to Raphael Leon Hassid.

Apart from this source, his involvement in the community would have been unknown. However it is clear that Mr Hassid was a man of substance as a seatholder and received honours at High Holy Day services from entries of money which he gave to the synagogue. He was unlike other seatholders in that he was always given the title 'Mr' or 'Esq'. His membership ran from 1905 until 1929. Another active member on the synagogue Committee was Samuel Roseman. In 1913 he was elected Exeter's representative for the election of a new Chief Rabbi as noted in the Jewish newspapers. Otherwise, again little is known about him.

The quiet prosperous life for Exeter's local Jews would soon be affected by the outbreak of two world wars and one in which they would play their part and serve King and Country.

Eileen Samuels' marriage to Louis, 1938

Below: *Conrad Samuels' 70th birthday*

CHAPTER 8
TWO WORLD WARS

THROUGHOUT HISTORY and contrary to popular assumption the Jews of England have readily volunteered to serve in the British Armed forces to protect the country's coastline and borders from invasion. They have contributed to HM forces and fought for their country and that includes the Jews of Exeter. Some served in the Napoleonic Wars. As early as 1798 there was a call for volunteers to train for arms to guard the country against invasion. Jews in Exeter, Plymouth and Penzance enlisted into the Volunteer Companies.[194] Samuel Nathan of Teignmouth, son of an Exeter Polish Jew, served under Lord Raglan in the Crimea War at Balaclava, Inkerman and Sebastopol.[195] In the 1850s Solomon Elsner and three other Exeter Jews enrolled in the *First Exeter and South Devon Volunteer Rifle Brigade*. This is known because their enrolment sparked a debate and correspondence within the wider Jewish community, particularly amongst London's Jews who were concerned that Elsner and his colleagues were required to serve on the Sabbath. Exeter's Jews made a robust but measured response and reassured their co-religionists that they carried out drill on weekdays and were still able to attend synagogue on the Sabbath.[196]

With the outbreak of the First World War not a single Exeter Jewish family remained unaffected and its young men served in action in the Armed Forces. During

Morris Smith, WW1

Jewish Legion on Parade, Crownhill, Plymouth in WW1. COURTESY ERIC SMITH

---
[194] Lemon Hart of Penzance served in the Volunteers and raised The Ludgvan Volunteers when England was threatened by a French invasion. See also *The Lost Jews of Cornwall* (ed. Keith Pearce & Helen Fry).
[195] *Jewish Chronicle*, 28 September 1899.
[196] *Jewish Chronicle*, 25 November 1859.

the First World War the Exeter community was overseen by the three main families: the Samuels, Glynn and Gabrielson. Five of Charles Samuel's sons fought in the First World War and by a miracle all survived. Members of the Smith family also served in the war and again, all survived.

Joseph and Hyman Smith, WW1

Second World War

By the Second World War new Jewish families had settled in Exeter and joined the existing small Exeter Hebrew Congregation. Numbers swelled and included members of the Smith, Boam and Silver families who had relocated from other cities. These families became the backbone of the Jewish community during this period alongside a number of evacuees and hundreds of Jewish service personnel, including Americans and Canadians. After 1940 and into 1941 the community became reasonably active after a period of struggle at the turn of the century. Military personnel billeted in the area boosted attendance at synagogue services. President Charles Samuels became the link between the local Jewish community and Allied Jewish chaplains, and together they arranged religious services and oversaw the welfare of Jewish servicemen.[197] Samuels also rallied the local Jewish community to help with wider activities for the war effort and although he himself did not live to see the Allied victory in Europe because of his death, he knew that the Allies were on their way to victory after the successful D-Day landings in June 1944. Charles Samuels' eldest son Julius served as a Captain in the Home Guard. William and Julia Boam's sons Bill and Derrick both served in the RAF. Bill trained as a wireless operator/air gunner and towards the end of the war he was posted to Iraq for three years from 1944-1947. Derrick also served with the RAF in Iraq as a flight fitter. Although the two brothers were both stationed in Iraq, their paths did not cross there during the war.

There is one Commonwealth War Grave in the old Jewish cemetery belonging to Pilot Officer H. D Abrams, Air Observer of the Royal Canadian Air Force who died

Derrick Boam with colleague in WW2

Johnnie Kessler (left) at Nissen Creek, POW camp 276, WW2

on 3 August 1941 at the age of 24. He was a member of the crew of Bristol Beaufort L4478 from No.3 Operational Training Unit which crashed one mile north of Croyde in North Devon while on a practice dive bombing flight.[198] The cause of the accident was never determined conclusively but it appears that the pilot lost control. There was one survivor, Sergeant Coles, and another fatality Pilot Officer David Marcus Batley.

---

[197] *Jewish Chronicle*, 8 December 1944.
[198] Information provided by Peter Elliott, Senior Keeper, Department of Research & Information Services, Royal Air Force Museum, Hendon.

Record of the death of a local Exeter Jewish soldier was recorded in the *Jewish Chronicle* in May 1942 after Pte Abraham Yarrow of the Devonshire Regiment died in action.[199]

In the village of Pinhoe, now a suburb of Exeter, there was a prisoners-of-war camp called Camp No.276 or Nissen Creek. It was here that low risk German prisoners were held. The army authorities needed fluent German speakers to work in the camp. One of the soldiers there was Adolf Kessler, a German-Jewish refugee who had fled Hitler's regime and volunteered to serve in the British army. Kessler originated from Cologne and arrived in Britain as a refugee from Nazi oppression before the outbreak of war. In 1944 he enlisted in the 'alien' Pioneer Corps before being transferred to the Royal Electrical and Mechanical Engineers. He served as an interpreter in Camp No.276 at Pinhoe. Some of the German POWs were like many being held in other camps across England - young soldiers who had been drafted into the German forces at the very end of the war and were not true Nazis. Kessler showed them kindness and treated them as accorded by the British army uniform and one of the prisoners made him a box in appreciation. By the end of the war POW camps like No.276 began a programme of re-education in readiness for the POWs' repatriation to Germany.

During the war there were two Jewish Chaplains to the forces who gave help to the Exeter Jewish community. They were Rev. Michael Adler and Rev. J Weintrobe who regularly led services and community activities. They were often aided by Lennie Cohen of the Borough Jewish School who had evacuated with his pupils from South London. In early September 1940 as the Battle of Britain pilots battled over the skies of Southern England with Luftwaffe attacks, Exeter synagogue was crowded for a service of Intercession. At that time Britain stood alone against the might of the Nazi war machine. Lennie Cohen led prayers in the synagogue for victory and the deliverance of British pilots in battle. An address was given by Rev Michael Adler and the community collected for the City of Exeter Spitfire Fund.[200] At the end of that year the community gathered for a Hanukah service which was attended by many soldiers. By now regular services were being held in the synagogue every Sabbath, conducted either by Rev Adler or Lennie Cohen.

A wartime bar mitzvah for Brian Glass of London was celebrated at the end of January 1941 in Exeter synagogue. Amongst the congregation were some thirty servicemen, 'whose excellent singing during the service was particularly noticeable'. The sermon was delivered by Rev M. Adler and an address given by Mr Lennie Cohen. Afterwards refreshments were held in a local hotel.[201] In March 1941 the first Purim service was held in the community for 30 years at which Rev. Adler officiated. Afterwards there was a gathering at the house of Mr and Mrs Glynn:

> 'Servicemen and medical students were among those entertained. Mr Adler and Mr A. A. Taylor spoke about the arrangements that were being made for opening a centre for evacuees at which also the Seder could be held. Interested residents to write to Rev .Adler, 1 Salutary Mount, Heavitree, Exeter.'[202]

COURTESY ELEANOR KESSLER

Irene Silver

---

[199] *Jewish Chronicle* 15 May 1942. Mourned by his wife Mrs S Yarrow in Exeter.
[200] *Jewish Chronicle*, 13 September 1940.
[201] *Jewish Chronicle*, 7 February 1941.
[202] *Jewish Chronicle*, 21 March 1941.

Sydney Fainlight

That same week in the synagogue Rev. Adler addressed the Jewish Students' Society of the Royal Free Hospital (Women's) Medical School who have been evacuated to Exeter and spoke about "The Teachings of the Past for the Jewish Future".

In May 1941, the Jewish Communal Centre which had been the vision of Rev. Adler finally opened at Oddfellows Hall near the Cathedral.[203] Its aim was to provide a focal point for communal activities which could not be held in the synagogue and possibly also because the synagogue was not large enough to hold over a hundred people for some of their events. The inauguration was attended by a hundred residents and many servicemen. Rev. Adler addressed the gathering and summarized the objectives of the centre, and Mrs A. A Taylor outlined some of the forthcoming activities. It was reported that a large number of people enrolled that day. The centre's opening hours were Wednesdays and Sundays from 5.30pm. It was here in August 1941 that *Jewish Chronicle* Cookery expert Mrs L. J Greenberg gave a talk under the auspices of the Ministry of Food, over which Mrs Michael Adler presided. By November 1941 the centre was being used for religion classes and in December a service was given for members of HM Forces led by Rev. Adler and Rev. J Weintrobe CF. Afterwards a concert was given by Miss Stella Glynn.

As with Plymouth, the city of Exeter was heavily blitzed by German bombers during the war and the synagogue did not escape damage during an air raid. In June 1942 it was severely damaged when an incendiary device landed at the side of the building:

> 'The roof was badly damaged, but it is believed reconstruction will be possible later. Mr Charles Samuels who has watched over the interests of the small Exeter community for 55 years after the late Morris Hart, was able the following day to save the Scrolls of the Law, one of which is a rare leather manuscript and the valuable silver ornaments. Some of the latter are inscribed with the date 1813. The quaint ark and the Almemar (reading desk) are intact.'[204]

After the war damage the community struggled on, not really being able to use their place of worship. It was almost forty years before the first floor was rebuilt properly. The second floor which had once housed the mikveh was gone forever. The original arched windows of the first floor which were blown out in the bomb blast, were replaced by square windows.

Wartime weddings

During the Second World War there were five Jewish marriages which, with the exception of the fifth, all took place in the synagogue and was officiated by Rev. Michael Adler. On 17 November 1940 Sarah Rabinowitz (Robbins) married Reginald Lewis of Aylestone (Leicester), a photographer and Private in the Royal Army Pay Corps. Sarah's profession was milliners sales lady and she lived in Old Tiverton Road in Exeter. Her father was merchant and traveller, Jacob Rabinowitz. The wedding was witnessed by Charles Samuels and Harry Greenburgh. A few days later on 24 November the first ever double wedding took place in the synagogue when the son and daughter of Phillip Cohen (Beadle of the

Barbara Samuels' marriage to Sydney Fainlight, 1946

---
[203] *Jewish Chronicle*, 23 May 1941.
[204] *Jewish Chronicle*, 5 June 1942.

At Barbara Samuels' wedding, Exeter

synagogue) married their respective partners. Adelaide Cohen, a 22 year old dress machinist, married 26 year old Abraham Fire, a Private in 9th Royal Fusiliers. At the time of the marriage his regiment was billeted at Seaton House, Ickham in Kent. Adelaide's brother Michael also married in the same service. He was wedded to 19-year old Rose Boam, a saleslady in gowns who was living at Park Road in Heavitree, the daughter of Maurice Boam, commercial traveller. At this time Michael Cohen was serving as a Private in the Royal Army Service Corps and stationed at Clayton, Aldershot.

Two years later on 17 March 1942 Muriel Rosalind Glynn, a daughter of Saul Glynn, married George David, a Private in the army who was based at Bicester. At the time of the marriage Muriel was resident at 159 Sidwell Street where her father ran a drapers shop. The two official witnesses to the marriage were Conrad Samuels and Simon Roseman.

The last wartime wedding to take place under the auspices of the Exeter Hebrew Congregation was in February 1945 at the home of the bride's parents, Craigmillar, Croftslea in Ilfracombe, North Devon. Joan Fainlight, the daughter of jeweller David Fainlight of the town, married American serviceman Captain Stanley Friedman who was a dental surgeon by profession.[205] The officiating minister was Plymouth's Rabbi Benjamin Wykansky. Conrad Samuels was also present to formally witness the marriage. The following year Joan's brother Sydney Fainlight married an Exeter Jewish girl, Barbara Samuels, daughter of Julius Samuels and a granddaughter of Charles Samuel and the late Charlotte Samuels. At that time Sydney Fainlight was a Major in the Devonshire Regiment.

It was over fifty years before another marriage took place under the auspices of the Exeter Hebrew Congregation and that happened in 1997.

Evacuees

Amongst the evacuees to the South-West from the blitz of London were members of the Braham family, watchmakers in London. Also the young boy Lionel Blue, who later became the beloved Rabbi whose *Thought for the Day* on national radio drew many non-Jewish listeners. Lionel was evacuated to Devon to live with a non-Jewish couple. Of his time in Exeter he wrote in his autobiography:

'I found myself in Exeter with a family I really warmed to. I took to "Auntie" Poppy and "Uncle" Harold and they conscientiously tried to educate me and teach me manners. At the beginning we just didn't understand each other. It never occurred to me that children went to bed at fixed times, not just when they were tired. I was also scared of the bathroom. We never had one in the East End... I learnt a lot in Exeter. I did learn manners which were much admired in the ghetto when I got back later. I opened the door for ladies and was especially polite to skivvies and charwomen.'[206]

Above: *Dawlish Habonim, evacuees in WW2*

Below: *Teignmouth Habonim, evacuees in WW2*

---

[205] After the war Joan (née Fainlight) and Stanley Friedman lived in America. For more information on the Fainlights, see Helen Fry, *Jews in North Devon during the Second World War*.
[206] *Hitchhiking to Heaven* by Lionel Blue, p. 31-2.

In Dawlish, Teignmouth and Exmouth three hostels took in around a hundred evacuee and refugee children as part of the Habonim Youth Movement, a movement which trained young Jews for eventual emigration to a kibbutz in Palestine. At the hostels they received training and Zionist education in readiness for their new life. In the end, for many different reasons, many remained in England and never emigrated to Israel/Palestine. Local Jews around Exeter often supported these young evacuees/refugees and in June 1941, for example, the three hostels joined together for an evening of song, plays and dances, attended by many local Jews.

Smith family

The Smith family was affected by both world wars. Between the First and Second World wars the family was based in Plymouth and were members of the Plymouth Hebrew Congregation. Morris Smith originated not from Plymouth but the Russian/Polish border. As a young boy he came to Britain with his parents and lived first in Old Castle Street in the East End of London. It is thought the family arrived as a result of the Pogroms in the 1880s and anglicised their surname from Schmitt to Smith. Morris Smith served in the Jewish Battalion of the Royal Fusiliers in Palestine in a regiment which had been assembled and stationed in Plymouth. He was wounded and eventually shipped back to Plymouth. He liked the city so much that after his recovery in a military hospital he moved his family from London to Plymouth, bringing there his widowed mother Mary, three brothers Nathaniel, Hyman and Joseph, and sisters Esther and Hetty with Hetty's husband Saul Solomon Silver.[207] The three brothers all returned safely from army service in France to discover that their father had died form the Spanish Flu epidemic.

Morris Smith married Sarah Sadie Caplan who hailed from a strictly Orthodox background and was one of the daughters of an East End kosher poulterer. They had two sons, both born in Plymouth: Eric in 1931 and Cyril in 1934. Tragedy struck the Smith family during the Second World War when Mary Smith and daughter Esther Smith were the first civilian fatalities of bombs that fell on Plymouth during the blitz. They are both buried in the Plymouth Jewish cemetery in Gifford Place. A plaque in their memory still exists in the Exeter Synagogue and reads:

> 'A loving tribute to our darling mother and sister Mary Smith and Esta who were killed through enemy action at Plymouth July 10th 1940. Sadly missed by all her children, brothers and sisters-in-law and grandchildren.'

With other victims of the Plymouth Blitz, their names are inscribed on a window at the Ford Park Cemetery (Gifford Place), Plymouth.

The Smiths left Plymouth in 1941; their home and business in Union Street having been destroyed in the blitz. Morris and Sarah Smith moved to Exeter with their sons Eric and Cyril and settled with Morris's sister Hetty and Saul Silver. Sarah ran a shop in Paris Street. Then because of the heavy blitz on Exeter the family moved to Barnstaple, North Devon where Morris opened an emporium in Boutport Street and sold miscellaneous

Joseph Smith's trade card

Joseph, Nat and Morris Smith

---

[207] Mary Smith had been widowed in 1918/19 when her husband contracted Spanish flu.

Herchel Smith who patented the contraceptive pill

Hyman Smith (middle) at the local horseraces

goods including military badges. Sarah continued to travel daily to Exeter to run the shop in Paris Street until it too was destroyed in a German bombing raid. Eric and Cyril attended schools in Exeter before receiving schooling in Barnstaple. In 1946 Morris Smith died and Eric left Barnstaple Grammar School prematurely to return to Exeter to work for his uncle Joe (Joseph Smith), a bookmaker. Eric lived with his aunt and uncle at 3 Fairpark Road and worked for his other uncles at the various Devon Racecourses on race days. This he did until joining the army for National Service in 1949. During his time in Exeter from 1946-1949, Eric recalls that the Exeter Jewish community often joined with the Torquay Hebrew Congregation for services and special events. It was a close-knit community of just a few families. Eric was stationed in London during his National Service and on completion decided to stay in the capital. He worked first for a Racecourse Press Service, then a bookmaker friend of the Smith family who by then had acquired the firm Ladbrokes. Eric became their racecourse representative. Subsequently he joined a firm of Chartered Accountants and qualified. Tuberculosis interfered with his life and after a long stay in hospital he enjoyed a living and lifestyle as a Licensee and Director of two famous West End Members Clubs. In retirement he still occupies himself by monitoring the accounts of The Royal Society of Asian Affairs and The Society for Asian Affairs; two learned societies with which he has associated for over twenty-five years.

Eric's brother Cyril has since died, but during his varied career after National Service had worked for Burberry all over Europe at the American PX stores, Gieves Outfitters at Harrow School, Vidal Sassoon in Bond Street and managed the Pickwick Club for Wolf Mankowitz in London. He subsequently toured the world with groups like The Pedlars which culminated in him staging concert in the UK and Australia for Frank Sinatra, Marlene Dietrich and many others. He had one daughter Sarah from his marriage to actress Lynda Baron.

Of the other Smiths, Eric Smith's uncle Joseph Smith had married his first cousin Mary Shatles, a Russian-born opera singer who had travelled with the Yiddish Theatre. They had four children, two of whom died at a young age. Mary's nephew Major Sydney Cowan joined them at

Sol Silver's Bookmakers licence badge

Fairpark Road after a distinguished wartime career. He had been in Burma with the Royal West African Frontier Force, then settled in Exeter to work in the office for his uncle. In the early 1950s when Joe's son Harry was called up for National Service they finally left Exeter with their daughter Sheila for London.

Harry (Hyman) Smith was a bookmaker in Exeter. He undertook the administrative duties at the Synagogue and organised the visiting ministers for the High Holy Day Services, especially after the death of Charles Samuels in 1944. Hyman had a small tailoring/general store in South Street which he eventually gave over to his niece Irene Silver. He then occupied himself assisting a friend and fellow congregants Harold and Marie Harris with their upmarket ladies' wear shop *Marie Wilson* in Fore Street and Sidwell Street with fellow congregant Harold Harris. Hyman died in Exeter, was cremated and his ashes scattered at The Turf on the mouth of the River Exe. The Smith family had a cottage for a period adjoining the Turf Hotel.

Nathaniel (Nat) Smith may have been the first of the family to move to Exeter. He married a non-Jewish girl in Plymouth, Florence Hafercorn and they then lived at 7 St James Road, Exeter. A letter written after *Yom Kippur* circa 1955/6 from Nat to his sister-in-law Sarah (wife of Morris Smith) gives an idea of the religious activities in Exeter during that period:

Becky Smith and brother Joseph Smith

> 'Just a line to first wish you a happy New Year and you all fasted alright. There were a lot of people in the shul here. I did not know more than half of them. It went off very well.'[208]

Back row from left to right: Peggy Silver, Eric Smith, Irene Silver; front row from left to right: Hetty Silver, Sarah Smith and Zelda Caplan

[208] Letter lent to the author by Eric Smith.

Herchel Smith's wedding, Exeter

Nat Smith lived in Exeter until his death in February 1982 at the age of 89. His body was taken to Plymouth for burial in the Gifford Place Cemetery where other family members are buried. An obituary in the *Jewish Chronicle* described him as 'a man of unique character, a grand old timer.'

Nat and Florence had only one child, a son Herchel (1925-2001) who attended Hele School in Exeter. Herchel married circa 1953 at the White Hart Hotel in Exeter having met his non-Jewish wife in Switzerland whilst convalescing from tuberculosis. Herchel was a member of Exeter Synagogue, although he attended services infrequently. He made a name for himself as an internationally known chemist and philanthropist. He had patented the contraceptive pill and has thus revolutionized the lives of women. He died in 2001 and bequeathed the largest legacy to date to Cambridge University. In the United States, Harvard University was the main focus of his benefactions, His ashes were scattered in Plymouth Sound. He is survived by son Markus Smith.

Hetty and Saul Silver had initially set up home in Plymouth. They had two daughters Irene and Peggy and a son Harry, all born in Plymouth. They moved to Exeter after the blitz on Plymouth. Saul was also a bookmaker and had a pitch at Exeter Racecourse and other venues. Eldest daughter Irene served in the ATS during the Second World War. Peggy attended The Maynard School in Exeter before taking up nursing in London. Harry was an engineer and during the war worked for Metropolitan Vickers on important aircraft work.

All the Smith and Silver families were members of the Exeter Hebrew Congregation. The only living members of this part of the Smith and Silver families are Eric Smith, Cyril's daughter Sarah, Irene's daughter Sheryl, Herchel's son Markus, Joseph and Mary's granddaughters Estelle, Sally Deborah, Nicole and Zara.

Harold Harris

Harold Harris and his wife Marie evacuated to Exeter during the blitz on London. Harold served in the RAF for a time and his wife Marie ran a Ladies' Retail shop in Fore Street and High Street, Exeter, as well as a shop in Torquay. After the war numbers in the community declined, especially after the departure of troops who had been stationed in the area. The community felt the loss of Charles Samuels after his death in 1944, and Harold Harris and Harry Smith worked together to keep the community going. They looked after the synagogue

Herchel Smith's wedding at the White Hart Hotel, Exeter. From left to right: Harry Smith, Mary Smith (née Shatles), Hyman Smith, Polly Smith, Sarah Smith, Eric Smith, Irene Silver and Sarah Glynn

William and Julia Boam

Harry (Hyman) Smith and Harold Harris

which was still in a terrible state of disrepair from the bombing of 1942. As President of the synagogue Harold ran most of its business after the war and paid its expenses from his own pocket. He lived in Exeter until his death on 20 January 1980 at the age of 73 and is buried in the old Jewish cemetery.

Boam family

William and Julia Boam first came to Exeter from London in 1914 to avoid the air raids on London during the First World War. They had seven children: Eva (who died of diphtheria at the age of 6 and is buried in London), Deborah, Lily, Rebecca, Hetty, Josephine, Derrick and Solomon [known as Bill]. William Boam was a commercial traveller trading in rugs and picture enlargements. Later William kept a pub The Devonport

Dorie Boam

in Fore Street, Exeter. He died in 1963 at the age of 84. He was predeceased by his wife who died in 1951 at the age of 68. Both are buried in the old Jewish cemetery. Their two sons Derrick and Bill served significant periods as President of the synagogue and their wives contributed to various aspects of the life of the congregation. Bill married Bertha Davis of London after meeting her while she was studying English Literature at the University of

Julia Boam and Hannah

Exeter. Together they had two sons and a daughter. Bill worked as a ladies' hairdresser and then as a retail credit trader. He is still actively part of the community and oversees the old Jewish cemetery.

Derrick Boam married Ella Levy and also settled in Exeter where he worked as an advertising agent. He too was passionate about the synagogue and preserving it for the future. When Alfred Dunitz first visited Exeter from London in 1978 he recalls that, 'membership was down to seventeen and I found the president Derrick Boam down on his knees with a non-Jewish friend repairing the base of a column supporting the gallery. It was he who kept the *Ner Tamid* (eternal light) alight above the Ark. The building was in urgent need of repair. The flat above the porch (damaged in the war) was demolished.' Having given a life-time of service to the community, Derrick Boam died in 2007 and is buried in the old Jewish cemetery, as is his wife who passed away in 2011.

The contribution of the Boam family to the synagogue over the decades has been significant, not only in serving as President or treasurer. It was thanks to a donation from the family during the 1970s that the old Jewish burial ground was purchased and this precious site saved from urban development.

Holocaust Survivors

The events which unfolded across Europe with the rise of Adolf Hitler in Germany in 1933 had far-reaching ramifications which continues to affect every Jewish community across the world. The trauma of the Holocaust and annihilation of six million Jews in concentration camps in Germany and Poland continues to affect the survivors and their descendants. Exeter is no exception. The stories of members of Exeter synagogue who managed to flee the Nazi regime are included in short profiles below. They are Kurt Wilhelm, Anne Lesh, Hannah [surname withheld] and Golda Weinberg.

Kurt Wilhelm

Kurt was born in Vienna in 1906 to a family that had its own printing business. The business was swiftly confiscated by the Nazis in 1938 after Hitler annexed Austria. Kurt's father had fought for Austro-Hungarian empire in WW1 and been awarded the Iron Cross. He had not thought it would come to this. With other Jews, Kurt had been forced by the SS to scrub the pavements outside his apartment in Vienna. He fled the city after Kristallnacht, the Night of Broken Glass, when the Nazis burned synagogues and Jewish businesses on 9/10th November 1938. Kurt lost his mother and other members of his family in a concentration camp in Poland, presumed to be Auschwitz. He recalled, 'I was a lucky one to get out. Six million didn't get out. I have nobody. My mother was one of thirteen - all died.'

After coming to England and the outbreak of war Kurt volunteered for the British army and served in the 'alien' Pioneer Corps, having trained in Ilfracombe with other refugee soldiers.[209] He was eventually invalided out of the army and lived in Exeter during the war with his

Julia Boam

Bertha and Bill Boam

---

[209] The story of refugees in the British army in WW2 is told in *Churchill's German Army* and *Jews in North Devon during the Second World War*.

wife. Kurt attended services regularly at Exeter synagogue in the last years of his life after his marriage to his second wife, Etty. He was a gentle and cultivated man who regretted that he had had no children. He served for many years as Trustee and Treasurer of the congregation.

Anne Lesh

Anne was born in Thuringia, Germany and also experienced the horrors of Kristallnacht. Her mother managed to secure a visa for her to come to England whilst Anne's brother emigrated to Palestine. Anne lodged with her mother's cousins in Hampstead. At the age of eighteen she trained as a nurse and it was in a hospital that she met her future husband, a doctor, and they married in 1947. Anne never saw her mother again – she perished in one of the death camps. In retirement Anne and her husband Walter moved from North Wales to Exeter and became part of the Exeter Jewish community. Anne died in August 1998 but just prior to her death she donated money for the purchase of new carpets during the restoration of the synagogue.

Hannah

Hannah was born in Berlin Spandau, with a sister five years younger. Their mother and father came originally from Hungary and moved to Berlin for better job opportunities because her father was a scientist. Hannah and her family experienced the full brunt of the Nazi regime in Germany in the 1930s. She knew about concentration camps and witnessed brutality on the streets of Berlin. She could not escape the regime and appears to have spent part of the war in hiding in a cellar. After finally coming to England she moved to Exeter in 1952 where she raised a family.

Golda Weinberg

Golda Weinberg's fabric shop next to the Odeon cinema in Sidwell Street was a "Jewish landmark" in Exeter, especially during the Second World War, when American Jewish servicemen called to buy bargains and presents. Golda never discussed the great sadness in her life until towards the end of her life. Her husband died very young, leaving her to raise their only child Isaac. Isaac went to Bramdean, a private school in Exeter, then Taunton School and won a scholarship to Oxford University. He later went to America where he married and had a son and daughter. When the family was still young he died suddenly. The shock almost destroyed Golda.

Golda regularly attended synagogue services for the last years of her life and was much loved by the children of the community as a grandmother figure. She loved living in Exeter and often refused requests from other family members to move to London. Golda lost most of her extended family who perished in the Holocaust in Poland, some in the Lodz Ghetto and others in death camps. One relative Lola survived Auschwitz and a cousin survived Belsen. Golda herself lived to a great age and died in 1990.

Every year on 27 January the congregation participates in Exeter's events to mark Holocaust Memorial Day. Today in the Dunitz Room, to the right as one enters the lobby of the synagogue, there is carved sculpture by Marcus Vergette from an original oak timber found during the 1998-9 restoration project. On the wall nearby hangs a painting entitled *Yizkor* by artist Rikki Romain which commemorates the Holocaust.

Yizkor by artist Rikki Romain commemorating the Holocaust

CHAPTER 9
REVIVAL AND THE COMMUNITY TODAY

THE POST-WAR PERIOD brought its own challenges and attendance at religious services fell dramatically. Servicemen and evacuees had left the area and the community's membership centred once again around just a few families. For the next thirty years its future seemed uncertain. The main families involved in the synagogue were Boam, Smith, Harris, Glynn and Samuels. There was also jeweller Abe Quait who was a prominent member of the congregation for sixty years from 1933 until his death in 1993. A plaque of remembrance to him still exists in the synagogue today. Two other plaques hang on the wall of the synagogue for other people connected to the community during the 1950s. One is in memory of Francis Miriam Brock, dated 1955; and the other is dedicated to her husband John Brock [Jacob Nathan] of Plymouth for 'his generous gifts' to Exeter synagogue. War damage to the synagogue had not yet been repaired because reparations money had not come through. Harold Harris took care of synagogue affairs and was aided later by Geoffrey Karpel and members of the Boam family. Ralph Collett who had farmed in North Devon during the war, later owned a business in Exeter which supplied second-hand office equipment. He was a benefactor of the synagogue and acted as nominal treasurer in the 1960s and 70s. Finances were difficult for the community during this period and Ralph, like other members before and after him, paid the bills from his own pocket.

During the 1960s Malcolm Wiseman first became involved with Exeter in his role as Minister for Small Communities. His post involved travelling from London to provincial and small communities to offer practical support and provide some religious services. He was also engaged in visits to students at the university and the local prisons. The community became a little more active but there were no young people or children to provide sustained renewal.

By the 1970s membership had dwindled to such levels that the future looked precarious. The synagogue's future was probably saved by students at the University of Exeter who gave it new impetus and raised attendance at services alongside existing community members. In

Hanukah party

August 1972 Malcolm Wiseman attended the annual meeting of the congregation to give as much support as he could to the community's future. The meeting was held in the home of the then President Derrick Boam. On the agenda was a discussion about services, the autumn High Holy day and also how to provide adequate facilities for the Jewish students at the university who had been holding services on the campus, including a weekly Friday night service. It was also an opportunity to present outgoing President Mr G. Karpel with a gift of thanks before his move to London with his wife.[210] Today a plaque still hangs in the synagogue commemorating his service as President from 1965-1972.

Towards the end of 1976 an appeal was made to the wider Jewish community for funds of £3,500 to maintain the synagogue for use by the students. Three thousand pounds had already been raised out of a total of £6,500 that was needed. Malcolm Wiseman was behind a project to expand the facilities on the first floor of the synagogue to provide a bedsit and shower for students who needed accommodation. Funds for this project were raised by Alfred Dunitz JP who was also involved in maintaining the disused cemeteries in Devon and Cornish ports. Today the first floor room serves the community as a meeting place with a kitchen for catering purposes.

It was during the 1970s that the community became suddenly aware that the lease on their burial ground (now the old cemetery) had expired. The ground was at risk of development and having to transfer the graves to a new ground. Negotiations proved effective and the community was able to buy the burial ground outright with a substantial donation from the Boam family.

During the 1980s Derrick Boam served as President, Kurt Wilhelm as treasurer, Brana Thorn as Student Liaison and Bertha Boam as Social Organiser. At Yom Kippur 1981 Jerry Lucas responded to an advertisement placed by Derrick Boam in the *Jewish Chronicle* for someone to lead services over the High Holy Days and this was his first year. Harry Freedman entered the Exeter scene at this time and recalls:

'I attended Exeter synagogue for the first time that Yom Kippur. At the end I said to Derrick Boam, "see you next week" (meaning the festival of Sukkot). He replied, "what do you mean next week? Our service will be next year..." That was the catalyst for running regular services. I organised and ran services once a month from then on. Regular attendees included Derrick and Ella Boam, Bertha and Bill Boam, Mrs Davies (Bertha's mother), Golda Weinberg, Abe Quait, Ralph Collett, Derrick Nahum who travelled faithfully every time from his home in Yeovil, Kurt Wilhelm, Danny and Liz Morris and family from Okehampton, Ricky Romain and his family from Axminster, the Redstone family

(farmers near Totnes) and Uri Davis, an academic at the University of Exeter. We struggled to raise a minyan for services but when we held a Hanukah party we got over a hundred people. Bertha Boam began religion classes on Sunday mornings. Around this time some local Christian evangelists started to attend the synagogue services. This led to tensions. On one occasion a Hebrew copy of the Christian Bible was left in the synagogue.'

Services were led by Harry Freedman with one scheduled service a month. Occasionally Malcolm Wiseman, Minister for Small Communities, came down from London to officiate at services or special events, and Jonathan Gorsky a few times. However, tensions did not only exist with a handful of difficult local Christian evangelists. The community faced political differences and pressure to conform, as Harry Freedman recounts:

'Exeter synagogue was the venue for the bar mitzvah of Uri Davis's son Gilad. This proved controversial because Uri was a longstanding pro-Palestinian campaigner. We resisted pressure from the United Synagogue's Beth Din (Rabbinical Court) who wanted the ceremony cancelled.'

During September 1983 six services were held for Rosh Hashanah (New Year) and Yom Kippur led by Jerry

---

[210] *Jewish Chronicle*, 18 August 1972.

Sonia Fodor re-enacts a Jewish wedding with schoolchildren

Lucas from London, assisted by Harry Freedman. After Yom Kippur thirty people sat down to a communal meal to break the fast. The following month the congregation's newsletter advertised One World Week and the Week of Prayer for World Peace. A Hanukah party was held in the synagogue that December. On 18 March the following year the festival of Purim was celebrated in the synagogue with a party called *Meshugganah Hatters Tea Party*, followed by a trip to Plymouth synagogue to hear the reading from the Scroll of Esther.

The Exeter Jewish Women's Group first met on 15 February 1984 at the home of Brana Thorn and the following Sabbath held a Creative Erev Shabbat service in the synagogue led by Brana. It was attended by 25 people and followed by a meal. The newsletter for April 1984 reveals that the *brit* [circumcision] took place for Leo Thorn-Gent, the first child of Frank Gent and Brana Thorn. This month also saw a blessing/naming of Ruth Jackman, daughter of Nancy & Gilad Jackman. October 1984 saw the formation of religions classes again. Children aged 5-8 were taught at Bertha Boam's home and older children and adults had sessions at the synagogue led by Frank and Brana. That same month a Shabbat Camp/weekend retreat was held in a field in a rural part of Devon by newcomers to the community and consisted of an open-air Sabbath service and discussions, attended by eight adults and seven children. In November monthly services resumed at the synagogue and services were also held for Hanukah.

In February 1985 a weekly Torah study group was formed by Harry Freedman. Frank Gent delivered a lunchtime lecture at the Royal Albert Memorial Museum on Exeter Jewish silversmith Ezekiel Abraham Ezekiel. It was this month that saw the death of Bernard Rosenberg, a longstanding and faithful member of the community. Later that year some of the congregation participated in interdenominational 'One World Week', and High Holy day services were led by Jerry Lewis. Derrick Boam who had been president for many years and wanted to retire, became Honorary Life President. Frank Gent was appointed President with Bill Boam as treasurer and Josie Odoni as secretary. Services continued to be led by Harry Freedman.

Celebrating 250 years of Jewish Life in Exeter

During 1985 a number of activities took place to celebrate approximately 250 years of Jewish life in Exeter. In February an exhibition opened at Exeter Central Library on '250 Years of Jewish Life.' It attracted much attention with people visiting from Dorset and Cornwall. Following its success the Devon Library Service toured the exhibition around libraries, schools and other institutions in Devon. In October the community organised an evening festival at Devonshire House in the University of Exeter under the auspices of the Jewish Society. This included live music with Jewish and Israeli dancing, Israeli food, an historical exhibition and a puppet show for the young generation. The event was attended by over 200 people. The celebrations were concluded on Tuesday 5 November with a Civic service at the synagogue attended by the Mayor and Mayoress of Exeter and Councillors. Amongst those present were representatives of churches and the University of Exeter. Frank Gent paid tribute to Mr Alfred Dunitz who had raised £30,000 to extend the synagogue in 1980. Exeter City Council agreed to erect a sign marking Synagogue Place. Bertha Boam instigated a building/investment fund for future major repairs.

Bar Mitzvah of Leo Samson Thorn Gent
יהודה שמשון בן אפרים וברנה

Exeter Synagogue
5th Nisan, 5757
12th April, 1997

Order of service for bar mitzvah of Leo Thorn Gent, 1997

Frank Gent leading children's religion classes

Revival Continues

At an open meeting in October 1985 concern was expressed at the level of damp in the synagogue and major repairs needed to the roof as well as lack of space in the cemetery in Magdalen Street. It was decided to charge a fee for the growing number of school visits to the synagogue to help with minor renovation work. At the end of 1985 the Jewish Playgroup first met for children under the age of five.

January 1986 saw the passing of community member Dr Walter Lesh. The community also began to look at its deeds and gaining charitable status. In February the first meeting of West Country Jewish Women took place. That same month a talk on Soviet Jewry was given in synagogue by Melinda Simmons. The first *West Quest*, a conference to gather Jews of the South-West, convened in Bristol attended by six members from Exeter congregation: Frank Gent, Brana Thorn, Phoebe Davies, Bill and Bertha Boam, and Derrick Nahum. Weekly religion classes continued to be led on Sundays by Harry Freedman and Bertha Boam. In April Melanie Solomon took over from Brana Thorn as Student Liaison and Brana became the representative for West Country Jewish Women. In May the community marked Yom Ha-Shoah [Holocaust Day] in the synagogue. On 20 July a summer concert by the Exeter Children's Chamber Orchestra took place at the Barnfield Theatre to raise funds for Exeter Synagogue Restoration Fund. That September the High Holy Day services were led by Harry Freedman and Frank Gent. That month it was agree that building improvements to the synagogue during the next year should include redecoration, replacement of the flat roof and installation of electric radiant heaters. Frank Gent continued visits to the sick, and with Harry Freedman, also prisoners in Exeter Prison, Dartmoor Prison and Channings Wood. Members from Exeter and Torquay Hebrew Congregations joined in a successful picnic extravaganza. In December a tree was planted in the Jewish cemetery, dedicated to the dedicated to the memory of those who died in Holocaust.

In March 1987 Harry Freedman left Exeter for London but returned on occasion to lead services. He encouraged Frank to take over the regular synagogue services so Frank travelled to London frequently to attend classes at Jews College to order to perfect his singing for the services. High Holyday services were covered by Gerry Lucas from London and for many years by Barry Gould, a chazan from Leeds. Purim that year was celebrated at the home of Frank and Brana and attended by sixty-eight people. It included story-telling, a Jewish puppet-theatre and singing. The newsletter reported that, 'Superb kosher food was provided by Peter and Lili Fabian, caterers from London.' That May the congregation participated in the Exeter Festival and offered three events: an Open Day at the synagogue on 24 May, a Jewish Film Evening at St Luke's College on 31 May, and a musical event entitled 'The Music of the Synagogue' with Geoffrey Shisler at Barnfield Theatre on 7 June. Over 500 people attended the Open Day and 200 people for the concert.

High Holy Day Services in September 1987 were led by Barry Gould from Leeds. That month saw the deaths of Polly Smith, Sam Springer and Erwin Kauders. That autumn saw the first meeting of the Exeter Synagogue Music Group. By the end of the year monthly Friday night services were held for the first time in the community's living memory. It saw the arrival of new members to the community, with all ages becoming involved in synagogue life. A ten-week programme of Hebrew classes took place in conjunction with Devon Community Education. The community did not have its own *mohel* [for circumcisions] and circumcisions during this period were performed by local doctor, Dr Philip Carmen. By now the synagogue's income from subscriptions had increased significantly to form the largest part of the its income.

Communal Passover seder

During 1988 the Jewish Society at the University of Exeter continued to be actively involved with synagogue life and it was this year that the first meeting of the Exeter Jewish Socialist Group took place. In February 1988 radio and sports broadcaster Mitchell Alexander died as did member Ralph Collett in May 1988, leaving a bequest to the synagogue. At the end of the year over a 150 people attended the community Hanukah party which was held at the Friends Meeting House and a presentation was given to Harry Freedman in recognition of his contribution to reviving synagogue services. The AGM that month was followed by a meeting of the Exeter Jewish Literary Society which had been founded nearly a hundred and forty years earlier in 1850 at the suggestion of the then President Alexander Alexander. This period also saw the funerals of John Victor Marcus, David Henry Hackney, Jacob Gilboa and Kurt Wilhelm. As part of that year's Exeter Festival, a concert was held at the Barnfield to mark the 225th anniversary of the foundation of the synagogue and also a concert in the synagogue with poet Wanda Barford, accompanied by lute and soprano.

In 1990 redecoration of synagogue interior was undertaken with offer of financial support from descendants of the Ezekiel family living in America. During 1991 Jonathan Gorsky, an Orthodox Jew and educator, served as guest minister for services in February.

Frank Gent with a Torah scroll, Exeter synagogue

He continued to lead services periodically throughout the year. This year saw the deaths of Hetty Willhelm, Joan Cohen, Beckie Brodie, Karl Schiller and former president Geoffrey Karpel. By the turn of 1992 two services a month were being held in the synagogue. A West Quest meeting in June attracted over a hundred Jews from South-West England and Wales. Towards the end of the year Hilary Radnor was taking occasional services and a communal Hanukah party was again held at the Friends Meeting House. Frank Gent had had success in outreach through the monthly newsletters and since 1983 the number of families connected in some way to the congregation had risen from 20 to 150. In August 1993 the congregation reconnected with its past with the celebration of the Golden bar mitzvah of David Long of Pennsylvania, USA. It was 50 years after David's 13th birthday when he should have had a bar mitzvah. David was a descendant of founding member of the synagogue Abraham Ezekiel. David Long generously donated a £1,000 to the synagogue on the occasion.

During 1994 Shabbat services were held weekly but the monthly pattern had changed to become more inclusive of Jews of differing traditions. Two traditional services were led by Ellis Weinberger using the Singer Prayer Book and two Progressive services led by Hilary Radnor and Harold Miller. Visiting rabbis/ministers during this period was Francis Berry from Bristol and Harry Freedman from London. The religion classes were run by Rivka Glaser. During the late 1990s High Holydays services were led by Rev Barry Gould from Leeds, monthly Friday services by Harry Merkin and Saturday morning services by Frank Gent. In September 1999 the community kept abreast of the modern age by launching an official website.

The community was growing and witnessing a period of revival. Frank Gent officiated at numerous weddings, funerals, circumcisions and bar/batmitzvahs. He connected with older Jews who had had no contact with the community but in their senior years were aware of their mortality and requested to see a local Jewish leader. Some had married non-Jews around the wartime but had a desire to connect with their Jewish roots. Frank Gent visited them as their health deteriorated and then facilitated a Jewish burial after their death. He and wife Brana visited the elderly or sick until later demands of their own family life increased and Sonia Fodor took on the welfare and pastoral visits.

During the 1990s the community mourned the death of several prominent members which included: Holocaust survivor Golda Weinberg who passed away in August 1990, Abe Quait in May 1993, Mrs Davis, mother of Bertha Boam, in February 1996 and Derrick Nahum in January 1998.

Thorn-Gent family

Frank Gent and Brana Thorn arrived on the scene in Exeter in the 1980s and became actively involved in the synagogue's revival. Frank Gent and wife Brana had met in London after Brana had completed university. They married in St John's Liberal Synagogue, London in August 1983, eventually moving to Bideford in North Devon. With both having refugee parentage they had much in common. Brana grew up in Gant's Hill, Essex which during the 1960s was one of the largest Jewish communities in Europe. Frank's childhood was shaped by the Jewish community in Manchester. Brana comments:

'Having spent our early years as a couple in Israel on a kibbutz, in Devon we began to recreate our "Israel experience" in Devon. We made contact with Exeter synagogue and after a while managed to find out about services. I remember travelling on the bus, for an hour and half each way for a Saturday morning service where Harry Freedman was leading a service. The congregation comprised mainly people who had moved to Exeter during the Second World War and stayed there. It was the first time that I had ever sat through a whole Saturday morning service. I appreciated the welcome from the congregation, the beautiful synagogue and the sense of being able to be Jewish in what was otherwise a white, Anglo-Saxon, Gentile area of England. In Bideford I felt that as a Jew I was living in an alien community where I didn't quite understand the rules, also I looked foreign and had a different outlook to life and customs.

Adults from left to right: Sonia Fodor, Brana Thorn, Frank Gent, Stella Tripp, with Lily, Leo and Esther Thorn-Gent
Sonia Fodor at the Ark

In the 1980s there were very few minority ethnic groups in Devon, other than Indian and Chinese families who had restaurants, market stalls or occasional cornershop. Meeting Jews connected to the Exeter community provided Frank and Brana with a sense of identity with which they could feel comfortable. They began to contact other Jews in the area and attended services regularly. This led to the creation of a wide social network of Jews of all ages and backgrounds, often celebrating the Jewish festivals together or enjoying each other's company. Frank and Brana have three children: Leo, Lili and Esther whom they have raised with a strong sense of their cultural Jewish heritage. They found in the community other Jews who wanted to raise their children as Jews, or older Jews who wanted to re-discover their identity later in life. This mix formed part of the Exeter Hebrew Congregation from the 1980s/early 1990s. Brana started to give talks about Judaism to local churches, schools and branches of the Women's Institute. Frank took on the role of President of the synagogue and injected new energy and life into educational projects, some of which included non-Jews. He hosted many school groups at the synagogue, explaining Judaism firsthand to school children who had never met a Jew before. Over many years he undertook extensive and valuable research into Exeter's Jewish history, with a special interest in the Ezekiel family, Gabriel Treves and Exeter Jewish silversmiths. His research resulted in the organisation of an exhibition which was displayed in the Exeter Library.

Sonia Fodor at the Ark

Frank and Brana continued to attend services and organise social events at the synagogue. As the community grew other venues were found to hold the Seder (Passover meal), like school halls or the Priory or Palace Gate. Hanukah and Purim parties were held at the Quaker Friends Meeting House or on occasion Frank and Brana's hosted parties and socials events in their own home to welcome new people to the community. One of the first large events that they initiated and organised took place at the university in November 1986 to celebrate about 250 years of Jews living in Devon. Brana recalls:

'It was to be crucial in attracting people who identified as Jewish or were interested to discover more about their Jewish connections. Over 200 people attended. As well as Jewish food it was the first public appearance of a klezmer band with Joel Segal. The band, which has entertained at our community events, festivals and special occasions for over 30 years now has a caller so that people can learn the dances. There was a Jewish puppet theatre which proved popular. From this event many new Jews wanted to know more about the Community and subscribed to the Exeter Hebrew Congregation Newsletter which Frank wrote and produced for many years by Letraset in the days before computers.'

The community's revival led to the formation of a Cheder (religious study group) for children and adults on a Sunday morning in the synagogue. Adults were able to learn Hebrew while their children were given religious instruction or other activities. Frank taught some of the adult education classes in Hebrew and attracted a few local clergy to study too. Jewish women continued to meet with their children and also separately in Jewish Women's Groups. As the children in the community reached their bar/batmitzvahs special religions classes were held for them to learn to read from the Torah scroll. Students from the University of Exeter were welcomed and met for Friday night meals in the synagogue as well as attending community events. Frank organised many Jewish social and cultural events in the synagogue and in local schools, theatres with film shows, art talks and musical evenings. Alongside these events other groups met: the Jewish Socialist Group and co-counselling group. Exeter synagogue also hosted events for the South-West Jewish Communities, all of which contributed to a vibrant community.

In October 1985 Frank was elected President of the congregation to replace Derrick Boam who was retiring after 13 years in the post. At this time Frank was employed as education officer at The Royal Albert Museum in Exeter. In January 1989 Exeter Cathedral hosted the Anne Frank Exhibition during which Frank led schoolchildren and students around the exhibition. Three hundred schoolchildren visited on its opening day alone.[211] By the time the exhibition closed on 6 February it had had thousands of visitors and over a hundred groups. The exhibition made an impact on the wider Exeter community, with vigils held in the High Street in memory of victims of the Holocaust. From 1987 Frank Gent joined Television South West's Religious Advisory Board and was occasionally asked to speak on 'Pause for Thought' on Radio Devon.

After nearly twenty years of actively running services and religious events, a turn of ill health forced Frank to retire from synagogue life. Now he undertakes charitable work for Cavernoma Alliance UK and sits on its Board of Trustees. Brana remains active in groups in Exeter, in particular the Jewish Women's Group and the Second Generation Survivors. Brana reflects on this period of revival from the 1980s: 'Some of the highlights for me looking back at the development of the Jewish Community were times when we attracted about 100 people celebrating the festivals. There were people of all ages, backgrounds, levels of faith and observance who came together to celebrate being Jewish as well as welcoming their non-Jewish partners and friends.'

Sonia Fodor

In 1979 Sonia and Michael Fodor arrived in Exeter from London.[212] From 1960-62 Sonia and Michael had lived in Karachi in Pakistan with their children Karen, Martin and Neil. It was there that Sonia founded the British School and Michael worked for UNESCO developing a literacy in Kashmir, Ceylon and Iran. They returned to London in 1962 where Michael took up employment with the Central Office of Information. After they moved to Exeter in 1979 Sonia had not linked up to the Jewish community until she attended the exhibition which had been organised by Frank Gent at the Central Library. She had had a religious upbringing in Dundee, Scotland and later became a school teacher working with children receiving home tuition. Michael, who originated from Hungary before the Second World War, had lived in London but was not a practising Jew. He was educated in a Quaker Boarding School and when in Exeter identified more closely with the Quakers but supported Sonia in her work in the Jewish community. In 1989 Michael and Sonia volunteered to act as stewards for the Anne Frank Exhibition at Exeter Cathedral. As a result Michael became one of Exeter's Red Coat tourist guides and Sonia began her more active involvement with the Exeter Hebrew Congregation. There were many elderly Jews in

---

[211] *Jewish Chronicle*, 27 January 1989.
[212] I am grateful to Brana Thorn and Renee Smithens for agreeing to visit Sonia Fodor to obtain information from her memories of serving the Exeter community during the 1980s and 90s. The material in this section comes from their interview with Sonia on 1st June 2011.

Brana Thorn-Gent with Sonia Fodor, 2011

the congregation, like Kurt Wilhelm and wife Hettie, and Golda Weinberg who were Holocaust survivors. The Jewish community then had a very low profile. Outside the synagogue, few people knew of its existence. The turning point was the community's major celebratory event organised at the University of Exeter in 1986. Sonia took over the organisation of Hanukkah and Purim parties and the annual communal Passover seder. Having joined the synagogue as Minutes secretary, she then served for a number of years as President after Frank Gent's retirement from office.

The local Council of Christians and Jews

In 1990 Frank was approached by a local Roman Catholic priest Father David Julian Friend, whose mother had been Jewish, to start a local Council for Christians and Jews (CCJ) in Exeter. Together they chaired the local group which was inaugurated in a special event at Exeter Cathedral in the summer of 1991. The guest speakers were Malcolm Wiseman and Revd. Marcus Braybrooke who were both actively involved on a national level with the CCJ. Helen Fry attended the inaugural meeting at the invitation of her friend Father David Friend and was inspired by the vision of the CCJ and subsequently joined the committee. With Frank Gent, David Friend, Sonia Fodor, Jane Nethsingha and David Hill she actively worked together to bring an interesting educational and social dimension to the local CCJ. Meetings usually took place on a monthly basis and often at the synagogue. On 16 June 1991 the synagogue hosted an Open Day to promote the new CCJ branch. The CCJ was indicative of a new era in which the community was confidence in itself to be given wider publicity in society. Having led a low profile for so long, it felt confident to embark on wider inter-faith relations with other faiths in the South-West and took part in an inter-faith society which was founded at the university during the 1990s. During the Iraq War when there was much fear of Muslims in

Bill Boam, 2012, courtesy Jonathan Fry

Britain, the Exeter Jewish community offered its solidarity with Exeter's Muslims after the mosque was attacked.

A measure of the special relationship which had developed between Jews and Christians locally was shown when CCJ committee member David Hill was diagnosed with terminal cancer and passed away at the age of only 36 in 1995, with a wife and three young children. Because around 500 mourners were expected to attend (and did) Crediton's Anglican Parish Church gave permission for a full Roman Catholic Mass to take place in the church for the funeral. It was particularly moving to see many members of Exeter's Jewish community seated in a row together at the funeral who might otherwise feel uncomfortable about being in a church. On that occasion they were ironically united with other Christian denominations in being able to attend but not participate in the Catholic rite (Mass). During the Mass the Biblical reading during the set-liturgy for that Easter week included a difficult passage from the New Testament which made some Christians bristle because it was one of the so-called 'anti-Jewish texts of the New Testament. The local Jews seemed much more relaxed about it than some of the Christians. It was after all, a time to remember David's life but also an apt reminder of the significance of the work of Christian-Jewish relations and inter-faith understanding.

During the early foundations of the local CCJ it was not without its tense moments when it attracted missionary Christians for a while who misunderstood its aims as a non-missionary organization. This situation was dealt with by the committee with some diplomacy. Uncomfortable and possibly embarrassing as it was for other Christians, the fact that Exeter synagogue members did not feel threatened by the missionaries perhaps showed how confident it had grown in its own self-identity and heritage.

An exhibition of the Jews of Devon and Cornwall

During 1998 and 1999 Helen Fry worked with Evelyn Friedlander, director of the Hidden Legacy Foundation (London) on an exhibition entitled *The Jews of Devon and Cornwall*. Evelyn, wife of esteemed scholar and Reform Rabbi, the late Rabbi Dr Albert Friedlander, had undertaken a number of projects to catalogue and preserve Jewish heritage in Germany and England. The South-West of England particularly interested her because Exeter and Plymouth are the oldest extant Ashkenazi synagogues in the English-speaking world and had unique artefacts which could be borrowed for an exhibition. Evelyn's vision was to tell the history and religious life of these communities through the artifacts, which also included items and material from the once-functioning Cornish Jewish communities of Falmouth and Penzance. During 1999 two pairs of Exeter synagogue's Rimmonim were sent for repair to enable them to form the main centre pieces of the Exeter artefacts for the exhibition.

The exhibition opened in Penlee House Art Gallery and Museum in Penzance on 7 February 2000 until 1st April. From there it travelled to the Royal Albert Memorial Museum, Exeter and was on display from 13 May 2000 until 17 June 2000. It was subsequently shown at three other venues: Falmouth Art Gallery, Plymouth City Museum and Art Gallery, and the Museum of North Devon in Barnstaple. Its success at each venue was marked by the large number of visitors which it attracted and its coverage in the local. For the Exeter Jewish community it marked an important statement about how far the community had come in terms of feeling comfortable in its Gentile surroundings. Although it remained security conscious, it was proud of its heritage and had become much more outward-looking and confident.

The New Millennium

At the turn of the millennium the Exeter congregation had a membership of forty families and a flourishing religion school. From 2000 Malcolm Wiseman relinquished his work with Exeter because of help from a new colleague, Anglo-Jewish scholar Elkan Levy, also of London. It was in 2004 that Elkan first came to Exeter to

Hidden Legacy Exhibition on the Jews of Devon and Cornwall, Exeter

take traditional services, often accompanied by his wife Celia and together they made some special and lasting friendships in the community. Elkan worked as part of the team of Malcolm Wiseman, ministering to small communities. He ensured that the services at Exeter were warm and inclusive and comments about that period: 'I regard a measure of my success as the large number of friends that we have in the Exeter community right across the religious spectrum.' Elkan officiated at one wedding and took a bar mitzvah as well as participating in some wonderful parties and functions. He also taught in the very advanced and high-level adult education programmes and ran some successful pre-Passover seminars. He was in post until 2010 when he and Celia emigrated to Israel.

Living in a provincial community where numbers are often small, the congregation has sought to accommodate Jews from across the religious spectrum. In February 2006 the community held its first Reform service led by Jess Gold and attended by thirty-four people.[213] Today there are other 'satellite' Jewish communities in the South-West at Totnes and in Somerset. Unfortunately Torquay Hebrew Congregation which had so many evacuees and members in the Second World War, as many as 2,000 according to some estimates, has ceased to exist in recent years. The Plymouth Hebrew Congregation which keeps strictly to the Orthodox tradition has dwindling numbers and yet seeks to keep alive the beautiful synagogue and preserve its heritage as the oldest Ashkenazi synagogue in Britain.

It is clear from the newsletters that the 1980s marked a particularly active and vibrant period in the Exeter synagogue's long history. What emerges from this revival is a community that externally was confident in its identity and knew its place alongside other faith communities in the area. Internally it had moved forward to achieve so much and become all-inclusive. Its success was succinctly summed up in an article by Harry Freedman in which he wrote: 'Ten years ago the community was on the verge of extinction, the shul was closed, and had it not been for Derrick and Ella [Boam] it would still be closed. Now we have services every three to four weeks, the students have a meal every Friday night and there is a growing social calendar.'[214]

The dynamism of that period laid the foundations for today's community which continues to exist and thrive thirty years later when some provincial Jewish communities have closed. Today the Exeter Jewish community has around a hundred adult members and organises regular services and activities. it is also a community which is active and looks to the future. It holds weekly Sabbath services and celebrates all the Jewish religious holidays. Some services are Traditional, others are Progressive to be open to all on the religious spectrum. The community takes part in inter-faith activities as a member of the Exeter Interfaith and Belief Group. Within the community itself, there is a regular Yiddish Group. Different groups have met over the years but today there is still a significant core group of Jewish women who are meeting regularly after 30 years to discuss books and films. Latterly there has been a group of women meeting as Second Generation Holocaust survivors. The community is confident of its place within the wider community but its identity is by no means static. Exeter Hebrew Congregation is one which by the very nature of its provincial life is being redefined in each generation. It is also a community that is conscious of its unique heritage, with one eye on its past and the preservation of its beautiful Georgian synagogue. Eddie Sinclair's report during the 1996-8 restoration of the synagogue succinctly sums up the situation:

'It is encouraging that as Exeter becomes increasingly proud of its heritage, so it is begins to recognise the Synagogue as a valuable resource. As a result, the role of the Synagogue is changing. As well as being a place of worship, it is now attracting a wide audience, of countless educational groups of all ages, as well as at last being put on the 'Leisure and Tourism' map. All of which bodes most positively for the Synagogue's survival in the next century. It is therefore no longer just a question of the survival of a place of worship with its ingrained history, of importance for a minority group. This Synagogue, the building and its contents, at last seem to be gaining the recognition that they deserve. It is of vital importance that those features that are the very essence of the place be preserved for the future.'

Silver Kiddush cup, no hallmark, but bears the date 1732 and initials R.S, on loan to the Jewish Museum London.
PHOTOGRAPH COURTESY FRANK GENT

---

[213] *Jewish Chronicle*, 17 February 2006.
[214] Newsletter, 4 February 1984.

Throughout its history the Jewish community of Exeter has been used to periods of decline and revival. The latest revival has lasted beyond forty years and is one in which the community remains focused on growth and education under a dedicated leadership and committee. As a Grade II listed building there is every hope that as an historic building this gem of a synagogue will survive. In terms of religious life, there is no reason to doubt that a worshipping Jewish community will be functioning in Exeter in another 250 years. The future for Exeter's Jews remains a positive one and whilst demographics change and new comers arrive, Exeter has always kept a nucleus going even when numbers had dwindled. Its history has shown that through decline and revival it has always had dedicated members who have cared enough to protect its future.

APPENDIX 1
LIST OF TOMBSTONES IN THE OLD JEWISH CEMETERY

The list of the tombstones in the old Exeter Jewish cemetery was originally compiled by Michael Adler in 1940, with Hebrew transcriptions and notes added by Rabbi Dr B. Susser in 1963. The list has been updated in 2012 by the author to include all burials since 1940 and a few pre-1940 which were not on the original survey.

Against the wall - next to mortuary
1. 1827, Isaac (?)
Front Row
2. No name. Surface illegible: all Hebrew. 12 lines. 1807
3. Jacob David, 15 December died 15 December 5602 [1842], aged 55
4. John Jacobs, 1911
Against Left Wall
5. Indistinct. Sunk in earth. No date
6. 1839: Hannah relict of Moses Ancona, and daughter of the late Moses Vita Montefiore. 25 April 5599, aged 71
Row 2
7. Grave of B.L. died [?]
8. Levy Alexander, 21 November 5615/1855, aged 99 years and 7 months
9. Fanny Alexander, died 29 September 5612/1852, aged 89

Old tombstone, now illegible

Levy Alexander's headstone, died aged 99 and 7 months

Tombstone of Fanny Alexander

Tombstone of Hyman Cohen

Headstone of Eleazar Lazarus

LIST OF TOMBSTONES IN THE OLD JEWISH CEMETERY

10. Betsy Ezekiel, relict of Henry Ezekiel, died 16 September 5611/1851, aged 68
11. Priscilla Ellen Myers, died June 1852, aged 17
12. Elizabeth Levy, wife of late Emanuel Levy, died 28 September 1852, aged 91 and 9 months
13. Isaac Solomon, died 22 June 5614/1854, aged 82 years
13b. Behind this lies three children of Myers and Deborah Solomon
 (Apart)
14. Samuel Levy, 1824, Hebrew only on the tombstone, design of a ewer and basin

Row 3

15. Betsey Lazarus, wife of David Lazarus, 12 July 1848, aged 44
16. Esther Jacobs, sister of Jacob Jacob of this City, aged 60, died 9 April 5608/1848
17. Mr Hyman Cohen of this City, died 14 April 5607/1847, aged 78, design of hands of Cohen on the tombstone
18. Phoebe Cohen, died January 1848, aged 80
19. Elizabeth Davis, died 20 January 5608/1848, aged 48
20. Eliezer Lazarus, died 26 Heshvan 5605, 4 November 1845, aged 56

Row 4

Two mounds of graves, no headstones
21. Catherine Lazarus Cohen, died 1840, aged 69
22. Miriam Davis, died November 1838, aged 52
23. Amelia, daughter of Abraham Ezekiel, 13th Sivan 1839, aged 60 [death certificate says 6th June = 23rd-24th Sivan]
24. Catherine, daughter of Abraham Ezekiel, died 3 July 1837, aged 69
25. Judith Phillips, died 28 December 559[?], aged 89 (?)
26. (Small, indistinct), Hebrew poem. No date

Row 5

27. Rachel Davis, died 10 Eyor 5597/1835, aged 84
28. Aaron Samuel Paris, 1836, erected by lamenting parents.
29. Lazarus Cohen, died 14 Tishri Motzei Shabbos 5595/1836, aged 71
30. Julia Lazarus wife of Eleazar Lazarus of this City, died 2nd Av 5596/1836
31. Jacob Jacobs, died 17 December 1836, aged 57
32. Henry Ezekiel, 10 November 5596/1836
33. Judith Davis, 10 January 1837, aged 73 years
(2 grave spaces)
34. Samuel son of Joseph Marks, 1870, aged 12

Row 6

35. Moses Johnson, died 26 August 5592/1832 aged 76
36. Sarah Solomon, died 29th May 5592/1832 aged 82
37. Moses Horvitz Levi, Minister of this Congregation 42 years, died 5594 [1834], aged 80
38. Catherine wife of Moses Levy, died 7 October 1834, aged 59[?] years

Row 7

39. (Small, indistinct) David Cohen, son of Andrew and Lavinia Cohen [no date]

Headstone of Elizabath Levy, wife of silversmith Emanuel Levy

Grave of Julia Lazarus

Barent Gompertz, unusual tombstone

Left: *Tombstone of Jacob Jacobs*

LIST OF TOMBSTONES IN THE OLD JEWISH CEMETERY

40. Moses Alexander, 1835, aged 8 months
41. (No English) 1829
42. Same gravestone shape as No.40 and no English, 1832, mother of Baruch Jonas.
43. 1831, aged 68 (No English), Probably Abraham Cohen brother of Lazarus Cohen

Row 8

44. Sacred to the Memory of Mrs Dorothy Lyons, died 13 February 5585/1825, aged 52
45. (No English), 5587/1827
46. Juliet the beloved wife of Gershon Levy (of Guernsey), aged 72, died 13 August 5586/1826
47. Barent Gompertz, died 9 September 5584/1824 (Altar Tomb). The marble top chipped off. Text of inscription supplied by Sir T. Colyer Fergusson and printed in his brother Isaac's book of poems, called *Devon*.

Row 9

48. Lazarus Moses Johnson, died 5581/1821, aged 86
49. Samuel Benedict, 5581/1821, aged 81
50. Gershon Levy of Guernsey, 5582/1822
51. Israel Myers, 1827, aged 14

Row 10

52. (Indistinct) 1816
53. Nancy Lazarus wife of Moses Lazarus, died Sunday 2[0?] Shevat, 1810
54. Moses Lazarus of this City, died 2nd Adar 5571/1811
55. (Indistinct) 1816
Five further tombstones indecipherable
A tombstone apart: with 15 Hebrew lines, indistinct

Row 11

[From back]
56. Rosina Elsner beloved wife of Solomon Elsner, 1863
57. Harriet Jacobs, 1862
58. David Lazarus, 1862
59. Solomon Aarons aged 102, 1864
60. Fanny Aarons, 1861
61. 1861

Headstone of Solomon Aarons, died aged 102 in 1864

62. Isabella wife of B. Myers, died November 1859, aged 56
63. Naphtali Solomon, died 15th March 5618/1858, 85 years
64. Fogel Solomon, 31 October 5617/1857, aged 80 years
65. Fogel beloved infant of Myers and Deborah Solomon, died 3 May 1859, 3 weeks and 13 days
66. Louisa Schultz, 1866, aged 74
67. Catherine Aarons, 1864
68. Ann Jacobs, died 27 Tamuz 1864, aged 60[?] years

Row 12

69. Laura Gabrielson, died 12 March 1937, aged 55
70. Harriet Gabrielson, died 22 February 1924, aged 78, wife of Morris Gabrielson
71. Simon Silverman, 25 July 1919, aged 78
72. Eugene Joel, died 14 February 1918, aged 85

From Back

Row 8

73. Fanny Milcah daughter of Myers and Deborah Solomon, died aged 11 years and 4 months, 27 Tamuz 1871
74. Henry M Hynes, aged 55 [?], died 29 May 1871
75. David Franklin, 1869, aged 84
76. Henry Lazarus, 1867 aged ?

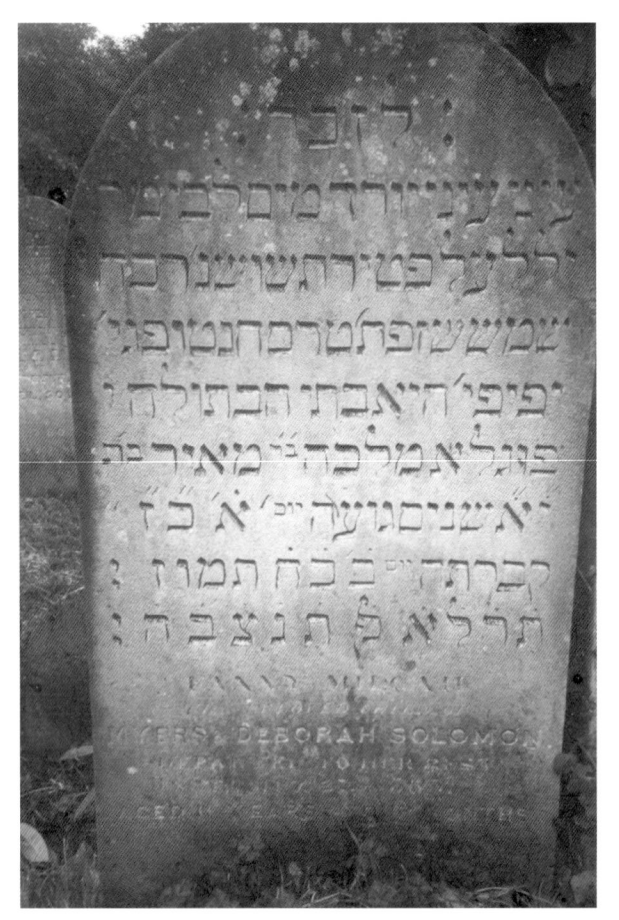

Grave of the child Fanny Solomon, daughter of Myers & Deborah Solomon

Headstone of Emanuel Jacobs

Row [?]

77. Mr Jonas Walter, died 1888 aged 65 [Brother of Catherine and Henry Walter and Ann Cohen of Lyme Regis and New Oxford Street, London]
78. Gustave son of Charlotte and Samuel Gittleson, died 24 August 1893, aged 8 months
79. Morris Gabrielson, died 5 January 1905, aged 60
80. Emanuel Jacobs, died 6 June 1903, aged 83
81. Alexander Alexander, died 22 February 1887, aged 83

Row 3

82. Aaron Joshua Nunez (Indistinct), 1846[?]
83. (Indistinct)
84. Florence Miriam Goodman, died 1897, aged 34
85. Harriet Aarons, died 22 January 1897, aged 64
86. Priscilla Zamoisky, died April 1908, aged 87
87. Everetta Glynn, died Adar 1910 [14 March 1910], aged 34

Row 2

88. Aaron Solomon, died 5610 [1850]
89. Elizabeth Abraham, 24 October 5503, aged 51

Row 7

90. Aaron Israel, died 20 September 1874, aged 72
91. Aaron Aarons, died 1874, aged 48
92. Louis Schultz, died 19 December 1873, aged 94
93. Katherine wife of Joseph Abrahams, died 23 September 1873, aged 84

Row 6

94. Lawrence A. Alexander, died 13 Sept 1881, aged 43
95. Abraham Solomon Palmer, died 13 March 1879, aged 85
96. Betsey Jonas, died 25 November 1878, aged 85
97. Esther widow of Jacob Jacob, died 21 October 1874, aged 85

Solomon Cappelle who died September 1874, aged 35, location of grave no longer known, probably never had a headstone

Row 5

98. Barnet Jonas, 23 January 1885, aged 79
99. Jonas Levy, died 19 February 1884, aged 85
100. Alfred Kennard, died 17 December 1883, aged 36
101. (No English) Benjamin son of Joel who died at the ripe old age. His days were lengthened to 82 years. He died on the first day of the week and was buried on the same day 27 Shevat 5643 [1883]
102. Andrew George Jacob, born at Falmouth, Cornwall, died at Exeter, March 1900
103. Golda wife of Aaron Raphael, died 11 August 1915
104. Rev. Abraham Rosenberg, Minister of the Hebrew Congregation of Exeter, died 12 May 1913, aged 61

Row 1

105. Aaron Raphael, died 12 January 1918, aged 42

Tombstone of Morris Gabrielson  *The chapel (ohel)*

Narrow Section to the Right of Main Path
From front row, front of cemetery
106. Charlotte Hannah, wife of Charles Samuels, died 16 September 1933, aged 67
107. Charles Samuels, died 20 November 1944, aged 82
108. Isidore Samuels, 12 October 1941, aged 51, husband of Maie and father of Jane and Susan
109. Julius Samuels, died 27 September 1947, aged 59, husband of Josephine and father of Barbara and Pamela. Also in memory of Josephine Irene (née Woolf), wife of Julius (1896-1977)
110. Conrad Samuels, died 25 May 1952, aged 73
111. Edgar Samuels, died 23 May 1958, husband of Joy and father of Felicity and Amanda

Only Hebrew inscription on the tombstone of Benjamin son of Joel, died 1883

Grave of Charlotte Samuels, wife of Charles Samuels

Samuel family burial section

LIST OF TOMBSTONES IN THE OLD JEWISH CEMETERY

Post-1940 Section

This has been compiled by starting with the front row of the post-1940 section (behind the old section, Row 11), then listing the headstones behind each subsequent row and backwards towards the rear wall of the cemetery. It goes along the rows from left to right. In some places there are mounds from burials but no surviving headstone to say who is buried there.

Row 1
112. Asser Oscar Heinemann, died April 1941, aged 63
113. Annie, widow of Joseph Finegold, died 31 January 1941, aged 72
114. Lisi Friedlander, died 16 December 1940
115. Annie Solomon, died 3 May 1941

Row 2
116. Yetta Kapelman, died 19 September 1941, aged 47
117. Viktor Gross, died 19 June 1942, aged 62
118. gap
119. Pilot Officer H D Abrams, Air Observer, Royal Canadian Air Force, died 3 August 1941 aged 24

Row 3
120. Rachel, wife of Aaron Caplin of Leytonstone, London
121. Rachel Gooding, died at Exeter, 5 February 1945, aged 70
122. Samuel Eidlestein, died 29 January 1945, aged 75
123. Bronche Bas Tuvyeh, Mrs B Kennedy, 16 November 1944
Large gap
124. Major Gordon Cecil Kennard, MC, born 20 June 1884, died 7 December 1943
125. Ada Stoloff, wife of Rev. W Stoloff, died 3 March 1945

Row 4
Large gap before tombstones begin
126. Miriam Harris, died 4 March 1950, aged 83; and Isidore Abraham Harris, died 20 March 1950, aged 81
127. Agnes Martha Levine, died 10 November 1948, aged 47, wife of Israel Levine
128. Millicent, wife of Abe Hollander, died 9 June 1945; and of Abe Hollander, died 15 May 1962
129. Elizabeth Barnard, died 6 June 1945 aged 84
130. Andre Blok, died 16 June 1941, aged 71, husband of Clara. Headstone on left hand side of path, parallel to Hetty Wilhelm

Row 5
131. Harriette Cohen, daughter of the late Rev Manasseh and Martha Cohen, died 14 January 1954, aged 85
132. J. Loewy, 6 May 1901 – 27 February 1951, a loving husband and father
133. Name illegible, 1875-1953, in loving memory of my dearest auntie
Gap
134. Julia Boam, died 30 December 1951, aged 68
135. Morris Rosenberg, died 28 November 1951, aged 75; and wife Eva Rosenberg who died 26 December 1968, aged 85

Row 6
136. Coleman Philipson, MA, LL.D. LITT.D. 1875-1958
137. Woolf Daniels, died 24 April 1956, aged 71

Headstone of Annie Finegold

Headstone of Conrad Samuels

Headstone of Gerard Klein

Headstone of Derrick Michael Nahum

Headstone of Josephine Beavis

Headstone of Elly Pollak-Weil

138. Isaac Jack Kurlander, died 25 March 1957, aged 69
139. Isaac Philip Hyams, son of Barnet Bairal, died 23 November 1956, aged 56
140. Charlotte Weise, 1905 - 1956

Row 7
Large gap before tombstones begin
141. Elliot Alpern, died 30 March 1961, aged 19
142. William Woolf Boam, died 30 December 1963, aged 84
Gap
143. Samuel Palley, born 2 June 1896, died 12 November 1970
144. Rose Sabel, died 22 September 1971, aged 71

Row 8
145. Louis Sabel, died 19 July 1975, aged 77
146. Heya Golda Schwartz, died 31 March 1965, wife of Jacob Schwartz who died 2 June 1951
147. Isaac Goldman, 1871 - 1962
148. Elizabeth Levy, died 6 February 1976, aged ?
149. Harold Harris, died 20 January 1980, aged 73
150. Mathilda Hyams, died 1979 (??)
151. Margaret Fink, died 30 November 1979, school teacher
152. Richard Asher Ellenbogen Ellis, born 3 November 1915, died 18 September 1981, son of doctor Abraham Ellis and Rebecca Ellis

Row 9 (by back wall)
153. Malcolm Isbitt, died 12 July 1977, aged 37
154. Jeannie Chariton, died 2 March 1977, aged 83

Narrow Section to the Right of Main Path
From back row towards the front
155. David Stanley Seigal, 1924-1984
156. Bernard Rosenberg, died 26 January 1985, aged 74
157. Maurice Frederick Mitchell Alexander, died 31 December 1987, aged 71, local reporter for the Express & Echo
158. Golda Weinberg, died 2 August 1990
159. Golda Zulman, died 16 December 1990, aged 86
160. Hetty Wilhelm (née Baron), died 5 May 1991
161. Phoebe Davis, born 16 February 1901, died 23 February 1996
162. Abe Sydney Quait, born 5 May 1912, died 17 May 1993, husband of Margaret
163. Barbara Algar, 19 August 1933 – 8 July 1997
164. Derrick Michael Nahum, 24 December 1916 – 22 January 1998
165. Bertha Rose Boam, 1930-2002
Large gap
166. Theresa Samuels, died 3 July 1976, aged 76

Along wall next to chapel, from left to right
167. Derrick David Boam, 1918-2007 and his beloved wife Ella (neé Levy), 1925-2011
168. Elly Pollak-Weil, born 3 December 1913 Vienna, died 17 August 2005 Devon; also in memory of her parents Samuel Bock died 20 June 1942 Vienna and Hermine Bock, died 26 May Maly Trostinec
169. Josephine Beavis (née Boam), 1922-2008 and Leonard Beavis, 1920-2000
170. Deborah Adams, 1906-2002, beloved sister of the Boam family and cousin of Raymond and Lee Lyons
171. Lilian Ryan, died 7 March 1998, sister of the Boam family
172. Gerard Klein, born 12 April 1923 Berlin, died 18 November 2003 Exeter
173. Israel Gershon Harris, 1881-1950, 'A man against men' (older tombstone)
174. Rachel Shortland 'Rae', 20 May 1916 – 5 June 1999 [middle of grass under a tree, near the chapel]

APPENDIX 2
LIST OF TOMBSTONES IN THE NEW JEWISH BURIAL GROUND, EXWICK MUNICIPAL CEMETERY

The list below is correct as of 1 July 2011. Note: where the date of death is unknown, the date of burial has been given.

JS 0001	Rosemary Deborah Joseph, 11 January 1927 – 21 January 1992, aged 65, resident of Shillingford St George, Exeter
JS 0002	Dael Eugene Smith, date of burial 19 February 1992, aged 42, of Plymouth, no headstone
JS 0003	Elizabeth Loewy, aka Ella or Elizabeth Conway, 1908-1994, aged 86, buried 20 June 1994, resident of Exeter
JS 0004	Annie Rose Fern, 1921-1995, wife of the late Alfred Fern, aged 74, buried 6 April 1995, resident of Torquay
JS 0005	Ruth Marjorie Joseph, 30 Sept 1923 – 25 July 1996, died Neumarkt, Germany, aged 72, resident of Shillingford St George, Exeter
JS 0006	Michael Leigh Algar, buried 4 October 1999, aged 63, resident of Holcombe near Bath, no headstone
JS 0007	Barbara Larah, 1956 – 2001, daughter of Esther and Monty Larah of Manchester, died Barnstaple aged 44, resident of Bickington, Barnstaple
JS 0008	Cyril Pentel (Betzalel ben Shabsai Lev), 1924 – 2007, died 27 April 2007 aged 83, resident of Budleigh Salterton
JS 0009	Marjem Chatterton, died 28 January 2010 aged 93, resident of Exeter, no headstone
JS 0010	Empty
JS 0011	Tamara Griffith, nee Loberman, 23 Oct 1924 – 4 March 2002, died aged 77, resident of Horsham, West Sussex
	Also: David Henry Griffiths, 15 June 1953 – 18 April 2005, aged 51, beloved son of William and Tamara, husband of Morag; resident of Topsham, Exeter. Notes: ashes.
JS 0012	David Mark Foot, 16 March 1917 – 18 February 2009, aged 91, resident of Exeter. Notes: ashes
JS 0013	Empty
JS 0014	Empty
JS 0015	Isaac Bachar, died 2 December 2002 aged 65, resident of Exeter, wife of Isabella, children: Aliza, Rachel and Miriam
JS 0016	Reserved
JS 0017	Empty
JS 0018	Esther Grynwald, died 3 June 2008 aged 88, resident of Exeter, no headstone

LIST OF TOMBSTONES IN THE NEW JEWISH BURIAL GROUND, EXWICK MUNICIPAL CEMETERY

David Mark FOOT
16th March 1917
18th February 2009

TAMARA GRIFFITH nee LOBERMAN
23 OCT 1924
4 MARCH 2002
A LOVING WIFE, MUM & NAN
relaxing at last

מיחדת לכולנו
אהובה מאוד
וחסרונה
מעציב מאוד

DAVID HENRY GRIFFITHS
15 JUNE 1953 – 18 APRIL 2005
BELOVED SON OF WILLIAM & TAMARA
DEVOTED HUSBAND OF MORAG, LOVING BROTHER & DAD
I've so many precious memories Dave

Jewish section, Exwick Municipal cemetery

APPENDIX 3
CENSUS RETURNS FOR JEWS IN EXETER: 1841–1901

In this appendix, spellings as transcribed from the original Census Returns have been retained and some street names or numbers were not often decipherable on the original entries. On occasion, the entry only contains the street name and not the number of the property.

1841 Census

Synagogue Place:

ISRAEL, Aaron	36	jeweller	b. Poland
ISRAEL, Esther	28		b. Poland
ISRAEL, Sarah	5		b. Poland
ISRAEL, Rebecca	2		

b. Poland
1 female servant

Synagogue Place:

DIMOND, Caroline	40	jeweller	b. Devon
DIMOND, Aaron			b. Devon

Synagogue Place:

RALPH, Susan	45	independent	b. Devon
RALPH, Elizabeth	20	dressmaker	b. Devon
RALPH, William	15	tailor's apprentice	b. Devon
RALPH, Eliza	10		b. Devon

High Street:

ALEXANDER, Alexander	36	optician	
ALEXANDER, Tryphenia	30		b. Devon
ALEXANDER, Fanny	10		b. Devon
ALEXANDER, Moses	7		b. Devon
ALEXANDER, Eliza	3		b. Devon
ALEXANDER, Lawrence	4		b. Devon
ALEXANDER, Jacob	2		b. Devon

Shared house with:

ALEXANDER, John	44	optician	
ALEXANDER, Isabella	32		b. Devon
ALEXANDER, Lewis	5		b. Devon
JOHNSON, Eliza	61	independent	

3 servants

CENSUS RETURNS FOR JEWS IN EXETER: 1841-1901

Fore Street:

SILVERSTONE, Israel	37	watchmaker	b. foreign
SILVERSTONE, Paulina	28		b. foreign
SILVERSTONE, Rosina	10		b. Devon
SILVERSTONE, Bella	8		b. Devon
SILVERSTONE, Sarah	7		b. Devon
SILVERSTONE, Rebecca	5		b. Devon
SILVERSTONE, Isaac	3		b. Devon
SILVERSTONE, Clara	1		b. Devon

Fore Street:

HART, Moses	55	watchmaker	b. Devon
HART, Ester	45		b. Devon
HART, Mordecai	25		b. Devon
HART, Grace	20		b. Devon
HART, Saul	18		b. Devon
HART, Leah	16		b. Devon
EZEKIEL, Benjamin	55	independent	b. Devon

Fore Street:

MARKS, Joseph	35	silversmith	
MARKS, Julia	32		b. Devon
MARKS, Isaac	7		b. Devon
MARKS, Sarah	5		b. Devon
MARKS, Charles	2		b. Devon
MARKS, Josiah	2mths		b. Devon
JOSEPH, Moses	18	shop boy	
1 female servant			

Fore Street:

AARON, Caroline	35	jeweller	b. Devon
AARON, Priscilla	20		b. Devon
AARON, Harriet	15		b. Devon
AARON, Aaron	10		b. Devon

Fore Street:

LEVY, Georgina	25	hardware dealer	b. Devon
EZEKIEL, Selina	25	independent	b. Devon

Fore Street:

EZEKIEL, Betty	50	independent	
EZEKIEL, Ellen	20		b. Devon
EMANUEL, Lewis	55	watchmaker	
1 female servant			

Fore Street:

PRINCE, Henry	34	furrier	b. foreign
PRINCE, Esther	28		
PRINCE, Naptali	1		
BARNET, Jane	21	assistant	
ABRAHAMS, Isabella	8		

WOOLFE, Fanny   20   b. foreign
WOOLFE, Rose   11   b. Devon
WOOLFE, Esther   10   b. Devon
WOOLFE, Aaron   6   b. Devon
WOOLFE, Jacob   3   b. Devon

Sun Street:

SOLOMON, Nathan   55   jeweller   b. foreign
SOLOMON, Nathan (Mrs)   55   b. foreign

1851 Census

8 Synagogue Place:

ISRAEL, Aaron	head	50	jeweller	b. Poland
ISRAEL, Esther	wife	38		b. Prussia
ISRAEL, Sarah	dau	14		b. Exeter
ISRAEL, Rebecca	dau	12		b. Exeter
ISRAEL, Jacob	son	9		b. Exeter
ISRAEL, Abraham	son	6		b. Exeter
ISRAEL, Israel	son	2		b. Exeter

6 High Street:

ALEXANDER, Tryphenia	wife of head	40	optician's wife, assistant	b. Plymouth
ALEXANDER, Fanny	dau	19		b. Exeter
ALEXANDER, Eliza	dau	15		b. Exeter
ALEXANDER, Lawrence	son	13	scholar	b. Exeter
ALEXANDER, Jacob	son	11	scholar	b. Exeter
ALEXANDER, Miriam	dau	9	scholar	b. Exeter
ALEXANDER, Fanny	dau	7	scholar	b. Exeter
ALEXANDER, Alfred	son	5	scholar	b. Exeter
ALEXANDER, Sarah	dau	3	scholar	b. Exeter

3 female servants, unmarried, aged 22, 18 and 17

6 High Street:

ALEXANDER, Isabella	wife of head			b. Plymouth
ALEXANDER, Henry	son	9	scholar	b. Plymouth
ALEXANDER, Rebecca	dau	7	scholar	b. Exeter
ALEXANDER, Rachel	dau	5	scholar	b. Exeter
ALEXANDER, John	son	3		b. Exeter
ALEXANDER, Samuel	son	1		b. Exeter

201 High Street:

DAVIES, Hyman	head	50	general merchant	b. Middlesex
DAVIES, Rebecca	wife	37		b. Exeter
DAVIES, Colman	son	11		b. Birmingham
DAVIES, John	son	9		b. Exeter
DAVIES, Elizabeth	dau	2		b. Exeter

CENSUS RETURNS FOR JEWS IN EXETER: 1841-1901

95 Fore Street:

LEVY, Isaac	head	36	druggist	b. Exeter
LEVY, Sarah	wife	34		b. Mosley
LEVY, Parnell	son	3		b. Exeter
LEVY, Jenny	dau	1		b. Exeter

107 Fore Street:

SILVERSTONE, Israel	head	44	shopkeeper	b. Poland
SILVERSTONE, Pauline	wife	38		b. Poland
SILVERSTONE, Bella	dau	18	Honiton Lace mfr	b. Exeter
SILVERSTONE, Sarah	dau	16	Honiton Lace mfr	b. Exeter
SILVERSTONE, Rosina	dau	19	Honiton Lace mfr	b. Exeter
SILVERSTONE, Rebecca	dau	15	scholar	b. Exeter
SILVERSTONE, Isaac	son	13	scholar	b. Exeter
SILVERSTONE, Clara	dau	11	scholar	b. Exeter
SILVERSTONE, Maurice	son	8	scholar	b. Exeter
SILVERSTONE, John	son	6	scholar	b. Exeter
SILVERSTONE, Selina	dau	4	scholar	b. Exeter
SILVERSTONE, Abraham	son	2	scholar	b. Exeter
SILVERSTONE, Fanny	dau	7mths		b. Exeter

113 Fore Street:

MARKS, Julia	wife of head	43		b. Exeter
MARKS, Isaac	son	17		b. Exeter
MARKS, Sarah	dau	15		b. Exeter
MARKS, Charles	son	11		b. Exeter
MARKS, Josiah	son	9		b. Exeter
MARKS, Ellen	dau	8		b. Exeter
MARKS, Rose	dau	7		b. Exeter
MARKS, Isabella	dau	5		b. Exeter
MARKS, Henry	son	4		b. Exeter
MARKS, Alexander	son	2		b. Exeter
MARKS, Kate	dau	1		b. Exeter
LEVY, Daniel	np	16		b. Guernsey

173 Fore Street:

DAVIS, Morris widow	head	58	haberdasher, jeweller	b. London
DAVIS, Priscilla	dau	25	assistant	b. Exeter
DAVIS, Ann	dau	19	assistant	b. Exeter
DAVIS, Julia	dau	15	scholar	b. Exeter
DAVIS, Samuel	son	6	scholar	b. Exeter
ALEXANDER, Moses	unmarried	17	assistant jeweller	b. Exeter

4 Gentile lodgers and 1 female servant

125 Fore Street Hill:

SOLOMON, Isaac	head	75	retired jeweller	b. Prussia (blind)
SOLOMON, Rosetta	wife	70		b. Kent
SOLOMON, Caroline	dau	28		b. Exeter

8 & 9 Market Street:

JACOBS, Emanuel	head	29	unmarried stationer	b. Exeter

| JACOBS, Esther | mother | 60 | widow lady | b. Lyme, Dorset |
| DAVIS, Sophia | niece | 6 | scholar | b. Exeter |

Market Street:

LAZARUS, David widow	head	58	quill manufacturer	b. Exeter
LAZARUS, Ann	dau	26		b. Exeter
LAZARUS, Esther	dau	20		b. Exeter
LAZARUS, Julia	dau	12		b. Exeter
LAZARUS, Henry	son	5		b. Exeter

2 Crescent Row:

LEVANDER, James	head	50	Surgeon dentist	b. Westminster
LEVANDER, Julia	wife	48	dentist's wife	b. Westminster
LEVANDER, Esther	dau	23		b. Westminster
LEVANDER, Charlotte	dau	21		b. Exeter
LEVANDER, Edwin	son	17	dentist's pupil	b. Westminster
LEVANDER, Mary	dau	15		b. Exeter
LEVANDER, Frederic	son	11		b. Exmouth

New Golden Lion Inn, Market Street:

| LANDSPARG, Simon | lodger | 20 | traveller | b. Warsaw, Poland |

North Street:

HYNES, Kitty	head	45	unmarried	b. Exeter
COHEN, Louis	boarder	9	apprentice	b. Surrey
COHEN, Edward	boarder	5	scholar	b. Surrey
COHEN, John	boarder	3	scholar	b. Surrey
WOOLF, Alfred	boarder	1	scholar	b. Barnstaple

1 female servant, aged 19, b. Exeter

Southernhay:

LAZARUS, Isaac	head	34		b. Exeter
LAZARUS, Eliza	wife	36		b. Falmouth
LAZARUS, Lewis	son	6	scholar	b. Exeter
LAZARUS, Julia	dau	11	scholar	b. Exeter
LAZARUS, Caroline	cs	19	assistant	b. Exeter

1 female servant aged 17

Southernhay:

| SCHLESINGER, Caroline | lodger | 42 | | b. Hamburg |
| SCHLESINGER, Joanna | lodger | 16 | | b. Germany |

2 Bartholomew Street:

HOFFNUNG, Samuel	head	40	Reader of Synagogue	b. Poland
HOFFNUNG, Caroline	wife	38		b. Poland
HOFFNUNG, Bertha	dau	10		b. Exeter

1 female servant aged 18

CENSUS RETURNS FOR JEWS IN EXETER: 1841-1901

16 Bartholomew Street:

| SCHULTZ, Lewis | head | 60 | jeweller | b. Warsaw |
| SCHULTZ, Louisa | wife | 55 | | b. Poland |

22 Bartholomew Street:

| LEVY, Elizabeth | head | 89 | annuitant, widow | b. Exeter |
| ABRAHAM, Sarah | head | 49 | annuitant, widow | b. Exeter |

Waterbeer Place:

AARON, Caroline	head	45	jeweller's wife	b. Middlesex
ZAMOISKI, Priscilla	dau	25	married	b. Barnstaple
AARON, Harriet	dau	20	unmarried	b. Barnstaple
AARON, Fanny	dau	18	unmarried	b. Exeter
ZAMOISKI, Julia	granddaughter	5		b. Exeter
ZAMOISKI, Esther	granddaughter	3		b. Exeter

3 Paragon Place:

| ALEXANDER, Levy | head | 98 | | b. Germany |
| ALEXANDER, Fanny | wife | 89 | | b. Germany |

Elizabeth Stone, house servant, aged 44

14 Paragon Place:

| LAZARUS, David | lodger | 31 | watch dealer | b. Exeter |

Friernhay Street:

| SOLOMON, Rose | dau | 21 | unmarried lace mfr | b. Exeter |
| ROTHSCHILD, Rebecca | visitor | 19 | unmarried | b. London |

1 female servant, aged 17, b. Exeter

David's Hill:

| SOLOMON, Nathan | head | 75 | retired jeweller | b. Prussia |
| SOLOMON, Fanny | wife | 74 | | b. Prussia |

2 Clodes Court:

MOSCHZISKY, Laura	head	28	dependant on relatives	b. Oxford
MOSCHZISKY, Blanche	dau	3		b. Devon
MOSCHZISKY, Mathilda	dau	1		b. Middlesex

3 Rackfield Place

JACOBS, Henry	head	36	jeweller	b. Poland
JACOBS, Ann		wife	33	b. Poland
JACOBS, Esther	dau	8	scholar	b. Exeter
JACOBS, John	son	5	scholar	b. Exeter
JACOBS, Sarah	dau	4	scholar	b. Exeter
JACOBS, Leah	dau	1		b. Exeter

THE JEWS OF EXETER

Bullers Arms, 107 Blackboy Road:

WOLFE, George	visitor	34	trav stationary	b. Exeter
WOLFE, Rachel	visitor	33	trav stationary	b. Barnstaple
WOLFE, Henry	visitor	32	trav stationary	b. Exeter

3 Lansdown Terrace:

SOLOMON, Myers	head	29	optician	b. Prussia
SOLOMON, Deborah	wife	22		b. Exeter
SOLOMON, Julia	dau	9mths		b. Exeter

5 Lansdown Terrace:

LAZARUS, Moses	head	37	master watchmaker	b. Exeter
LAZARUS, Rebecca	wife	34		b. Poland
LAZARUS, Barnett	son	12	scholar	b. Exmouth
LAZARUS, Julia	dau	10	scholar	b. Exeter
LAZARUS, Joseph	son	8	scholar	b. Exeter
LAZARUS, Samuel	son	6	scholar	b. Exeter
LAZARUS, Eleazar	son	3		b. Exeter
LAZARUS, Nathan	son	2		b. Exeter

1 nursemaid aged 22; 1 female servant aged 18; both born Exeter

Oaksheaf Inn:

AARON, Solomon	lodger	82		b. Poland
COHEN, David		45	traveller	b. Poland

13 Holloway Street:

JACOBS, Harriet	lodger	57	pauper	b. Poland

(in household of William How and family)

King Street:

LEVY, Morris	lodger	28	hawker	b. Warsaw

Sun Street:

NATHAN, Solomon	lodger	86	traveller	b. Poland

2 Silver Terrace:

TURETZKY, Joseph	lodger	28	goldsmith	b. Poland

1861 Census

Synagogue Place:

ISRAEL, Aaron	head	55	hawker	b. Exeter
ISRAEL, Esther	wife	44		b. Exeter
ISRAEL, Abraham	son	15		b. Exeter
ISRAEL, Aaron	son	11	scholar	b. Exeter
ISRAEL, Julia	dau	9	scholar	b. Exeter

CENSUS RETURNS FOR JEWS IN EXETER: 1841-1901

ISRAEL, Fanny		2	scholar	b. Exeter
ISRAEL, Rachel		8mth		b. Exeter

Mary Arches Street:

FRANKLIN, David	lodger	49	traveller	b. Poland

2 Bartholomew Street:

MENDLESOHN, Myer	head	28	minister of Heb Cong	b. Prussia
MENDLESOHN, Rebecca	wife	25		b. Exeter
MENDLESOHN, Sydney	son	3mths		b. Exeter
MENDLESOHN, Emilie	sister	31		b. Prussia

1 female servant

6 High Street:

ALEXANDER, Alexander	head	54	optician	b. Sheerness
ALEXANDER, Fanny (Tryphenia)		50		b. Plymouth
ALEXANDER, Eliza	dau	25		b. Exeter
ALEXANDER, Alfred	son	15	scholar	b. Exeter
ALEXANDER, Sarah	dau	13	scholar	b. Exeter

1 general servant

60 High Street:

SOLOMON, Myers	head	39	optician	b. Prussia
SOLOMON, Deborah	wife	32		b. England
SOLOMON, Julia	dau	10	scholar	b. England
SOLOMON, Elezer	son	10	scholar	b. England
SOLOMON, Sarah	dau	7	scholar	b. England
SOLOMON, Esther	dau	5	scholar	b. England
SOLOMON, Samuel	son	3	scholar	b. England
SOLOMON, Fanny	dau	12mths		b. England

1 female servant

230 High Street:

ELSNER, Solomon	head	30	antiquary, gen dir	b. Prussia
ELSNER, Rosina	wife	29		b. Exeter
ELSNER, Dora	dau	6	scholar	b. Exeter
ELSNER, Jacob	son	1		b. Exeter
SILVERSTONE, Isaac	boarder 23		commercial traveller	b. Exeter

1 female servant

21 Paris Street:

ROTHSCHILD, Henry	head	36	commercial traveller, jewellery	b. Middlesex
ROTHSCHILD, Rebecca	wife	26		b. Middlesex
ROTHSCHILD, Rosina	dau	8	scholar	b. Exeter
ROTHSCHILD, Alexander	son	7	scholar	b. Exeter
ROTHSCHILD, Jeannott	dau	5	scholar	b. London
ROTHSCHILD, David	son	4		b. London
ROTHSCHILD, Sarah	dau	3		b. Exeter
ROTHSCHILD, Myre	son	7 weeks		b. Exeter
ISRAEL, Rebecca	domestic servant	20		b. Exeter

1 female servant aged 14

THE JEWS OF EXETER

167 Fore Street:

SILVERSTONE, Israel	head	53	jeweller	b. Poland
SILVERSTONE, Pauline	wife	45		b. Poland
SILVERSTONE, Sarah	dau	26	lace manufacturer	b. Exeter
SILVERSTONE, Clara	dau	21	lace manufacturer	b. Exeter
SILVERSTONE, Maurice	son	19	wholesale jeweller	b. Exeter
SILVERSTONE, John	son	17	assistant	b. Exeter
SILVERSTONE, Abraham	son	12	scholar	b. Exeter
SILVERSTONE, Selina	dau	15	scholar	b. Exeter
SILVERSTONE, Fanny	dau	10	scholar	b. Exeter

Inn, 161 Fore Street:

AARON, Solomon	lodger	93	hawker, formerly	b. Poland (blind)
SOLOMON, Nathan	lodger	96	hawker, formerly	b. Poland

Fore Street Hill, next to Devonport Inn:

ALEXANDER, Jacob	head	21	furnishing wholesaler	b. Exeter
ALEXANDER, Fanny	sister	29	assistant	b. Exeter
ALEXANDER, Lauren	brother	23	commercial traveller	b. Exeter
ALEXANDER, Tryphenia	sister	17	scholar	b. Exeter

1 female servant

5 Waterbeer Streer:

AARONS, Aaron	head	33	optician	b. Exeter
AARONS, Caroline	mother	57	general dealer	b. London
AARONS, Harriet	dau	35	milliner	b. Exeter
ZAMOISKI, Priscilla	lodger	38	milliner	b. Exeter
ZAMOISKI, Julia	dau	14	scholar	b. Exeter
ZAMOISKI, Etty	dau	13	scholar	b. Exeter
ZAMOISKI, Florence	dau	3	scholar	b. Exeter

1 Snells Buildings, Waterbeer Street:

LAZARUS, David	wid head	68,	quill manufacturer	b. Exeter
LAZARUS, Moses	son	32	optician	b. Exeter
LAZARUS, Esther	dau	29	dressmaker	b. Exeter
LAZARUS, Henry	son	15	scholar	b. Exeter
LEVY, Ann	lodger	35	general dealer	b. Exeter
LEVY, Betsy	dau	7	scholar	b. Exeter
LEVY, Hyman	son	5	scholar	b. Exeter

Preston Street:

HARDING, John	head	24	boot & shoemaker	b. Exeter
HARDING, Amelia	wife	25	boot & shoemaker	b. Exeter
HARDING, Mathilda	dau	3		b. Exeter
HARDING, Benjamin	son	3mths		b. Exeter

Mint Street:

DAVIS, Hyman	head	60	general dealer	b. London
DAVIS, Rebecca	wife	46		b. Exeter
DAVIS, John	son	19	assistant	b. Exeter

CENSUS RETURNS FOR JEWS IN EXETER: 1841-1901

DAVIS, Sophia	dau	16	assistant	b. Exeter
DAVIS, Elizabeth	dau	12	scholar	b. Exeter
DAVIS, Samuel	son	9	scholar	b. Exeter

Mint Street:

| SCHULTZ, Lewis | head | 78 | retired jeweller | b. Poland |
| SCHULTZ, Caroline | wife | 69 | | b. Poland |

173 ??? Street:

BARNARD, Asher	head	35	general merchant	b. Rochester
BARNARD, Rebecca	wife	34		b. Dover
BARNARD, Issacher	son	12		b. Ipswich
BARNARD, Benjamin	son	10		b. Ipswich
BARNARD, Daniel	son	9		b. Ipswich
BARNARD, Julia	dau	6		b. Exeter
BARNARD, Hannah	dau	4		b. Exeter
BARNARD, Joseph	son	3		b. Exeter
BARNARD, Solomon	son	1		b. Exeter

3 servants

South Street:

| JACOBS, Esther | head | 70 | | b. Lyme, Dorset |

1 servant

1 Cobourg Place:

| MOSCHZISHER, Laura | married, 38, wife of Francis Moschzisker teacher of languages | | | b. Oxford |
| MOSCHZISHER, Mathilda | dau | 11 | scholar | b. Pimlico, London |

Frierhay Street:

| JACOBS, Harriet | wid head, | 68 | | b. Poland |
| JACOBS, Leah | granddaughter | 11 | | b. Exeter |

Dolphin Inn, Market Street:

| LYON, Henry | lodger | 19 | commercial traveller | b. Prussia |

Marine Stores, Coombe Street:

| COHEN, David | unmarried, | 55 | traveller jewellery | b. Poland |

22 Paragon Place:

JACOBS, Henry	head	45	travelling jeweller	b. Poland
JACOBS, Ann	wife	43		b. Poland
JACOBS, Esther	dau	19	school mistress	b. Poland
JACOBS, Jacob	son	15	scholar	b. Exeter
JACOBS, Sarah	dau	14	dressmaker	b. Exeter
JACOBS, Leah	dau	12	scholar	b. Exeter
JACOBS, Nathan	son	7	scholar	b. Exeter

THE JEWS OF EXETER

1871 Census

8 Market Street:

LAZARUS, Moses	head	42	optician,	b. Exeter
LEVY, Ann	sister	45	jeweller	b. Exeter
JONAS, Barnet	uncle	65	retired jeweller	b. Topsham
LEVY, Bessy	neice	17	housekeeper	b. Topsham

6 High Street:

ALEXANDER, Alexander	head,	66	optician	b. Kent
ALEXANDER, Fanny	wife,	60		b. Devonport
ALEXANDER, Fanny	dau,	39		b. Exeter
ALEXANDER, Eliza	dau,	35	unmarried	b. Exeter
ALEXANDER, Lawrence	son,	23		b. Exeter
ALEXANDER, Frances	dau,	27		b. Exeter
CHARLES, Eustace	grandson,	5		b. Hackney
GIDLEY, Miriam	servant,	18		b. Christow, Devon

60 High Street:

SOLOMON, Myers	head,	49	optician & jeweller	b. Prussia, here 40 years
SOLOMON, Deborah	wife	42		b. Exeter
SOLOMON Elezer	son	18	commercial traveller	b. Exeter
SOLOMON Samuel	son	13	scholar	b. Exeter
SOLOMON Nathan	son	5	scholar	b. Exeter
SOLOMON, Julia	dau	20	assistant to father	b. Exeter
SOLOMON Sarah	dau	16	tutor in family	b. Exeter
SOLOMON Esther	dau	16	scholar	b. Exeter
SOLOMON Fanny	dau	11	scholar	b. Exeter
SOLOMON Ruth	dau	9	scholar	b. Exeter
SOLOMON Catherine	dau	7	scholar	b. Exeter
SOLOMON Eve	dau	1		b. Exeter

6 Synagogue Place:

ISRAEL, Aaron	head	67	attends to synagogue	b. Poland circa 1804
ISRAEL Esther	wife	57		b. Prussia
ISRAEL Israel	son	22	traveller	b. Exeter
ISRAEL Julia	dau	20	assistant at home	b. Exeter
ISRAEL Fanny	dau	13	scholar	b. Exeter
ISRAEL Rachel	dau	11	scholar	b. Exeter
SMITH, Julia		27	no occupation	b. Camborne, Cornwall

7 Hatchers Street:

AARONS, Aron	head	44	optician	b. Exeter
AARONS, Julia	wife	30		b. Exeter
AARONS, Cakoloion	dau	3		b. Exeter
AARONS, Beny	dau	2		b. Exeter
AARONS, Solomon	son	3 mths		b. Exeter

5 Paragon Place, South:

ZAMOISKI, Priscilla	head widow	44	assistant	b. Exeter
ZAMOISKI, Florence	dau	14	scholar	b. Exeter

CENSUS RETURNS FOR JEWS IN EXETER: 1841-1901

| AARONS, Harriet | visitor | 40 | dressmaker | b. Exeter |

Jubilee Place:

SHAPIRO, David	head	45	Reader to Hebrew Congregation	b. Poland
SHAPIRO, Esther	wife	45		b. Poland
SHAPIRO, Isaac	son	14		b. Poland
SHAPIRO, Victoria	dau	10	scholar	b. Jersey
SHAPIRO, Amelia	dau	8	scholar	b. Northumberland

King Street:

BUSTEIN, Abraham	head	50	pawnbroker	b. Poland
BUSTEIN, Rose	wife	40		b. Exeter
BUSTEIN, Phoebe	dau	15	scholar	b. Plymouth
BUSTEIN, Dinah	dau	13	scholar	b. Plymouth
BUSTEIN, Alice	dau	12	scholar	b. Plymouth
BUSTEIN, Sarah	dau	9	scholar	b. Plymouth
BUSTEIN, Joseph	son	7	scholar	b. Plymouth
BUSTEIN, Marcus	son	5	scholar	b. Plymouth
BUSTEIN, Rhoda	dau	3		b. Plymouth
BUSTEIN, Issac	son	11 mths		b. Plymouth

2 female servants aged 20

16 Bedford Circus [??]

BARNARD, Asher	head	46	no occupation	b. Rochester
BARNARD, Rebecca	wife	43		b. Dover
BARNARD, Benjamin	son	21		b. Ipswich
BARNARD, Daniel	son	30		b. Ipswich
BARNARD, Julia	dau	16		b. Exeter
BARNARD, Hannah	dau	14		b. Exeter
BARNARD, Joseph	son	12		b. Exeter
BARNARD, Solomon	son	10		b. Exeter
BARNARD, Samuel	son	8		b. Exeter
BARNARD, Henry	son	7		b. Exeter
BARNARD, Katie	dau	4		b. Exeter

3 servants

10 Russell Street:

WOOLF, Michael	head	45	traveller	b. Exeter
WOOLF, Mary	wife	45		b. Exeter
WOOLF, Priscilla	dau	15		b. Hampton Court

Mantle Grand, Heavitree:

PIOTROWSKI, Dionisi	head	64	income from foreign [???]	b. Poland
PIOTROWSKI, Isabella	wife	54	income from foreign	b. France
PIOTROWSKI, Mina	dau	26	income from foreign	b. France

11 Leiny Place:

| MOSES, Hana | head | 65 | independent | b. Plymouth, circa 1806 |
| CAYUNTER, Hanny | neice | 4 | | b. Exeter, circa 1867 |

THE JEWS OF EXETER

Courtney Arms, Mary Arches Street:

| TREADMAN, Woolf | lodger | 50 | hawker | b. Russia |

Dolphin Inn, Market Street:

JACOBS, Abraham		41	commercial traveller	b. Exeter
CUNITZ, Lewis		47	commercial traveller	b. Prussia
PRESTINBURG, William			commercial traveller	b. ??

West Street:

| SHILTZS, Lewis | boarder | 95 | no occupation | b. Warsaw, Poland |

South Western Hotel, Paul Street:

| PALMER, Abraham | widow, | 66, | lodger, commercial traveller | b. Warsaw, Poland |

....

1881 Census

6 High Street:

ALEXANDER, Alexander	head	76	optician	b. Sheerness
ALEXANDER, Fanny	wife	70		b. Plymouth
ALEXANDER, Eliza	dau	45	in shop	b. Exeter
ALEXANDER, Frances	dau	37	in shop	b. Exeter
ROWCLIFFE, Elizabeth	servant,	19	general domestic	

4 Northernhay Place:

| HAWKINS, Thomas | head | 49 | surgeon | |
| ALEXANDER, Eustace | | 15 | student of law | |

29 Bridge Place or Street:

AARONS, Julia	head	37	jeweller	b. Exeter
AARONS, Caroline	dau	13	scholar	b. Exeter
AARONS, Solomon	son	10	scholar	b. Exeter
AARONS, Annie	dau	8	scholar	b. Exeter
AARONS, Barnet	uncle	75	watch material dealer	b. Topsham

17 Parr Street:

WOOLF, Michael	head	55	traveller & pensioner	b. Exeter
WOOLF, Anna	wife	32		b. Honiton
WOOLF, Priscilla	dau	25	dressmaker	b. Hampton Court
WOOLF, Caroline	dau	18	dressmaker	b. Exeter
WOOLF, Rose	dau	2		b. Exeter
WOOLF, William	son	3 mths		b. Exeter

47 Mary Arches Street:

| SHEPPERD, ??? | lodger | 30 | hawker | b. Poland, Russia |

Alphington Street:

MYERS, Benjamin	head	80	widow, retired	b. Maldon, Essex
MYERS, Albert	son	37	no occupation given	b. London
MYERS, Edward	son	35	no occupation given	b. Cambridgeshire

1 housekeeper, 1 cook and 1 groom

1891 Census

4 St Leonard Place:

GITTLESON, Samuel	head	30	picture frame manufacturer	b. Germany
GITTLESON Charlotte	wife	25		
GITTLESON Julius	son	4		
GITTLESON Arnold	son	3		
GITTLESON Isidor	son	7 mths		
CHARD, Alice	servant	18		
SEWARD, Elizabeth	nursemaid	14		

172 Fore Street:

HART, Joseph	head	35	hardwareman	b. Suffolk
HART, Flora	wife	30		b. Middlesex
HART, Moses	son	5		b. Exeter, circa

2 servants

14 Elmside

WOOLF, Frederick	head	27	draper	b. Redruth
WOOLF, Jennie	wife	28		b. Devonport
WOOLF, Havelock	son	2		b. Plymouth

5 Yeovil Place:

WOOLF, Michael	head	64	assusage agent	b. Exeter
WOOLF, Anna	wife	42		b. Honiton
WOOLF, Rose	dau	12		b. Exeter
WOOLF, William	son	10	scholar	b. Exeter
WOOLF, Charles	son	7	scholar	b. Exeter
WOOLF, Leah	dau	4	scholar	b. Exeter
WOOLF, Alfred	son	2 mths		b. Exeter

44-45 Queen Street:

FELDMAN, Moses		60	commercial traveller	b. Poland

1901 Census

4 St Leonard Place:

SAMUELS, Charles	head	40	picture frame manufacturer	b. Russia
SAMUELS, Charlotte	wife	40		b. Islington
SAMUELS, J	son	14		b. Exeter
SAMUELS, A	son	13		b. Exeter
SAMUELS, J	son	10		b. Exeter
SAMUELS, L	son	9		b. Exeter
SAMUELS, J	dau	6		b. Exeter
SAMUELS, E	son	3		b. Exeter
SAMUELS, T	dau	1		b. Exeter
SAMUELS, T	dau	4mths		b. Exeter
SAMUELS, C	brother	23		
MITCHELL, J	gardener	34		
MITCHELL, M	wife	29		
MITCHELL, W	son	10mths		

2 servants aged 17

16 Oxford Road:

GABRIELSON, Morris	head	56	commission agent	b. Warsaw, Poland
GABRIELSON, Hetty	wife	52		b. Cracow, Poland
GABRIELSON, Amelia	dau	28	milliner	b. London
GABRIELSON, Everetta	dau	24		b. London
GABRIELSON, Madge	dau	19	dressmaker	b. Plymouth
GABRIELSON, Laura	dau	17	book-helper	b. Plymouth
GLYNN, Saul	singleboarder	26	draper	b. Moscow, Russia

51 Sandford Place:

WOOLF, Michael	head	75	Insurance agent	b. Exeter
WOOLF, Anna	wife	53		b. Honiton
WOOLF, Charles	son	17	salesman	b. Exeter
WOOLF, Leah	dau	14	assistant tailor	b. Exeter
WOOLF, Alfred	son	12		b. Exeter

51 Northernhay Street:

NORMAN, Alfred	boarder	22	jeweller	b. Gilna, Russia

125 Fore Street:

SILVERMAN, Simon	boarder	54	hawker	b. Russia, c.1847

2 Friary Hill:

BREEMAN, Henry	boarder	31	clergyman (Hebrew)	b. Nothaluratuck, Russia

11 Raleigh Road:

JOEL, Eugene	boarder	53	school modern languages	b. Paris, c.1848

APPENDIX 4
RABBIS AND MINISTERS

Rabbis and Ministers of Exeter Hebrew Congregation and their period of service:

Rev. Moses Horowitz Levy	1792-1837
Rev. Michael Levy Green	1839-1841
Rev. Samuel Hoffnung	1841-1853
Rev. Berthold Albu	1853-54
Rev. Myer Mendlessohn	1854-67
S. Alexander	1867-1869
Joseph Lewis	1869-1870
Rev David Shapiro	1870-1871
S. Bach	1871-1874
Rev. Mark Harris	1874-1874, 3 months
Rev. Marcus Manovitz	1875-1876
Lazarus	1876-1878
Rev. M Davidson	1879- ???
A Muller	1885- ???
I. Litovitch	1895-1897
J B Rittenberg	1898-1898, 6 months
Rev. S Pearlstein	1898-99
H. Bregman	1899-1904
Rev Daniel Caplan	??? - 1908
Rev. Abraham Rosenberg	1908-1913
Shinerock	1916-1917

APPENDIX 7
JEWISH CREDITORS AND CHRISTIAN DEBTORS IN MEDIEVAL EXETER

Jewish Creditors in the Exeter Vetus Cista 1237-1275

This provides a list of Exeter Jewish creditors who loaned money to Christians during the Medieval period. Between 1237 and 1275 the Jews of Exeter were owed a total of over a thousand pounds; a significant amount of money.

fil = son of

Jacob Copin	£357	0s.	0d.
Amite relicta Samuel	£198	0s.	0d.
Jacob Crespin	£114	0s.	0d.
Isaac son of Moses	£90	13s.	4d.
Deulecresse Capellanus	£75	16s.	4d.
Aaron de Caerleon	£26	0s.	0d.
Salomon fil Salomon	£26	0s.	0d.
Salomon fil Aaron	£20	0s.	0d.
Isaac son of Salomon	£20	0s.	0d.
Tertia relicta Lumbard	£16	10s.	0d.
Lumbard son of Salomon	£15	0s.	0d.
Moses son of Samuel	£10	0s.	0d.
Jacob son of Samuel	£10	0s.	0d.
Samuel son of Moses	£7	13s.	4d.
Aaron son of Josce	£7	10s.	0d.
Copin fil Lumbard	£6	6s.	8d.
Ursell fil Manser	£6	0s.	0d.
Moses fil Josce	£5	0s.	0d.
Abraham fil Milo	£4	4s.	0d.
Diay son of Samuel son of Moses	£4	0s.	0d.
Josce son of Benedict Bateman	£2	0s.	0d.
Lumbard son of Deulecresse	£1	0s.	0d.
Total lent by Exeter's Jews	**£1023**	**19s.**	**8d.**

Christian debtors in the Exeter Vetus Cista 1237-1275

The following is a list of Christians, including local clerics [clericus] who owed money to the Jews of Exeter during the Medieval period. The original spelling of names has been retained:

John fil Bernard	£169	10s.	0d.
Osanna relicta Edward Rudde of Dartmouth	£50	10s.	0d.
William de Middleton of Somerset	£40	0s.	0d.
Simon fil Guy	£30	0s.	0d.
Joanna relicta Jocelin de la Hele	£22	0s.	0d.
Robert de Bursy de Blakemore	£20	13s.	4d.
Egidius son of Thomas de Goshill	£20	0s.	0d.

Extract of Exeter's Medieval Archae

THE JEWS OF EXETER

William son of William de La Lade of Somerset	£20	0s.	0d.
Robert le Demeys Miles of Devon	£20	0s.	0d.
Hugo Cole de Suelcester	£20	0s.	0d.
Richard de Bontumbur	£20	0s.	0d.
Hugo Cissor of Honiton	£20	0s.	0d.
Roger de Cotton	£20	0s.	0d.
Richard Le Brade	£16	0s.	0d.
Henry Lunetrot	£15	0s.	0d.
Henry de Dumesmor	£14	13s.	4d.
Hugo de Morba	£13	6s.	8d.
Roger de Loyes	£12	0s.	0d.
John Hamelin, junior	£11	0s.	0d.
Willian de Horsham, neaqr Manaton	£10	0s.	0d.
Olivis de la Dere, cleric	£10	0s.	0d.
John de Ffurneus	£10	0s.	0d.
Geoffrey de Lucy	£10	0s.	0d.
John de la Leye	£10	0s.	0d.
William of Westcott	£10	0s.	0d.
Robert de Stowerigge	£10	0s.	0d.
Philip le Kuyt de Uppecote	£10	0s.	0d.
Richard le Brode	£10	0s.	0d.
John le Viteri	£10	0s.	0d.
John Malerbe	£10	0s.	0d.
Mauricius de la Herbe	£10	0s.	0d.
William de Oxton	£10	0s.	0d.
Wales de Sinteherne Toch	£9	6s.	8d.
Henry Buchard de Ralegh	£9	0s.	0d.
Henry de la Wyldechurche	£8	10s.	0d.
Adam de Cleyagh	£8	10s.	0d.
Philip de Bunewall fil William de Bunewall	£8	6s.	8d.
John Comyn of Exbridge	£8	0s.	0d.
Roger de Molins clericus of County Devon	£8	0s.	0d.
Philip of Sidenham (Sidenham Damarel)	£8	0s.	0d.
Richard Brode of the parish of Hylstington	£8	0s.	0d.
Randulph fil Randulph of Doddiscombsleigh	£8	0s.	0d.
Philipi de Colewyle	£7	10s.	0d.
John Quynel, Rector of the church of Shobrok	£7	0s.	0d.
Roger le White of Colyton	£6	16s.	0d.
John de Regny of County Somerset	£6	13s.	4d.
Robert Cusin	£6	13s.	4d.
Michael de Columbar	£6	0s.	0d.
William de Wyteslegh Aurifaber	£6	0s.	0d.
Robert de Strong	£6	0s.	0d.
Baldewin de Raddon of County Dorset	£6	0s.	0d.
Jordanus de Neweton Civis Exeter	£6	0s.	0d.
Philip Benyng of Okehampton	£5	8s.	8d.
William de Denlis of County Somerset	£5	6s.	8d.
Richard de Warewyke	£5	6s.	8d.
Philip de Columbar de Scotland	£5	0s.	0d.
Roger Launtelere	£5	0s.	0d.
John de Haldehaye	£5	0s.	0d.
Thomas de Clune	£5	0s.	0d.
Isabella de Colewille relicta Philip de Colewill	£5	0s.	0d.
Hugo Ereward de Suelsester	£5	0s.	0d.
Alan Tinctor of Exeter	£5	0s.	0d.
Geoffrey Hasumund of Okehampton	£5	0s.	0d.
Serlo de Morkeshull	£5	0s.	0d.

Lamentius de Prato of Samford Peverel	£5	0s.	0d.
Randulph Aurifab fil Adam de Morton Civis Exeter	£5	0s.	0d.
Randulph of Doddiscombsleigh	£5	0s.	0d.
Alexander de Viteri	£5	0s.	0d.
Roger de Cameslegh	£4	13s.	4d.
Nicholas de la Cnolle	£4	6s.	8d.
Jordan de Pleybroke	£4	0s.	0d.
Richard de Wormore fil Hugo de Marba	£4	0s.	0d.
William Sanguin of Whimple	£4	0s.	0d.
Nicholas de la Sale of Exeter	£4	0s.	0d.
Roger of Beancombe Capellanus	£4	0s.	0d.
William de Bynnewall	£3	6s.	8d.
John de Cordyngton	£3	6s.	8d.
Ernulphus de la Vale	£3	6s.	8d.
Reginald of Deancombe Capellanus	£3	5s.	0d.
Reginald Bakestar	£3	0s.	0d.
Richard Beneg fil Philip Beneg	£3	0s.	0d.
Anna de la Wynard fil Randolph of Kent	£3	0s.	0d.
Robert le Franceys de Brimyl	£2	13s.	4d.
John Spark fil Walter Spark	£2	0s.	0d.
William primus fil Henry Garettar of Mueltestr	£2	0s.	0d.
John de Oxton	£2	0s.	0d.
Edward Corbyn	£2	0s.	0d.
Arnulphas, clericus de Hunegost	£2	0s.	0d.
Richard Bullock Goldsmith	£2	0s.	0d.
Ernulphus de la Valle	£2	0s.	0d.

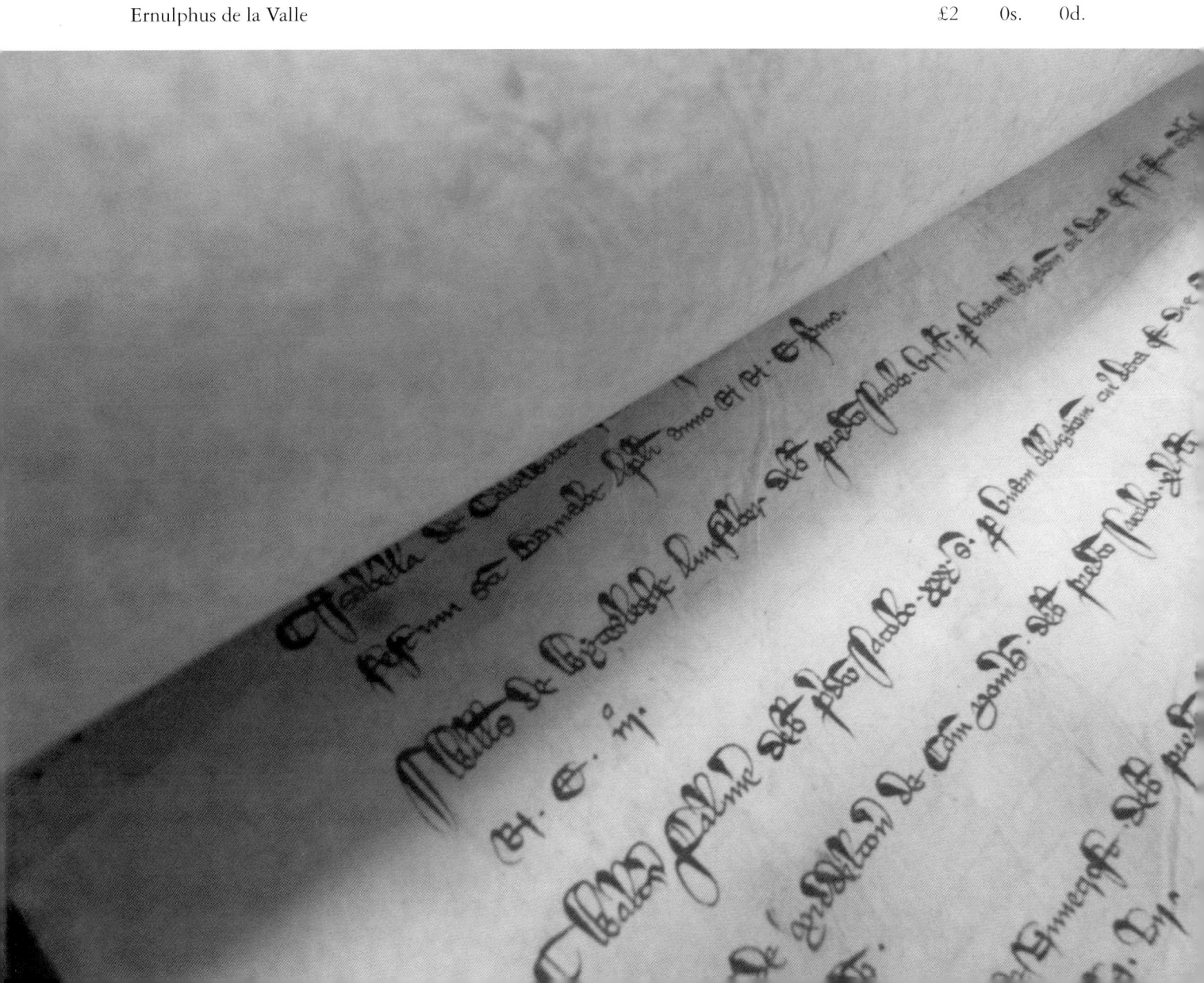

Matilda de Crofte relicta de William de Crofte	£2	0s.	0d.
Geoffrey Avienel	£2	0s.	0d.
Thomas Dunekan	£2	0s.	0d.
John de Middleton of County Devon	£2	0s.	0d.
Robert le Sanger de Brunneford	£2	0s.	0d.
Alexander son of Nicholas de la Cnolle	£1	13s.	4d.
Walter Palme	£1	10s.	0d.
William Chare de la Sele	£1	10s.	0d.
Randulph de la Stone de Pont de Clift	£1	10s.	0d.
Paul de Neweton	£1	10s.	0d.
John le Draker de Cockeleye	£1	10s.	0d.
Richard Russel ulicta Exeter	£1	6s.	8d.
Nicholas de la Pole	£1	6s.	8d.
Adam, clericus de Exeter	£1	6s.	8d.
Roger Russel de Braneys	£1	6s.	8d.
Andrew de la Hille	£1	4s.	0d.
Randolph de Sonehampton	£1	0s.	0d.
Robert Ballard	£1	0s.	0d.
Thomas de Relbe	£1	0s.	0d.
Walter Coleman	£1	0s.	0d.
David Duncepoi de Brameys	£1	0s.	0d.
Roger le Chewaler de Okehampton	£1	0s.	0d.
Adam de Keneford	£1	0s.	0d.
Thomas Wode	£1	0s.	0d.
Robert de Cockington	£1	0s.	0d.
Richard fil Albert Faber of Exeter		10s.	0d.
Roger Gaygne		10s.	0d.
John Blannpayn		10s.	0d.
Total owed to Exeter's Jews	£1023	19s.	8d.

Jewish Creditors in the Exeter Nova Cista 1285-1290

Abraham	£58	6s.	8d.
Cuntasse	£33	6s.	8d.
Amite	£20	0s.	0d.
Symme fil Lumbard and Josce fil Isaac	£20	0s.	0d.
Auntere	£10	0s.	0d.
Cok Moses	£7	6s.	8d.
Isaac fil Josce	£6	13s.	4d.
Jacob le Frere Peres	£6	13s.	4d.
Isaac	£6	13s.	4d.
Abraham and Cok	£6	13s.	4d.
Total	£175	13s.	4d.

Christian Debtors in the Exeter Nova Cista 1285-1290

William de Bysenham	£20	0s.	0d.
William de Coleford	£20	0s.	0d.
Alienora de Wotton	£15	0s.	0d.
John fil Roger de Poteford	£13	6s.	8d.
Matilda de Chilton	£10	0s.	0d.

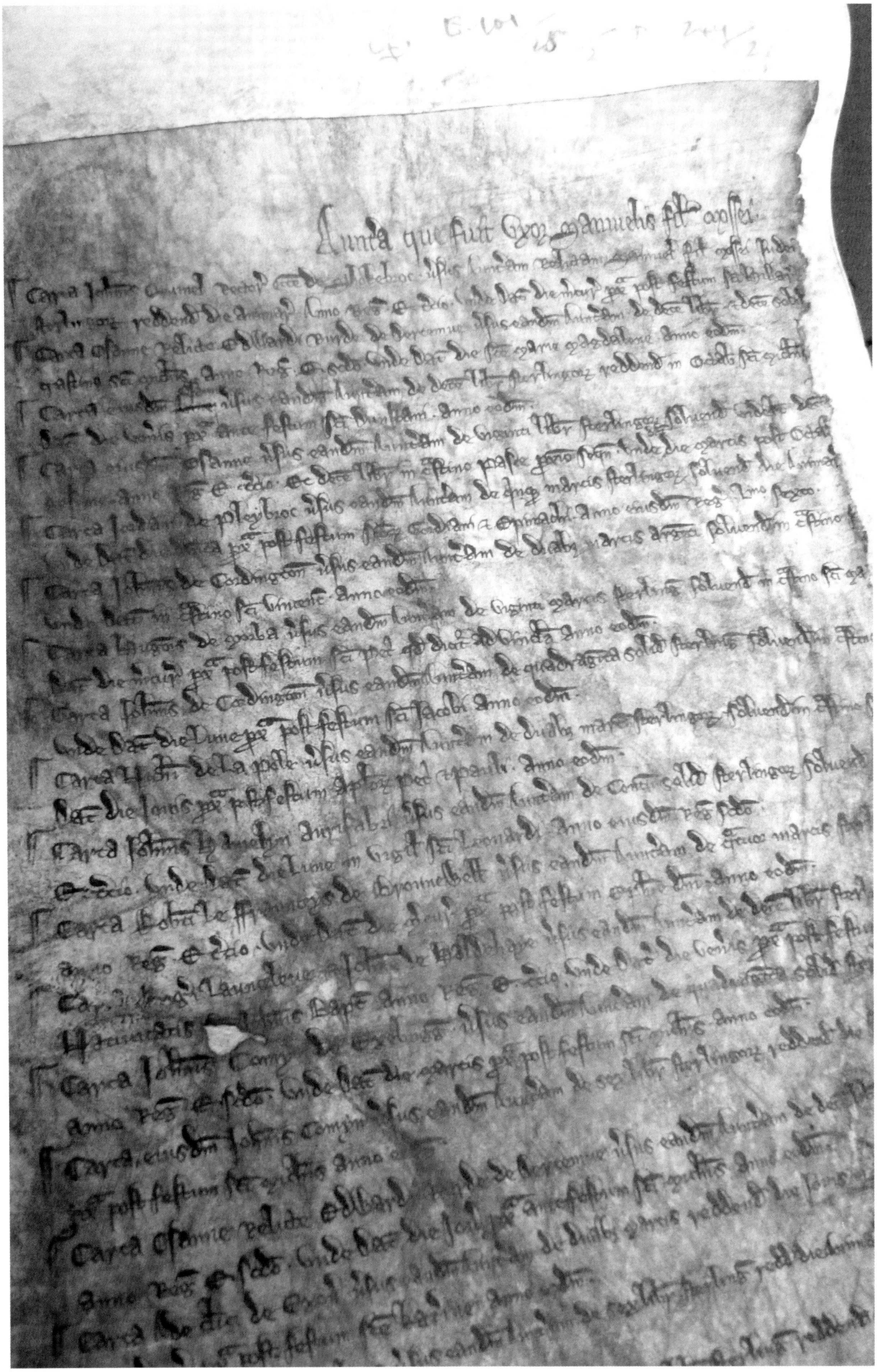

Nicholas Tri de Jude	£10	0s.	0d.
Rogeer de Poteford Miles	£10	0s.	0d.
William de Cheyne	£10	0s.	0d.
William Bathel	£6	13s.	4d.
William de Cableford	£6	13s.	4d.
Gilbert Gladeware	£6	13s.	4d.
Nicholas de Terry de la Lud	£6	13s.	4d.
Joel de Huddespyte	£6	13s.	4d.
Randulph Aurifaber de Sotton	£6	13s.	4d.
Roger de Wallebere	£6	13s.	4d.
William de Soysetock (Bailiff of the hundred of Tavistock)	£6	13s.	4d.
Jacob de Mohun	£6	13s.	4d.
Geoffrey de la Stone de Taunton	£6	13s.	4d.
Warin de Fifastre (Parson de Weyre)		13s.	4d.
Total	£175	13s.	4d.

Jewish Creditors who were owed for tallies in the Exeter Nova Cista 1285-1290

Certain Exeter Jews	£13	16s.	8d.
Isaac de Campeden	£4	13s.	0d.
Abraham	£4	0s.	0d.
Anterre and Leon	£3	0s.	0d.
Cok, Auntetot and Abraham	£2	13s.	0d.
Abraham fil Isaac	£1	12s.	0d.
Cok Moses	£1	5s.	4d.
Isaac	£1	3s.	6d.
Isaac fil Josce	£1	2s.	10d.
Cok	£1	0s.	8d.
Auntetot and Abraham		8s.	0d.
Leo fil Josce		7s.	0d.
Jacob fil Peter		6s.	8d.
Cuntasse		2s.	0d.
Total	£35	10s.	8d.

Christian Debtors with Tallies in the Nova Cista 1285-1290

Roger de Poteford	£3	13s.	4d.
William de Poteford	£3	13s.	4d.
John de Stonehenge	£3	7s.	6d.
William de Boyskok	£3	6s.	8d.
Jacob de Moun	£3	5s.	10d.
Alice Knoyl	£3	0s.	0d.
Nicholas Terry de la Lade	£2	13s.	0d.
Roger de Poteford	£2	0s.	0d.
Richard Bailiff de Stanborough	£1	12s.	0d.
William de Cheyny	£1	4s.	0d.
Gilbert Gladewynne	£1	3s.	6d.
William Tyrel	£1	2s.	10d.
Philip de Huddeapyte	£1	0s.	0d.
William Baghel	£1	0s.	0d.
Lucas Fraunceys		13s.	4d.
John de Poteford		13s.	4d.
Warin de Fishaherte (Parson of Weyre)		10s.	0d.
William de Hysenham		8s.	0d.

Thomas Starlet	7s.	0d.
Henry de la Pomay	6s.	8d.
Richard del la Legh	4s.	0d.
John Walweyn	2s.	0d.
Walter Anng	2s.	0d.
Philip de Ryston	2s.	0d.
Total	£35 10s.	8d.

Surviving names of the Chirographers of Exeter 1224-1290

Jewish Chirographers	Dates of office
Moses le Turk	1224-33
Ursell, son-in-law of Amiot	1224
Hak (Isaac) son of Deudoné	prior to 1244
Josce Crespin	1224-66
Bonenfant, son of Leo	1244
Lumbard Episcopus	1260-66
Leo of Burg	prior to 1266
Jacob Copin	1266-80
Jacob Crespin	1275-90

Christian Chirographers	Dates of office
Lawrence Cissore	1244
Henry Picot	1224-3
Richard Bollock	1266-77
Thomas de Langedon	1266
David Taylor	1277

APPENDIX 8
LIST OF EXETER HEBREW CONGREGATION 1896–1999

1896
President – Charles Samuels
Treasurer – S. Fredman
Minister – Rev. I Litovitch

1945
President – Conrad Samuels
Hon. Secretary & Treasurer – Edgar Samuels
Registrar – Julius Samuels

1947
President – Conrad Samuels
Hon. Secretary – Miss Theresa Samuels
Registrar – Julius Samuels

1949
President – Conrad Samuels
Hon. Secretary – Major S. Cohen
Treasurer – J. Smith

1953
President – Harold Harris
Hon. Secretary – Major S. Cohen
Treasurer – J. Smith

1963
President – Harold Harris
Secretary – Mrs R. Sabel

1969
President – G. Karpel
Secretary – Mrs R. Sabel

1971
President – G. Karpel

1983-1999

June 1983
President – Derrick Boam
Treasurer – Kurt Wilhelm
Services Harry Freedman
Student Liaison – Brana Thorn
Newsletter – Frank Gent

September 1983 - August 1985
President – Derrick Boam
Treasurer – Kurt Wilhelm
Services Harry Freedman
Student Liaison – Brana Thorn
Newsletter – Frank Gent
Social Organiser – Bertha Boam

September 1985
Honorary Life President - Derrick Boam
President – Frank Gent
Treasurer – Bill Boam
Services Harry Freedman
Student Liaison – Brana Thorn
Newsletter – Frank Gent
Social Organiser – Bertha Boam

October 1985 – February 1986
Honorary Life President - Derrick Boam
President – Frank Gent
Treasurer – Bill Boam
Secretary – Josie Odoni
Services Harry Freedman
Student Liaison – Brana Thorn
Newsletter – Frank Gent
Social Organiser – Bertha Boam

April 1986 – August 1986
Honorary Life President - Derrick Boam
President and newsletter editor – Frank Gent
Treasurer – Bill Boam
Meetings Secretary – Josie Odoni
Services Harry Freedman
Student Liaison – Melanie Solomon

LIST OF EXETER HEBREW CONGREGATION 1896-1999

Social Organiser – Bertha Boam
West Country Jewish Women – Brana Thorn

September 1986 – September 1987
Honorary Life President – Derrick Boam
President and newsletter editor – Frank Gent
Treasurer – Bill Boam
Services – Harry Friedman

September 1987 – January 1991
President and newsletter editor - Frank Gent
Treasurer - Bill Boam

February 1991
President - Frank Gent
Vice President - Ellis Weinberger
Treasurer - Bill Boam
Meetings Secretary - Sonia Fodor

June 1991
President - Bill Boam
Vice President - Ellis Weinberger
Social Organiser and Synagogue visits - Sonia Fodor
Newsletter editor - Frank Gent

January 1992
President - Ellis Weinberger
Vice-President - Frank Gent
Treasurer - Neil Saxon
Social Organiser and School visits - Sonia Fodor

March 1994
President - Ellis Weinberger
Vice-President - Hilary Radnor
Treasurers - Neil and Shelley Saxon
Newsletter editor - Frank Gent
Social Organiser and Synagogue visits - Sonia Fodor
Religion School - Rivka Glaser

September 1994
President - Ellis Weinberger
Vice-President - Michael Elan
Treasurers - Neil and Shelley Saxon
Newsletter Editor - Frank Gent
Social Organiser and Synagogue visits - Sonia Fodor

March 1995
Acting President - Frank Gent
Vice-President - Michael Elan
Treasurers - Neil and Shelley Saxon
Newsletter editor - Frank Gent
Social Organiser and Synagogue visits - Sonia Fodor

September 1997
President - Sonia Fodor
Vice-President - Frank Gent
Treasurer - Susan Foot

September 1999
President - Sonia Fodor
Vice-President - Frank Gent
Treasurer - Susan Foot

אנכי ה׳
לא יהיה
לא תשא
זכור את
כבד את
לא תרצח
לא תנאף
לא תגנב
לא תענה
לא תחמד
PRESENTED BY MR & MRS H. GRANT
IN MEMORY OF
THEIR BELOVED DAUGHTER HELENE

BIBLIOGRAPHY

Archives

The Devon Record Office, including records of Exeter Hebrew Congregation and Susser Archive deposited there; Exeter Cathedral Archives; The Westcountry Studies Library; British Library newspaper Library; the Jewish Museum (London); archives of the Chief Rabbi and Beth Din at The Metropolitan Archives (London); Lansdowne MSS at the British Museum; and the Royal Archives at Windsor. Also the National Archives, ref: TNA: E/101/250/2 for material on Jews in Medieval Exeter. See also Rigg, *Calendar of the Plea Rolls of the Exchequer of the Jews*, Vols. I, II and Jenkinson, *Calendar of the Plea Rolls of the Exchequer of the Jews*, Vol. III. Copies available in The National Archives.

Newspapers and Journals: *Transactions of the Jewish Historical Society*, *Jewish Chronicle*, *Exeter Flying Post*, *Trewman's Flying Post* and *Western Morning News*.

Books & articles

Adler, Michael. 'The Medieval Jews of Exeter', in Transactions of the Devonshire Association, 1931, vol. l, xiii, pp.221-240

Berger, Doreen. *The Jewish Victorian: Genealogical Information from the Jewish Newspapers 1861-1870*, Robert Boyd Publications: 2004

Berger, Doreen. *The Jewish Victorian: Genealogical Information from the Jewish Newspapers 1871-1880*, Robert Boyd Publications: 1999

D'Blossiers Tovey. *A History of the Jews of England: from 1066-1738*, Weidenfeld & Nicolson: 1990

Fry, Helen. *Jewish Cemeteries of Devon*, Amazon: 2012

Fry, Helen. *Jews in North Devon during the Second World War*, Halsgrove: 2005

Fry, Helen. 'The Jews of Barnstaple and Bideford', in *European Judaism*, autumn 2001, p.4-13

Hidden Legacy Foundation. *The Jews of Devon and Cornwall*, Redcliffe Press: 2000

Green, Geoffrey. *The Royal Navy and Anglo-Jewry, 1740-1820*, Naval & Maritime Bookshop: 1989

Jamilly, Edward. *The Georgian Synagogue: an architectural history*, Jewish Memorial Council: 1999

Kadish, Sharman. *The Synagogues of Britain and Ireland*, Yale University Press: 2011

Kadish, Sharman. *Jewish Heritage in England: An architectural Guide*, English Heritage: 2006

Pearce, Keith & Helen Fry (ed). *The Lost Jews of Cornwall*, Redcliffe: 2000

Roth, Cecil. *The Rise of Provincial Jewry*, The Jewish Monthly: 1950

Samuel, Judith. *The Jews of Bristol,* Redcliffe: 1997

Sinclair, Eddie. 'Interim Polychromy Report. Exeter Synagogue: Ark Polychromy, unpublished survey, 1998

Sinclair, Eddie. 'The Restoration of the Ark Paintwork. Exeter Synagogue: Polychrome Survey,' unpublished survey, 1996

Susser, Bernard. *The Jews of South-west England: The Rise and Decline of their Medieval and Modern Communities*, University of Exeter Press: 1993

Susser, Bernard. *The Decennial Census*, Studies in Anglo-Jewish History, 1995, privately published

Weiner, A. 'Jews in Exeter before 1290,' in the *Jewish Chronicle*, 28 December 1906

---

[i] *Trewman's Flying Post*, 1 July 1841.
[ii] EHC Minute Book, 1838, p.72.

INDEX

Aarons, Aaron 39, 61, 71
Aarons, Caroline 38, 61
Aarons, Harriet 61
Aarons, Priscilla 38
Aarons, Solomon 39, 53, 61
Abel, Isaac 39
Abel, Jacob 39
Abrams, Pilot Officer H D 53, 58, 62
Abrahams, Joseph 23
Albu, Revd Berthold 35, 38, 39, 41-2, 47, 68
Alexander, Alexander 9, 35, 36, 37, 38, 39, 41, 42, 43, 47, 56, 59, 63-66, 71, 73
Alexander, John 36, 63, 66
Alexander, Solomon 39
Alexander, Revd S. 43
Archae (Exeter) 12, 13-15, 19-21

Bach, Revd S. 43
Barnard, Asher 36, 37, 38, 62
Bendix, Mr 30
Benedict, Samuel 24, 28
Bernum, Lionel 37
Birmingham 39
Block, Andrew 35
Boam family 88, 97-99
Boam, Bill (Solomon) 51, 88, 97, 99, 103, 109
Boam, Derrick 49, 88, 97, 99, 102, 103, 104, 108
Boam, William 88, 97
Bonenfant 12, 16, 17, 20
Bregman, Revd H. 45, 48
Bristol 14, 15, 17, 18, 21, 38, 43
Bristol Tallage 15-17, 40
Brock, John 101
Burstin, Mark 38

Caplan, Revd. Daniel 45
Cappelle, Solomon 59
Chirographers 13, 16
Christian-Jewish relations 36
Cohen, Lazarus 24
Collett, Ralph 35, 101, 105
Comitissa (Jewess) 13, 16, 20
Copin, Jacob 17-18, 19, 20
Council of Christians & Jews 109-110
Crespin, Jacob 16, 17, 18, 19, 20

Davidson, Revd M. 44
Davis, Abraham Solomon 24
Davis, Hyman 37, 47, 73

Davis, Morris 38, 64
Davis, Rosetta 38, 40
Deulecresse le Chapleyn 17, 18, 19
Deulecresse le Eveske 13, 14, 15, 16
Dimond, Caroline 61
Dunitz, Alfred 49, 50, 99, 102, 104
Dyte, Maures 39

Edward I 17, 18, 19
Elsner family 69-70, 73
Elsner, Rosina 35, 69
Elsner, Solomon 35, 36, 37, 38, 39, 47, 65, 69, 70, 87
Exchequer of the Jews 13, 17
expulsion (from England) 17, 19-21
Ezekiel, Abraham 23, 25, 26, 28, 31, 53, 55
Ezekiel, Amelia 26, 28, 29
Ezekiel, Benjamin 25
Ezekiel, Betsy (née Levy) 28, 29, 38
Ezekiel, Catherine (Kitty) 26, 28, 29
Ezekiel, Ezekiel Abraham 26-28
Ezekiel, Ezekiel Benjamin 55
Ezekiel, Georgiana 28, 38
Ezekiel, Henry 25, 26, 28-9, 37, 38, 45, 55
Ezekiel, Sarah 26, 28
Ezekiel, Selina 29, 38
Ezekiel, Solomon 55

Fainlight, Sydney 90
Falmouth 9, 35, 59, 63
Fodor, Sonia 49, 52, 103, 107, 108-109
Franklin, David 71
Fredman, Samuel 44, 74, 75
Freedman, Harry 45, 102, 103, 105

Gabrielson family 77, 79-80, 84, 88
Gabrielson, Maudie 39
Gent, Frank 33, 45, 49, 59, 103, 104, 105, 106-108
Glynn family 84-86, 88, 91
Glynn, Saul (Solomon Glinternick) 74, 84-86
Gompertz, Barent 24, 53, 58
Green, Revd Michael 37, 38, 40-1

Habonim 92
Harris, Harold 48, 95, 96-97
Harris, Revd, Mark 43-4
Harris, Nathan 59
Harris, Simon 33, 34, 35
Hart, Arthur Wellington 29, 38

Hart, Moses Mordecai 30, 68
Henry II 11, 12, 14
Henry III 15, 16, 17
Hoffnung, Revd Samuel 41, 48
Hort, Abraham 40
Hort, Caroline 40
Hyman, A 44
Hynes, Henry 62
Hynes, R 62

Jacobs, Emanuel 37, 56, 64
Jacobs, Esther 38, 39
Jacobs, Harris 41
Jacobs, Henry 39
Jacobs, Jacob 23, 24, 38, 55
Jacobs, Kitty 25, 31
Jacobs, Morris 55, 62
Jacobs, Samuel 24
Jacobson, David 39
Jewish Parliament 16-17
Joel, Bernard 24
Johnson, Lavinia 38
Johnson, Moses 39
Jonas, Barnet 39
Jonas, Benjamin 28, 55
Jonas, Jonas 55
Jonas, Samuel 23

Israel, Aaron 43, 61, 73

Karpel, Geoffrey 101, 102, 106
Kauffman, David 67
Kessler, Adolf (Johnnie) 88, 89
Kestenberg, Abraham 38

Laurance, Barnet 62-63
Lawrence, Lionel 48
Lazarus, David 36, 42, 63
Lazarus, Eleazar 38, 45, 47, 62-63
Lazarus, Deborah 67
Lazarus, Isaac 63
Lazarus, Julia (wife of Eleazar) 38
Lazarus, Julia (daughter of David) 39
Lazarus, Moses 36, 37, 38, 41, 55, 58, 62, 64, 70
Lazarus, Nancy 38
Lazarus, Revd 44
Lazarus, Samuel Joyful 38, 62
Lesh, Ann 50, 99, 100
Levander, family 70-71
Levi, John 28, 38
Levy, Abraham 38
Levy, Elkan 45, 110-111